Production Activity Control Reprints
Revised Edition, 1989

© 1988, American Production and Inventory Control Society, Inc.

International Standard Book Number: 1-55822-013-5
Library of Congress Catalog Number: 88-082787

American Production and Inventory Control Society, Inc.
500 West Annandale Road
Falls Church, Virginia 22046-4274

Stock No. 05012, 7/90, 3200

PRODUCTION ACTIVITY CONTROL REPRINTS
REVISED EDITION, 1989
Table of Contents

Foreword

This compilation of articles from APICS publications has been selected as representative of the body of knowledge in production activity control by the Production Activity Control Committee of the Curricula and Certification Council. We recognize that there are many fine articles which could have been selected and welcome recommendations for future inclusions. The committee may be contacted through the APICS Society Headquarters.

To help in studying for the PAC certification exam, the reprint articles have been cross-referenced to the major topical outline areas found in the Examination Study Guide. These topical outline areas are:

  I. Organization and Objectives
  II. The Production Environment
  III. Scheduling Techniques
  IV. Data Requirements
  V. Shop Capacity Control in the Short Term
  VI. Production Authorization
  VII. Lead Time Determination and Control
  VIII. Priority Control and Dispatching
  IX. Production Reporting and Status Control
  X. Production Measurement and Control
  XI. Production Activity Control Relationships

PAC Reprint Articles and Outline Areas

Reprinted from the APICS 1983 Conference Proceedings.

CONTROLLING WORK ORDERS ON THE SHOP FLOOR

Gary L. Bartholomew, CPIM
WABCO/Construction and Mining Equipment Group of American Standard

OBJECTIVE

You've implemented an MRPII System--Now What Do You Do?!!

Many companies find that even after they have implemented an MRPII System, the real challenge is to control the shop floor so that it responds in a timely manner. Even with a new "Formal System", many companies rely on an "Informal System" to expedite material through their shop. This informal system may be a remnant of the old informal system or a newly created "Hot List" which uses information generated from the MRPII System. In either case, what is being done in practice is a lot different from what is described in theory.

The objective of this presentation is to outline some of the theories that are applicable to Shop Floor Control and describe what one company is doing to plan and control work order priorities and capacities in their job shop environment. This paper will outline the process a work order goes through from the point that it is first planned until it is completed. The techniques used throughout this process will be discussed at each step. There will also be a discussion of how an On-Line Data Collection System is used to support this planning and controlling process.

OVERVIEW

Plan and Control Priorities and Capacities

For more than a decade it has been recognized that a company can achieve on-time delivery at minimal cost if it can plan and control its order priorities and then plan and control the capacity required to produce the schedules extrapolated from the priority process.[1] During this same time period, a body of knowledge has been formulated called SFC(Shop Floor Control). In addition, each month there are numerous articles published which describe how to better control the "Shop". All of this has helped the practitioner to better control his environment. But the fact remains that he continues to seek better solutions to increasingly complex situations. We must recognize that we have only begun to change the manufacturing environment.

To better understand what is required to control the shop floor we need to first review what we have learned in the last ten years.

PRIORITY PLANNING

Effective priority planning is the cornerstone from which shop schedules(Priority Dispatch Lists) and time-phased load(Capacity Requirements) are derived. This planning process does not begin in the shop. It begins with management decisions as to what, when, and how much should be produced. This plan must then be exploded so that all items that are required are ordered with enough time to produce or procure them. If there is not enough time allowed, the plan may fail despite heroic attempts to execute it.[2]

Priority planning on the shop floor tells the foreman what work he should work on next. This priority scheduling works best when each operation on a work order can be scheduled through each work center. The priority(ranking) of the operation should be derived from the due date assigned to the work order by MRP and calculated from a Critical Ratio technique.[3] A forward scheduling technique is used to develop an "Expected Ship Date" while a backward scheduling technique starting with the "Promise Ship Date" is used for setting operation start dates.[4]

CAPACITY PLANNING

Once priorities are determined a capacity plan can be established by extending the time-phased priority operation schedule by the standard time required to perform the operation. This load profile should be expressed in a time-phased format that can be used by management. That means that the shop foreman needs to know if he needs to schedule overtime or transfer employees today. The superintendant needs to know if he should hire or reduce employees in the next two to four weeks. The Production Control Manager needs to know if he needs to find outside suppliers to supplement the shops' capacity in the next two to ten weeks. And the Production Planning Manager needs to know what capacity is required in the next three to eighteen months as he plans what product will be produced where, when and in what quantity.

WHAT NEXT?

Now that we have made our priority and capacity plans, how do we execute them? How do we get feedback that tells managers how well the shop is performing to plan? How do we control work orders on the shop floor? The answers to these questions are just beginning to be addressed. There are some techniques that have been used successfully. There are some new techniques that still remain to be tested. The following section reviews some of these techniques.

PRIORITY CONTROL

Priority control means working on the "right" things first. For the shop floor this means working on the "right" work order. There are numerous reasons why this might not happen. Most shops do well on those work orders that the boss is checking on. But the others (even those with greater priority) will be pushed aside if this happens. To remedy this, what is needed is a measurement of how many of the "right" hours are worked.

One of the best new techniques measures the "Number of Days of Overdue Load" of all work orders at a work center. Another version recognizes only work orders that are available to be worked on at the work center. This technique provides a normal distribution from which a standard deviation can be calculated. Standard deviations from each work center can then be grouped in a priority sequence indicating which centers are "bottlenecks". Another new technique measures the "Priority of Orders Worked". This technique measures when an order is worked compared to the number of days late or ahead of the scheduled run date. The standard deviations from each work center can then be compared to the "Number of Days of Overdue Load" report. If the standard deviations vary significantly it might indicate that high priority work is not being worked.

CAPACITY CONTROL

Capacity control means working the "right" number of hours in a given time period. For the shop floor this means having the required number of men and machines in the "right" work centers at the "right" time. In a job shop environment this can be a complicated process. Changing manpower and machines is often a costly proposition. Management needs a measurement of how many of the "right" hours at the "right" work centers are worked at the "right" time.

Input/Output Control is the technique that has been widely used to indicate to management if decisions made concerning the placement of men and machines were executed and were the right decisions. If not, corrective action can then be taken. Another technique which can help identify if the "right" number of hours are being worked is called the "Ideal/Current Booking Rate".[4] By comparing the Ideal to the Current, management can determine if changes in men or machines are needed.

With these tools, it would appear that controlling the shop floor would be a manageable task. Unfortunately, there is a gap between what we know and how well we apply these techniques.[5] If American business is to remain competitive in the future, we need to do a better job of bridging the gap.

The following sections describe how one company is controlling work orders on its' shop floor. But first, a discussion about the job shop environment and the "people-side" of manufacturing control systems.

JOB SHOP ENVIRONMENT

More than half of the manufacturing organizations in North America have developed a multipurpose factory called a "Job Shop". These factories are designed to manufacture a variety of products. To do this the factory is designed around the manufacturing process. The cut and form shop is in one area, the weld shop in another area, the machine shop in yet another area, and assembly in still another area. This results in a complex routing environment which is extremely difficult to schedule and control.

With a small investment any company can have the hardware and software required to control the shop floor. But without PEOPLE the software and hardware will control nothing. The difficulty is that what many people are doing today will have to change significantly. The operator and foreman will have to work without piles of work-in-process ahead of each work center. The general foreman and industrial engineers will have to design quick set-ups that support the manufacture of smaller lot sizes. Production Control will have to manage the flow of work through the shop and reduce the amount of expediting. Factory management will have to have a flexible work force that can be easily adjusted from one area to another. It must also recognize that using labor productivity ratings as a means of measuring labor efficiency is not as effective as measuring the on-time shipments. Organizations who make this change actually find that labor productivity improves.[6]

American business does not have a history of embracing changes. But change will be as critical to survival in the 1980's and 90's as proper management of cash flow. All levels of employees must learn to constantly try new ideas and concepts with the recognition that all changes will not fully succeed and additional changes may have to be made.

BACKGROUND

The remainder of this paper focuses on the changes made to control work orders on the shop floor at WABCO-Construction and Mining Equipment Group of American Standard, Inc. at their Peoria, Illinois facility. This group produces off-highway trucks from 35 to 250 ton capacity. This product is usually assembled to customer order but because of lead time requirements most components are ordered based upon forecasted requirements.

In July 1978 authorization was given to implement a new "Materials Management System". This system included a closed-loop MRPII system based upon purchased software. In June 1982 the loop was closed with the implementation of the Production Control Module. This module included Priority Dispatch and Capacity Requirements reports.[7] Since then the project emphasis has continued and additional improvements made to the system.

WORK ORDER CYCLE

To understand how we control work orders it is necessary to first review the complete cycle through which an order goes. (See Figure 1) To control a work order there are seven statuses at which the order can be scrutinized. Each status is date oriented. These dates are calculated by back scheduling from the MRP calculated due date by the length of the production lead time, then the picking lead time, the releasing lead time and the firming lead time.

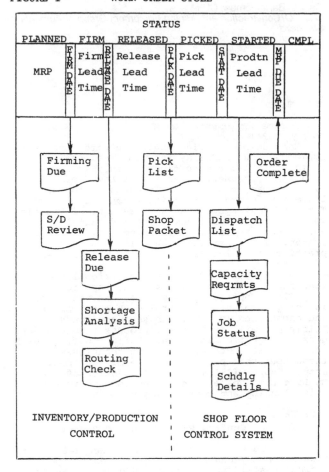

FIGURE 1   WORK ORDER CYCLE

The first status occurs while MRP is controlling the quantity and the due date within the parameters allowed by the parts' order policies. When the planning date equals the firming date a Supply/Demand Review report on the part is printed along with a listing of orders due for "Firming". This list is then used as a turnaround document for batch updating of the status of the work order. A listing of orders for which no component parts are found is also printed. This indicates that a possible Bill of Material error has happened. Prior to "Firming" the order the Planner/Scheduler reviews the inventory policies, order quantity and the possibility of combining orders to reduce set-up costs.

Once an order is "Firmed", MRP can not change the order quatity or the component part linkages. A review of the routing is then initiated by sending a copy to the Routing Department. After it has been reviewed and updated, if necessary, the status on the order is batch updated to the next status.

When the planning date equals the releasing date and the order has been "Firmed" an "Order Due for Releasing" message is printed. The Planner/Scheduler reviews the order for material or component shortages and then releases the order to the shop once any shortages have been rectified. At this point, shop documentation is prepared and job packets distributed to the shop. The control of the work order now passes to the Production Control System which is discussed in the section below on "Priority Control".

Although the PC system is controlling the order additional status updates are transmitted to the Inventory Control System. When labor is first reported to the work order the status is changed to a "Started" status. Then when the quantity remaining at the last operation with labor units is zero, the production operation details are eliminated and the status changed to "Complete". The order is not removed from the data base until a document from the dispatching system is received indicating that all operations are complete.

The next five sections describe some of the functions performed by management and employees to control work orders while they are on the shop floor.

PRIORITY PLANNING

Demand Management

A group of Order Analysts review customer orders and major component schedules. They are responsible for the management of the upper level independent demands and seperately scheduled items. Working from a Master Schedule each analyst is responsible for a specific type of order, i.e. Service Parts. Orders for the seperately scheduled items are not rescheduled by MRP if their status is "Firm" or greater. This allows the analyst to control the due dates, order quantities and component requirements on these items.

Rescheduling Assumption

One of the strengths of the system is an automatic rescheduling feature for work orders. With a Bill of Material seven to eleven levels deep and running MRP once a day, it takes seven to eleven days to effect an upper level schedule change to work orders for parts at the lowest levels. To overcome this time lag after MRP is run at each level a rescheduling program automatically reschedules the due date on work orders for parts at that level. These, in turn, revise their demand dates on their components where MRP recalculates the requirements. This process continues through all the levels until all work orders are rescheduled. These new due dates are then used to produce Priority Dispatch Lists and Capacity Requirements that are valid and timely.

PRIORITY CONTROL

Supply Management

The Planner/Scheduler is assigned to a department(s) and is responsible for the complete Work Order Cycle of all parts whose first operation is in one of their assigned departments. This provides accountability when an item is not completed on time or when an order encounters other difficulties. There is one person who is responsible for the order from beginning to end.

Work Order Control

A previous section has described the seven statuses through which a work order passes. In addition to these a work order on the shop floor is subject to additional scrutiny by both Production Control and Factory Management, especially if it is not progressing according to schedule.

Because the Planner/Schedulers are reviewing each work order for shortages prior to releasing, any work order required for an upper level order and not completed on time will have corrective action taken prior to its' parent order release. This approach keeps attention focused at all levels not just the end item level. In addition, since each Order Analyst is responsible for a group of Customer Orders, they are constantly reviewing work orders and working with the Planner to correct any orders falling behind schedule. All of this effort attempts to release work orders to the shop in a timely fashion so that they can complete the item on schedule. (See Figures 2,3&4)

Work orders are also controlled by an on-line data collection system which is discussed in a seperate section below and by a shop management system which is described in the following section.

FIGURE 2   RELEASING DUE

ORDER NO	DATE	QTY	DESCRPT	DIS PT
LE68709035	06 10 83	10	Plate	55B120
SJ8908898	06 11 83	5	Rod	65G090
TK3827865	06 11 83	25	Tube	65K899
TK4566899	06 11 83	150	Sq Cut	45M900
JG8655999	06 15 83	30	Pin	45M060
TD4534564	06 15 83	5	Wheel	50D004
JG6753987	06 20 83	20	Round	50D004

FIGURE 3   SHORTAGE ANALYSIS

PART NO	D/S ORDER	DUE DATE	QUANTITY DMD	QUANTITY SPLY
TL5409	FB223329758	08 19 83	2*	
5 OH	FB223435263	08 20 83	2*	
	ARPA00110567	08 23 83	12	
	TL540945363	08 23 83		20
	FB223435264	08 25 83	4	
VD7586	FB223329758	08 19 83	1*	
2 OH	FB223435263	08 20 83	1*	
	FB223435264	08 25 83	2	
	PORD00P23433	08 26 83		10

FIGURE 4   COMPLETION OVERDUE

ORDER NO	DUE DATE	DESCRPT	QTY OS	DIS PT
SVPT004090	06 20 83	Spacer	10	600000
SVPT011221	06 21 83	Fan	5	100000
SVPT093345	06 25 83	Flange	1200	65P020
SVPT087732	06 30 83	Pad	200	55K080
SVPT546644	06 30 83	Valve	20	65J002

Shop Management Responsibility

A critical part of work order priority control on the shop floor is the responsibility that factory management has in getting the work done on time. To accomplish this task, they work from several reports.

The primary report is the "Priority Dispatch List". (See Figure 5) This is a listing in priority sequence by work center of orders scheduled through the center over a specified horizon. From this report the foreman assigns work to the operator and takes any required action such as requesting tooling. The foreman marks on this list any pertinent information concerning the order (i.e. working, waiting on tooling, complete). An additional feature of this report is that it tells the foreman the work center where each order is currently working. This allows him to "pull" the order into his department.

FIGURE 5   PRIORITY DISPATCH LIST

WORK CNTR:5050		QUANTITY		TIME	REQRD	CURNT
ORDER NO	OP	OS	AVAL	RUN	AVAL	CNTR
TK449423743	05	6	5	2.4	2.0	1005065
TB545834563	05	10	0	12.0	0.0	1006333
TV095645332	10	20	20	20.0	20.0	1005050
TV095645332	15	20	0	15.0	0.0	1005050

Another report that is used by the foreman is an abbreviated microfiche copy of the released work order data base. This gives him an overall view of the operation status of a work order from which he can make decisions regarding possible work availability. (See Figure 6)

FIGURE 6   JOB STATUS REPORT

ORDER NO	DESCRPT	QTY	ROUTING/CMPLT
TN61425272	Plate	12	100-12,100-12,100-12,315-00,066-00
TM97295344	Bar	10	066-05,334-00,334-00,066-00

Finally, a prioritized abbreviated released work order data base is printed for the Plant Manager, Superintendents, and General Foremen. This report carries a last labor reported date. If there is no labor reported within a specified time frame the Superintendent or General Foreman will investigate and take corrective action. If there is no labor within a slightly longer time frame, the Plant Manager will contact the Superintendent or General Foreman requesting that corrective action be taken. This usually insures that the order starts moving again. (See Figure 7)

FIGURE 7   JOB STATUS PRIORITY

ORDER NO	DESCRPT	QTY	LAST LBR
TL37567471	Brkt	74	08 04 83
	100-74,100-74,315-00,318-00,066-00		
TK77714536	Plate	50	06 30 83
	100-50,101-00,315-00,066-00		
JG89527508	Tube	10	08 04 83
	315-00,318-00,319-00,066-00		

In the last few years, shop supervision has come to live by the following rule: "It's your responsibility until it leaves your department." It is this attitude that helps to improve work order control on the shop floor.

CAPACITY PLANNING

There are three levels of capacity planning. First a rough-cut plan is laid out by Production Planning. This report is based upon a time-phased estimate of labor units required to produce base model equipment with factoring to account for additional load such as service parts requirements. Planning uses this report to adjust their long-term production schedules. (See Figure 8)

FIGURE 8   ROUGH-CUT CAPACITY REQUIREMENTS

DEPT	01	02	03	04	05	06	07
100	2890	3390	3233	3380	4890	5680	6580
120	560	600	670	550	480	700	890
124	7680	7880	6740	5600	6500	7850	7970
315	2150	2450	3120	3320	3415	3555	4100
TOTAL	10679	14320	13763	12850	15285	17785	19540

At the second level a capacity report is produced as part of the MRPII system. This report has a three month horizon and is used by Production Control and the General Foremen to plan manpower and machine requirements. The report is divided into three separate sets of time buckets. The first grouping is four-five day buckets. This allows for close monitoring of load for scheduling overtime and shifting existing manpower. The second grouping is three-ten day buckets. This allows management to view capacity requirements that determine our future manpower needs. The last grouping is two-twenty day buckets which gives management an indication of future trends. A special feature of this report is that work centers are combined based upon labor groups. This facilitates calculating staffing requirements and transfers between work centers within the same group. (See Figure 9)

FIGURE 9   CAPACITY REQUIREMENTS

DEPT WKCT		08/05	08/12	08/19	08/26	09/02
100 5050						
	Load	250	240	180	100	300
	Lbr Capc	200	200	200	200	400
	Mach Capc	400	400	400	400	400
	Lbr Cum Dev	50-	90-	70-	30	130
	Mac Cum Dev	150	310	530	830	930

Finally, at the end of each work center schedule is a summary total of set-up hours, run hours, and work available hours. (See Figure 10)

FIGURE 10   SCHEDULING DETAILS
WORK CNTR:3952   HORIZON FROM:081283

		QUANTITY			TO:083083
ORDER NO	OP	OS	AVAL	STRT DATE	CURNT CNTR
TK67898283	25	10	05	08 12 83	100 5650
JG67589484	30	20	0	08 15 83	315 6765
TJ78905644	20	50	50	08 22 83	315 3952
JG98776253	30	5	5	08 30 83	315 3952

Because of the ability to control and reschedule priorities on all work orders in a single processing run the capacity reports reflect the the latest schedule changes for all work centers. This gives the system current valid capacity requirements.

CAPACITY CONTROL

A weekly review of the capacity reports is held with each General Foreman, his Foremen, Production Control and any other individuals as required. During this half-hour meeting, changes to labor capacities are discussed and agreed upon, changes to work center factors are communicated, possible bottleneck work centers acted upon (See Figure 11) and other items concerning the production plan for the week are discussed. At the next weekly meeting action agreed upon the prior week is reviewed and any additional changes agreed upon. In this manner capacity is continuously monitored and follow-up action instituted.

FIGURE 11   PRIORITY DISPATCH CAPACITY REQ

		TIMES REQUIRED		
PRIORITY	SET-UP	RUN	TOTAL	AVAIL
LESS THAN 0	40.00	86.00	146.00	76.00
BTWN 0 AND 1	5.65	32.80	38.45	26.45
GRTR THAN 1	12.58	53.60	66.18	10.90

NOTE: Figures 2 through 11 are representations of actual reports which contain additional detail.

DATA COLLECTION

The Shop Floor Control System described above is supported by an on-line data collection system for time and attendance reporting and labor reporting. This system is integrated with the host system. There are thirty-three terminals on the shop floor and two CRT's.

All released work orders are on this system including production, tooling, maintenance and expense jobs. Depending upon the type of job, a series of validations occur as labor is reported. For example, an employee reporting production labor must have a valid badge, work order number, operation number, work center(asset) number, and the quantity reported must not exceed the total authorized or the quantity reported at the prior operation. There are similar validations for other types of jobs. For production and many standard expense jobs prepunched cards are provided. If necessary routines are available to key-in data.

The system also has several update capabilities. Work orders can be changed, deleted or added on-line. Fields that can be changed include: for operation detail--operation number, operation description, department, bay or location, work center, scrap quantity, run units, set-up units, and rework indicator; for header detail--order status part description, unit of measure, authorized quantity, due date, start date, order account code, job number, job dash, total scrap quantity, total completed quantity, rework indicator and rework department charged. In addition to these fields, the foreman has the ability to do limited inquiry and updates through the data collection terminal.

Besides having production work orders on the system, all "Time-Sheet" operation details also are on the system with many of the same validation checks and update characteristics listed in the above section.(A "TS" operation breaks a long operation into measureable elements.)

This on-line, updateable system has provided for a level of data integrity without which the Shop Floor Control System would only be partially successful. It is on-line data collection that has closed the loop on work order control on the shop floor.

FUTURE FEATURES

Although this system has improved managements' control of the shop floor, there are several areas that can be improved. First, to improve our priority planning, a method of calculating slack time through all levels of the Bill of Material needs to be developed. This will give orders required for current shipments priority over orders for components for future shipments. Second an operation sequencing technique needs to be implemented. This will give better visibility of potential "bottleneck" work centers so correcting action can be taken. Third, the on-line data collection system needs to be expanded to capture material movement reporting. This will enable the foremen to have information as to what is currently in queue at each work center and it will give management more information regarding material handling work loads and performance. Fourth, maintaining "shop paper" and an electronic data system is a redundacy that needs to be eliminated. This will require additional hardware and software support but will provide cost savings in personnel and clerical expenses while providing more accurate information. Finally, management needs to have improved reporting of areas that deviate from planned parameters. Reports described in the first section on Priority Control (i.e. Number of Days of Overdue Load) will eliminate much of the clerical effort now done by management while providing more consistent information.

SUMMARY

The "Key Point" to remember when developing a Shop Floor Control System to support an MRPII system is that it must provide the shop with:

- CURRENT VALID PRIORITIES
- CURRENT VALID CAPACITY REQUIREMENTS
- ON-LINE INQUIRY
- MANAGEMENT CONTROL MECHANISMS
- FEEDBACK MECHANISMS

In short, it must provide shop supervision with the current information they need to do their job and a means to alter the plan if required.

REMEMBER--
SHOP MANAGEMENT WORKS IN A REAL WORLD.
IF A SHOP FLOOR CONTROL SYSTEM IS TO
WORK IN THIS SAME ENVIRONMENT,
IT MUST PROVIDE THE INFORMATION AND
FEEDBACK MECHANISMS REQUIRED
OTHERWISE INFORMAL SYSTEMS WILL DEVELOP
TO TAKEOVER WHERE THE FORMAL SYSTEM HAS
FAILED.

REFERENCES

[1]Wight, Oliver W., Production and Inventory Management in the Computer Age, CBI Publishing Company, Inc., Boston, Massachusetts, 1974.

[2]Gue, Frank, "Shop Floor Control/Capacity Planning in a Job Shop", American Production and Inventory Control Society, Mid American Seminar and Technical Exhibit, 1983 Conference Proceedings, p.43.

[3]Wight, op. cit., p. 124.

[4]Gue, op. cit., p. 45.

[5]Lankford, Ray, "Job Shop Scheduling: A Case Study", American Production and Inventory Control Society, 1982 Conference Proceedings, p. 97.

[6]Gue, op. cit., p. 46.

[7]Bartholomew, Gary L., "Controlling the Shop Floor from MRP to CRP-A Case Study", American Production and Inventory Control Society, 1982 Conference Proceedings, p. 411.

ABOUT THE AUTHOR

Gary Bartholomew is Manager of Production Control and Scheduling at WABCO-Construction and Mining Equipment Group of American Standard. He has a BS degree from Bradley University and a Master's degree from the University of Illinois. While at WABCO he has been a Foreman, General Foreman, and Project Manager. He is currently teaching evening classes in the Business School at Illinois Central College.

Reprinted from the APICS *1984 Conference Proceedings.*

ON-LINE COMPUTERIZED SHOP FLOOR CONTROL—
A PRACTICAL SOLUTION FOR EXECUTING THE
MANUFACTURING PLAN

Wesley J. Froehlich, CPIM
Burroughs Corporation

OBJECTIVE

The objective of this presentation is for the author to share his experiences as a Project Manager responsible for the development of a wide-ranging application software system specifically designed to execute a manufacturing plan in the factory on a timely basis and to monitor the progress of work orders through the production facilities. It will cover the characteristics and detail functionality of an on-line, data base oriented solution to shop floor control that could support virtually all areas of plant operation and provide manufacturing management with the information necessary to more effectively control factory resources.

Functionally, the On-Line Computerized Shop Floor Control System, hereafter referred to as the System, was a totally integrated application divided into eight major application modules:
- Order Scheduling
- Order Release
- Production Reporting
- Order Monitoring
- Time and Attendance Reporting
- Work Planning and Assignments
- Performance Monitoring
- Material Control

These interactive modules were related to each other. They shared a common data base--one set of data used by all functional departments and serving as the foundation for operational control on the factory floor. Each of these modules will be discussed in more detail.

ORDER SCHEDULING

To meet a production plan, work in the factory must be scheduled and controlled effectively. Order Scheduling helped determine capacity needs and provided detailed operation scheduling. In addition, Order Scheduling allowed for replanning --as priorities continually change, the System was flexible enough to reschedule either the complete order or individual operations.

Order Scheduling Transactions

Determining capacity needs and scheduling of work could easily be accomplished by using:
- Update Transaction: established the foundation for the order scheduling process. Work order, operations and work center data could be added, modified or deleted.
- Backward Scheduling Transaction: started with the order due date from the planning system or as specified by the production planner. The System calculated the "date" for starting the order by subtracting the sum of the operation lead times from the order due date. In addition, start and due date of each operation was determined.
- Priority Scheduling Transaction: provided the capability to review the shop's work load in a "what if" mode. The System maintained a separate trigger file which contained the necessary data to model the work-load environment on the shop floor as changes to the due dates of orders were made. In this manner, it was possible to assess the effect of rescheduling orders and to make changes to status of work centers without disrupting the current system data base.

Order Scheduling Displays

Order Scheduling provided the following displays and reports for people responsible for planning work into the shop and maintaing work schedules:
- Work Order Schedules: based on due dates and operation lead times.
- Work Center Loads: schedules loaded onto individual work centers showing the capacity requirements for the planning horizon.
- Maintenance Results: newly created, or modified existing, work order, operation or work center records.

ORDER RELEASE

Order Release provided the connection between the inventory management and the System. The primary output of the inventory management system consisted of planned orders. The function of Order Release was to change the status of the order from "planned" to "released".

The intent of Order Release was for the release of work orders only when needed material was available. The result was to minimize the number of orders physically staged, to reduce production lead times caused by lack of material and to reserve material on a priority basis.

Order Release Transactions

Order Release identified planned orders to the plant floor with sufficient time to meet delivery schedules. It provided the means to:
- Determine Orders to be Released: scanned the planned orders and determined which items were candidates for release by the production planner.
- Check Component Availability: checked inventory records for material held in central stores locations, warehouses, bins and other stocking locations.
- Change Order Status: status of the order changed from "planned" to "released" in the System data base.
- Reserve (Allocate) Material: required components were reserved to specific released orders.
- Produce Shop Paper: created the "shop packet" accompanying a released order on the shop floor.

Order Release Displays

The System provided the following displays and reports during Order Release:
- Planned Orders: those planned orders subject to production planner review were displayed to ensure that the orders were released on schedule in an orderly fashion while neither overloading the shop floor nor requiring expediting.
- Material Requirements: a check of component availability before orders were released to determine what required materials were physically available and where, and possible creation of a shortage list.
- Work Order Reservations: depicted what materials had been committed to previously released work orders.
- Shop Documentation: created the following required documentation to accompany the released order:
  - Routing (Work Order Operation) List
  - Kit Picking List
  - Engineering Drawing List
  - Work Order/Operation Reporting Cards
  - Material Move Tickets

PRODUCTION REPORTING

A key module of the System was the Production Reporting Module, which provided timely and accurate order progress information for improved control of jobs on the shop floor.

Production Reporting Transactions

Using easy-to-operate terminals at or near their work areas, employees could report the various transactions necessary to control work in process. These transaction included:

- **Setup**: when setup personnel are ready to start a new job, they could select the next highest priority job available and inform the System of the beginning of setup activity. On completion of setup, setup personnel perform a "setup end" transaction.
- **Part and Assembly Production**: before an employee began working on a job, the System was informed that the operator was beginning this activity. When an operation is completed, the operator notifies the System by a "processing complete" transaction. Under certain circumstances, it is necessary to enter a "processing partially completed" transaction even though work on the operation continues, for example, end of shift. This is also used on long-running jobs where some of the completed parts are moved to the next operation and work is begun on them (overlapped operations).
- **Job Completed**: the completion of an operation is indicated to the System by the operator recording a "processing completed" transaction.
- **Scrap**: the System provided the capability to report scrap after the operation was completed.
- **Rework**: in a manufacturing environment it is often necessary to record the activity of reworking parts. The recording of rework in the System was done in the same manner as in recording part production activity.
- **Non-Production Activities**: during the performance of a job in a plant, a situation could occur to cause an interruption for some period of time. These needed to be recorded in the System because they adversely affect efficiency. There are three types of interruption: (1) those that relate to the job such as waiting for materials, etc.; (2) those that relate to the work station such as machine trouble; (3) and those that relate to the employee such as medical, etc. The transaction for non-production activities consisted of entering the appropriate transaction code. To restart the operation, normal operation reporting transactions were used.

The System accumulated labor and machine hours for payroll and cost purposes as well as for shop efficiency reporting. All transactions were edited for completeness, accuracy and reasonableness.

Production Reporting Displays

The following displays provided an up-to-date status of all work order operations reported from the factory:

- **Operation Status**: a list of all operations sorted by work order number, based on the most current activity status code. In this manner, it was possible to get an overview of current shop activities. The activity status code allowed displaying all operations which had the same status (material at work center, setup started, setup completed, processing started, processing partially completed and processing completed).
- **Operations Affected by Scrap Reason**: at operation reporting time, employees reported a scrap quantity and the reason (scrap reason code). These codes could be used to display a list of all operations, sorted in work order sequence, which had caused one type of scrap within a specified time period. In addition, the System provided a summary of all operations which had

produced any type of scrap over a specified time period.

ORDER MONITORING

Order Monitoring provided for the ability to keep work order information up-to-date. It also provided for the ability to inquire into the current status of any work order and to close the work order after all operations were completed.

Order Monitoring Transactions

- **Modify Work Orders**: in view of the fact that many changes can affect a job between the time it is released to the shop and before it is completed, the System provided the ability to handle:
  - Routing changes
  - Engineering changes
  - Order quantity changes
  - Lot splitting
  - Reworking
  - Order concellations
- **Monitor Work Order Status**: kept track of the status of all orders as they moved through the plant and highlighted those orders that were behind schedule so that corrective action could be taken. Also, facilitated better customer service by enabling prompt and accurate answers to customer inquiries concerning the status and likely completion dates of orders.
- **Furnish Work Order History**: periodically reviewed all completed orders, initiated appropriate closing information and deleted the records from the active work order file. Information about closed orders could be made available to Accounting and other functional departments.

Order Monitoring Displays

The following displays in the Order Monitoring module covered the processing of changes to the work order, inquiry into its status, and the final processing of a completed work order:

- **Changed Work Orders**: the data base could be updated with changes to released work orders that were initiated by functional departments (cost, engineering, etc.) and become effective consistent with change order policy.
- **Copied Work Orders**: this function was very important if there were repeat orders, similar type orders, split orders or orders for replacement parts. It made the time consuming data entry operation for these types of transactions unnecessary.
- **Work Order Status**: the status of all work orders was maintained by the System and was available, on request, to any authorized person who needed the information.
- **Completed Work Orders**: when all operations were completed, closed orders could be displayed or listed and the information communicated to Accounting and other functional departments. The completed orders could be deleted from the active file.

TIME AND ATTENDANCE REPORTING

The System provided real-time time and attendnace reporting for recording each employee's time at work. With Time and Attendance Reporting, the user could reduce the amount of clerical time required to keep track of employee and team attendance. It furnished vital information for payroll and cost purposes, for shift planning and analysis and for shop efficiency reporting.

Time and Attendance Transactions

Specific Time and Attendance transactions were:

- **Identify an Employee or Team**: the System

assumed that each employee or team could be identified with a badge, permanently encoded or punched, with his or their number. Shop floor terminals read these badges and transmitted the employee/team identification data to the System.

- Record the Arrival/Departure for Each Employee or Team: provided for the clocking in on a shop floor terminal at the beginning of a shift, and clocking out at the end of a shift. It also provided for the clocking out and in again upon departure and return to the plant during the shift.
- Record Individual and/or Team Attendance Plan By Shift: for workload planning purposes, the System included a transaction to be used to enter future dates for scheduled absences, such as vacations.
- Record An Actual Absence By Employee: when an employee was absent, the System provided for that information to be entered for workload planning as well as employee records and payroll activity.
- Calculate the Total Time at Work By Employees: the System could be used to adjust the actual arrival and departure time to agree with normal shift start/stop time. Elapsed attendance time is then calculated, which could be balanced with the detailed transactions accumulated in Production Reporting.

Time and Attendance Reporting Displays

The System provided a choice of time and attendance displays as follows:

- Employee Attendance/Absentee Data: Showed which employees are available for work per shift by department, or by shift for the entire plant.
- Clock-In/Clock/Out Transactions: Provided a display of each employee's clock-in/clock-out transactions to satisfy any inquiry by plant supervisors.

WORK PLANNING AND ASSIGNMENTS

Effective planning of jobs and their timely release into the shop requires up-to-date information along with the means for transmitting changes quickly and easily from the shop floor to production control and management personnel. With the System, production supervisors and schedulers could use on-line terminal devices to enter or review the following:

- Activity status of machines and employees: Decisions can be made on shifting work based on employee availability, machine downtime, and other non-production activities.
- Work sequence displays or listings for each work center: Shows the prioritized jobs presently at the work center and those scheduled to arrive in the next few days.
- Assignment of machines or workers (or teams) to individual production operations: Allows the foreman to meet overall scheduling and work load leveling objectives.

Work Planning and Assignments Transactions

Work Planning and Assignments provided for the planning of work and its release into the shop. Included in this module are the following transactions:

- Employee Status: at shift start, or periodically throughout the day, the department supervisor or scheduler could request the status of a particular employee or the status of all employees in the department. In addition, the supervisor or scheduler could use the shop floor terminal to review all employees engaged in a particular activity.
- Machine Status: the System provided the capability to retrieve the status of a particular machine, or machines, in the same manner as described for determining employee status. Either the status of a particular machine, or the status of all machines in a work center could be requested. Furthermore, a global inquiry for all machines with the same status could be requested.
- Dispatching Jobs to a Work Center: A work sequence (dispatch) list is available in the System and can be displayed for each work center. It lists, in priority sequence, all of the work orders by operations now in the work center or in transit to the work center. Up to five previous work centers are also noted on the dispatch list.
- Assign Employee/Machine to an Operation: This transaction enables the supervisor to assign or reassign an employee or machine to an operation by using an on-line terminal. If team assignments are required, the supervisor must first assign or reassign the employees to a team and then assign the team to an operation as described above.

Work Planning and Assignments Displays

The System provided a variety of displays which showed the current shop floor environment as well as employee and machine assignments. Thus, the user could be constantly abreast of job progression, resource utilization and the differences between planned and actual shop floor activities. Displays available to choose from are:

- Shop Floor Organization: the System provided a series of displays for providing up-to-date information about the plant organizational structure. The user could:
  - Display all departments, work centers or work stations (machines) defined in the factory.
  - Display all employees, teams or shifts defined in the factory.
- Dispatch List: another major System function was to provide a work sequence (dispatch) list for each foreman to help him assign jobs in the proper priority sequence.
- Employee Status/Machine Status: the System furnished employee/machine status available on-line as needed. With this information immediately available, the production supervisors could be able to react to change much more quickly and could realize assignment of employees and machines much easier.

PERFORMANCE MONITORING

The Performance Monitoring module provided, on demand, a wide range of displays and reports to assist the supervisors in measuring their department's performance. These important information tools offered a means to assist in analyzing productivity efficiency and pinpointing areas where attention and action were needed.

Performance Monitoring Transactions

The transactions included some of the traditional methods for measuring the productivity of a department. These were:

- Employee Productivity: the department supervisor was able to inquire as to the work activities of a particular employee or for the entire department.
- Work Center Utilization: the System provided analysis of work center workload (actual utilization versus planned availability) providing the department supervisors with a tool to measure performance to plan in the shop.

Performance Monitoring Displays

Performance Monitoring displays provided for the analysis of work center utilization and department and employee productivity reporting. Examples were:

- Daily Labor Acitivity: provided a summary of work activities for a shift by department
- Work Center Utilization: provided information pertaining to work center's capacity. How busy are your machines and where are the "bottlenecks" were questions answered here.
- Employee/Machine Activity History: provided an analysis, for a time period specified by the user, of all activities performed by the employees of a department and for each work center and work station of a department.

MATERIAL CONTROL

Two key elements of all shop floor operations addressed by the System were:

- Location and status control of all production inventories held in stores.
- Control of movement of work-in-process inventories.

Up-to-the-minute information of what is "physically on the shelves" was available with the Material Control module. To accomplish this, the System provided the power required to maintain and monitor inventory data.

Material Control Transactions

- Update: the user was provided with all of the transactions for rapidly creating, displaying, changing and deleting of material data records. The following were easily maintained:
  - Parts data: for each manufactured, assembled or purchased part.
  - Work-in-process data: for each released work order in the System.
  - Location data: for physical locations such as building, plants or warehouses, and for item stocking data, such as bins.
- Material Reporting: for people who are responsible for keeping control of inventories, having current inventory status information and the means for keeping records accurate is of paramount importance The material reporting transactions which could be entered into an on-line terminal and interactively processed by the System were:
  - Issues and Receipts: receipts into stock from sources such as inspection and production, and issue from stock to the factory or customers.
  - Transfers Between Locations: transfers from one location within the company (building, plant, warehouse, etc.) to another, or between bin locations.
  - Cycle Counts: performing inventory counts on a periodic or cyclical basis.
  - Inventory Adjustments: adjustments to inventory record balances to reflect actual quantities on hand, so that you can get a valid stock status reading at any time.

Material Control Displays

The following are examples of Material Control lists and reports that could be displayed at any time with up-to-the-minute accuracy:

- Updated Data: Newly created, or modified existing, parts data, work-in-process material data or location data.
- Inventory Status: on-hand, on-order, reservations--determine material availability.
- Inventory Locations: report of all inventory locations (bins, warehouses, etc.) by part number.

- Shortages: highlighted--for a part or for a work order.
- Cycle Count: display of all parts due or overdue to be cycle counted. Also, capability for entering results of latest physical inventory count.

SUMMARY

In summary, let's review what an On-Line Computerized Shop Floor System can provide as tools to achieve better control of shop floor control activities:

- Up-to-date work order status providing...
  - Shorter lead times due to early awareness of bottlenecks requiring immediate attention
  - Improved communications with customers on expected delivery dates
  - Same status data available to all departments--sales, cost accounting, engineering, production control, inventory control, etc.
- Current and projected workload efficiency and utilization: considering personnel and facilities--to help plan, replan and optimize resource utilization through more efficient operations.
- On-going cost performance of work orders: tracking of actual cost performance to the estimate as it occurs--provides the ability if required, to make changes to improve the product's posture right then and there... not after the fact.
- Impact of Scheduling Changes: "What if" capability on the current plan to help in rescheduling, taking into account both employees and machines.
- A System designed for factory personnel: a practical solution for executing the manufacturing plan that was designed for factory operators recognizing that their primary function is concerned with their manufacturing duties and not shop floor reporting. Provided a man-machine interface that did not require data processing expertise.

ABOUT THE AUTHOR

Wesley J. Froehlich is a Senior Manufacturing Line of Business Consultant at Burroughs Corporation located in Radnor, Pennsylvania. In this capacity, he is responsible for the specification development of both new and enhanced manufacturing systems applications software.

Immediately prior to joining Burroughs, Mr. Froehlich's position was that of Manufacturing Industry Marketing Manager at Sperry Corporation Computer Systems where he was program manager responsible for the development of, and bringing to the marketplace, an on-line interactive shop floor control system.

Recipient of a Bachelor's Degree in Accounting from the University of Illinois, Mr. Froehlich has also undertaken graduate work in Industrial Management at Temple University. He is a Past President of the APICS Central Montgomery Chapter, was Publicity Director for Region IX and is currently the Assistant Vice President for that Region. In addition, Mr. Froehlich has served as General Chairman for Congress for Progress VIII, is recognized as a CPIM by APICS, and is a holder of the Data Processing Management Association Certificate in Data Processing.

Reprinted from *Production and Inventory Management*, Fourth Quarter, 1987.

A PROCEDURE FOR IMPLEMENTING INPUT/ OUTPUT CONTROL: A CASE STUDY

TIMOTHY D. FRY
Department of Management Science, College of Business Administration, University of South Carolina, Columbia, SC 29208

ALLEN E. SMITH
Department of Management, East Tennessee State University, Johnson City, TN 37614

Many manufacturers suffer from problems due to out-of-control lead times. These include poor customer service, long backlogs, inability to set realistic delivery dates, and excessive work-in-process (WIP) and finished goods inventory. The relationship of planned lead times to WIP has led to the popularization of the "Lead Time Syndrome." In [1], Oliver Wight explains that as planned lead times increase, orders are generated sooner, thus increasing backlogs in the shop. A means to control lead times, thus reducing the severity of the associated problems, are input/output (I/O) controls.

As explained by Wight, I/O can be stated simply as: the input to a shop in a given time period must be equal to or less than the output of the shop over the same time period. The key to I/O control is thus through the control of shop inputs. The easiest point to control such inputs is at the gateway operations, which are the first operations to be performed in the manufacture of a part [1]. It makes little sense to have large queues of WIP piling up after these gates. Therefore, if a queue at a particular downstream work center is building up, the gate to this work center should not continue producing work.

The remainder of this article will discuss a six-step procedure necessary for the implementation of I/O control. The method is demonstrated through a case study of the actual use of this procedure at a tool manufacturer.

ABC TOOL

ABC Tool is a southeastern manufacturer of various tools such as pliers, wrenches, adjustable wrenches, and various automotive tools such as torque wrenches. Yearly sales are about $25 million with an inventory of finished goods and WIP of $12 million. The plant layout is a typical job-shop layout where similar pro-

cessing is done in distinct areas. In two previous years, the profit and loss statement indicated that ABC Tool had lost hundreds of thousands of dollars. Inventory turns were averaging about one per year while customer service, measured as percent of dollars shipped on time, was below 75%. A backlog of orders existed in the plant of $1.2 million, with quoted lead times of about 120 days. Scrap and rework was high and was seldom worked on, since workers chose other easy jobs in order to increase their "earned hours." Earned hours was an efficiency measure used to determine the amount of actual output compared to expected output based on production standards. Production runs were typically twice the setup times, which resulted in a WIP inventory of over $5.2 million.

In an effort to reduce lead times, reduce inventories, and improve customer service, the management at ABC decided to implement simple I/O controls. It was decided that these controls would be tested on only one product line to evaluate the effectiveness of I/O before implementing in the entire shop. The product line chosen was pliers, which represented about 40% of total sales with a finished goods inventory of $1.4 million and a WIP inventory of $1.9 million. This product line was chosen due to the relatively standardized product flow. In Figure 1, a BOM and routing is presented for a typical plier, and in Figure 2 the routing is indicated on a partial plant layout diagram for the pliers product line.

A PROCEDURE FOR IMPLEMENTING I/O

The following six-step procedure was used at ABC Tool to implement I/O controls; any implementation of I/O would involve a similar, if not identical, procedure.

Step 1. Management must shift from local efficiency performance measures to global throughput measures. At ABC Tool, workers were being evaluated by their "earned hours" produced for the day—little thought was given to system throughput until quarterly financial statements became due. This led to a frequently

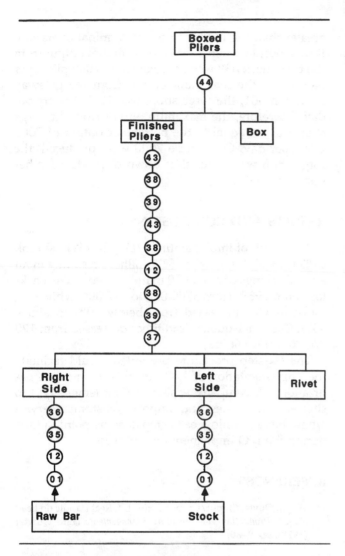

FIGURE 1: Sample BOM and routing

were found: at work station 038, where the pliers were edged and polished, and at work station 051, where dies were supplied for the various machining and stamping operations. A decision was made to eliminate the bottleneck at workcenter 051 by increasing the investment in dies. This made control easier, since only work center 038 remained a bottleneck.

Step 3. Set maximum inventory levels between work stations. At ABC Tool, this was accomplished by asking each work center foreman how much inventory he felt was necessary to insure that his work center wasn't starved. Whenever the inventory at a work center reached this level, the workers at the feeding station were then assigned to other work or sent home.

Step 4. Reduce production lot sizes. This had the direct effect of reducing inventory and allowing for a more level final assembly schedule. At ABC, where production runs were typically twice the setup time, the quantity produced was often greater than a year's

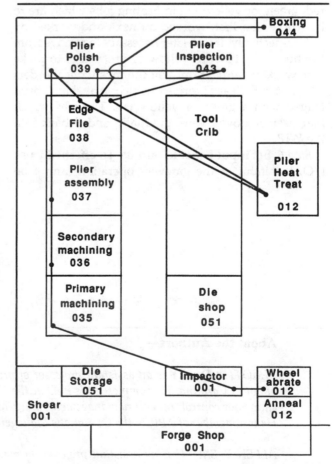

FIGURE 2: Plant layout

observed phenomenon in manufacturing firms called the "hockey stick," illustrated in Figure 3. As seen, throughput increased dramatically as the financial period end approached. During the early part of the period, performance was based on local efficiency measures and as a result, throughput suffered. As the end of the period approached, management emphasis shifted from worker efficiency to more global measures such as throughput. Thus, the main concern of management changed to getting the product out the door.

Step 2. Identify all bottlenecks to determine the maximum system throughput. This was accomplished by a careful analysis of the product routing to determine bottleneck work centers where the product was delayed most often. Bottleneck work centers generally have a higher-than-average WIP queue than nonbot-

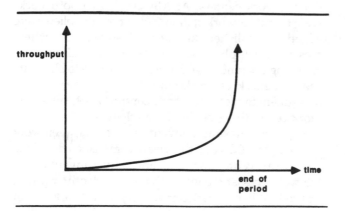

FIGURE 3: Hockey stick phenomenon

supply. It was decided that lot sizes would in all cases be less than a three-months' supply.

Step 5. Work only on the correct items. Workers tended to work on those items which increase their earned hours. At ABC, jobs were tagged with either a red, green, or yellow tag indicating jobs which are to be worked on first, worked on next, and worked on last, respectively. It was later necessary to remove from the floor all jobs with yellow or green tags to make sure workers worked only on the most critical orders and not the "easy" orders which may have been tagged with a green or yellow tag. The jobs which had been removed were gradually added back into the WIP.

Step 6. Set input equal to output. To effectively use I/O, the input at the gateway operation cannot be greater than the output from the terminal operation. It was found in Step 2 that the maximum output from the bottleneck 038 was approximately 7000 pliers per day, while the maximum output from the gateway operation 001, the forge shop, was 12,000 pliers per day. Therefore, the maximum output from the forge shop was set equal to the bottleneck output of 7000 pliers per day. Once these 7000 were produced, the forge shop was either shut down or produced other nonplier products.

RESULTS AND CONCLUSIONS

As a result of implementing I/O, pliers WIP shrank 42% from $1.9 million to $1.1 million, resulting in an annual savings of $200,000 in holding cost. The backlog shrank 93% from $700,000 to $47,000, while customer service increased from below 70% to above 90%. Customer-quoted lead times decreased from 120 days to under 60 days.

The six-step procedure presented would facilitate the implementation of I/O controls for many organizations. A company wishing to implement I/O to shorten lead times and improve customer service would have to follow each step at some point in time during the I/O implementation process.

REFERENCES

1. Wight, Oliver, "Input/Output Control, A Real Handle on Lead Time," *Production and Inventory Management,* Third Quarter (1970), pp. 9–30.

About the Authors—

TIMOTHY D. FRY is an assistant professor of production/operations management at the University of South Carolina. He completed his PhD at the University of Georgia. His research interests include shop floor control, inventory management, multi-objective scheduling, and production control systems. He is a member of APICS, the Operations Management Association, and the Decision Science Institute.

ALLEN E. SMITH is an assistant professor of management at East Tennessee State University. Allen is currently working on his PhD in management information systems from the University of South Carolina. His research interests include artificial intelligence in manufacturing, expert systems, flexible manufacturing systems, and computer-integrated manufacturing.

Reprinted from *Production and Inventory Management*, Vol. 12, No. 3 (1971).

DELIVERY AS PROMISED

R. DAVE GARWOOD

Mallinckrodt Chemical Works, St. Louis, Missouri

Looking for a way to reduce lead times and make delivery promises fact not fiction? The theory of many has been solidified into an action oriented solution — Input/Output Control. Is I/O Control difficult, complex, or require a computer? No, but it works! Reductions in lead times of 24 to 4 weeks have been made while significantly improving promised delivery date integrity.

In today's competitive markets, on-time delivery based on shorter lead times is a prime factor in selecting suppliers. Late delivery and long lead times are not tolerated. However, *you* must *depend on delivery as promised from your plant* and *Vendors* in order for you to meet *your promised delivery dates*! But, do they?

Are you plagued with any or all of these symptoms?

- 40 to 60% of the open orders are late.
- Vendors quote 12 week lead times but deliver in three (3) days when the pressure is applied.
- Your expediters do nothing but try to meet the latest reschedule.
- Lead times often extend 4 to 16 weeks and reschedules to promised delivery dates increase exponentially when business increases.

And Vendors beware! Some of you are using expensive and ultimately tragic solutions to these symptoms. If you are quoting longer lead times, prepare for a smaller share of the market.

The Real Problem — Lead Time Instability

Every time business increases delivery date integrity decreases and lead time emerges as the focal point for argument. A basic premise of every inventory system, statistical order point or material requirements planning, is to place replenishment orders to cover demand over the lead time. Lengthening of lead times force inventory systems to look at demand over a longer period and consequently place more orders. For example, if lead time increases from 8 weeks to 12 weeks, Inventory Control places the orders they normally would have placed to cover demand over the next 8 weeks, plus the demand over another 4 weeks. Result: Inventory Control is predicting further out in the future what they need (the additional 4 weeks) and getting more inaccurate than ever! Greater inaccuracy in the determination of what is really needed generates more expediting or rescheduling to correct for the inaccurate delivery dates and keep inventories under control. Meanwhile, the backlog increases and requests to further increase lead time arise. The problem is again amplified by Inventory Control increasing lead time and our favorite national pastime — finger pointing — goes into extra innings! Inventory Control points at Purchasing or the plant and says, "You aren't meeting our required delivery dates." The plant or Purchasing points to Inventory Control and says, "You aren't giving us the full lead time and furthermore you are expediting to improve delivery in less than the standard lead time." The finger-pointing continues, but little is accomplished in solving the *real problem – lead time instability*.

Solution – Control Backlog and Stabilize Lead Times

Lead time instability is a direct result of serious shortcomings in our planning and control. The *key* to *stabilizing* and *reducing lead times* is *control* and *reduction* of *backlog*. Input/Output Control is a technique to control backlog and provide the opportunity for the practitioner to solve one of our oldest ills – fluctuating lead times.

Input/Output Control addresses two problems separately – *Capacity* and *Priority*. First, a family of items or parts which require a common production area are identified and *Capacity Requirements* are projected for the *total group*. *Capacity is reserved* and manpower and equipment requirements are planned accordingly. Capacity is a production rate expressed in production units per time period. Production units must be a common denominator for the family of items or parts utilizing the same capacity but requiring different manufacturing times. Examples of production rates are pieces per week, molds per month or standard hours per week. Previously a backlog was crested to level the work load. You were left with limited flexibility to juggle the orders in backlog (or queue) as your requirements changed, and provided no means to plan for future increases or decreases in capacity requirements. Required capacity based on the size of the backlog is usually not appreciably increased until the backlog becomes excessively large and late orders pile up until *something must be done*. Second, reduce the lead time by draining most of the wait or queue time out of the total lead time – leaving only order preparation, manufacturing time and transit time. The backlog is shrunk to include only those orders in process in the plant. Third, select the input to match capacity from the family of items or parts with highest priority. The important point – *capacity is reserved* and *committed* but the selection of specific items – *priority determination* is not made until the last possible moment.

The Input and Output must match the capacity or backlog will increase. If the backlog is allowed to increase, the spiraling lead time problems – expediting, missed deliveries, etc. – will emerge. The Input must not be less than the capacity or a work shortage will occur and the plant or Vendor will retreat to their old habits of building a backlog for security. *Input/Output Control* is *working most effectively when capacity* is *correctly established* and *Inventory Control* is *pulling work ahead to avoid future peak loads*. At that point we have placed ourselves in the enviable position of acting to stay out of trouble in place of reacting to get out of trouble.

The fourth step is to monitor the Vendor's or Plant's performance. Output, measured in the same units of measure as Input, must be maintained at the planned level to avoid late deliveries and increased backlog. The four steps are repeated in a planning – replanning session every week, month, or whatever planning time cycle is selected.

Application – Input/Output Control at Fisher Controls

In July of 1969, Fisher Controls initiated a system utilizing the principles of Input/Output Control with a cast iron foundry. The program was started during a time when the foundry's lead time was increasing from 12 to 24 weeks. We were successful in holding an average 10 week lead time and have now reduced it to 4 weeks. Expediting has been reduced from daily phone calls from our Buyers to bi-monthly phone calls from the foundry. The program has since been expanded to cover 75% of our foundry purchases with equally good results.

The scheduling and capacity determination in our Vendor's foundry is centered around the molding operation; therefore, we project capacity requirements and measure both Input and Output in terms of molds per month. Since pattern equipment is often constructed to give more than one casting or piece per mold, a "Conversion Factor" in pieces per mold is determined for each part based on the current pattern equipment construction. All part numbers purchased from the Vendor are identified. After a mutual examination with the Vendor of our pattern equipment records, each part number is assigned to a molding area (production area) in which each part is made and recorded on an Input/Output Control Worksheet.

Figure No. 1 is an example of the Input/Output Control Worksheet. In this example, 34 parts are purchased from Vendor XYZ and molded in the Squeezer Line. The RATE – last six month's average usage per month – ranges from 0 to 510 per month. The Conversion Factors range from 1 to 5 pieces per mold. For example, Item 16 (Part No. 4L6918) has an average usage of 90 pieces per month or 45 (90 ÷ 2) molds per month.

At the end of each month the Input/Output Control Analyst examines the inventory status of each part number and determines the *anticipated* future requirements – quantity and timing over the planning horizon. The quantities are logged into the appropriate month on the Worksheet. Assume today is January 31. The Analyst totals in molds the projected (but not on order) requirements through March. If the total molds are less than March's capacity commitment (established from last month's projected requirement), the Analyst reaches out into the future time periods and pulls the requirements forward until the total commitment is filled. If the total required molds are greater than his capacity commitment established last month, he has four alternate courses of action:

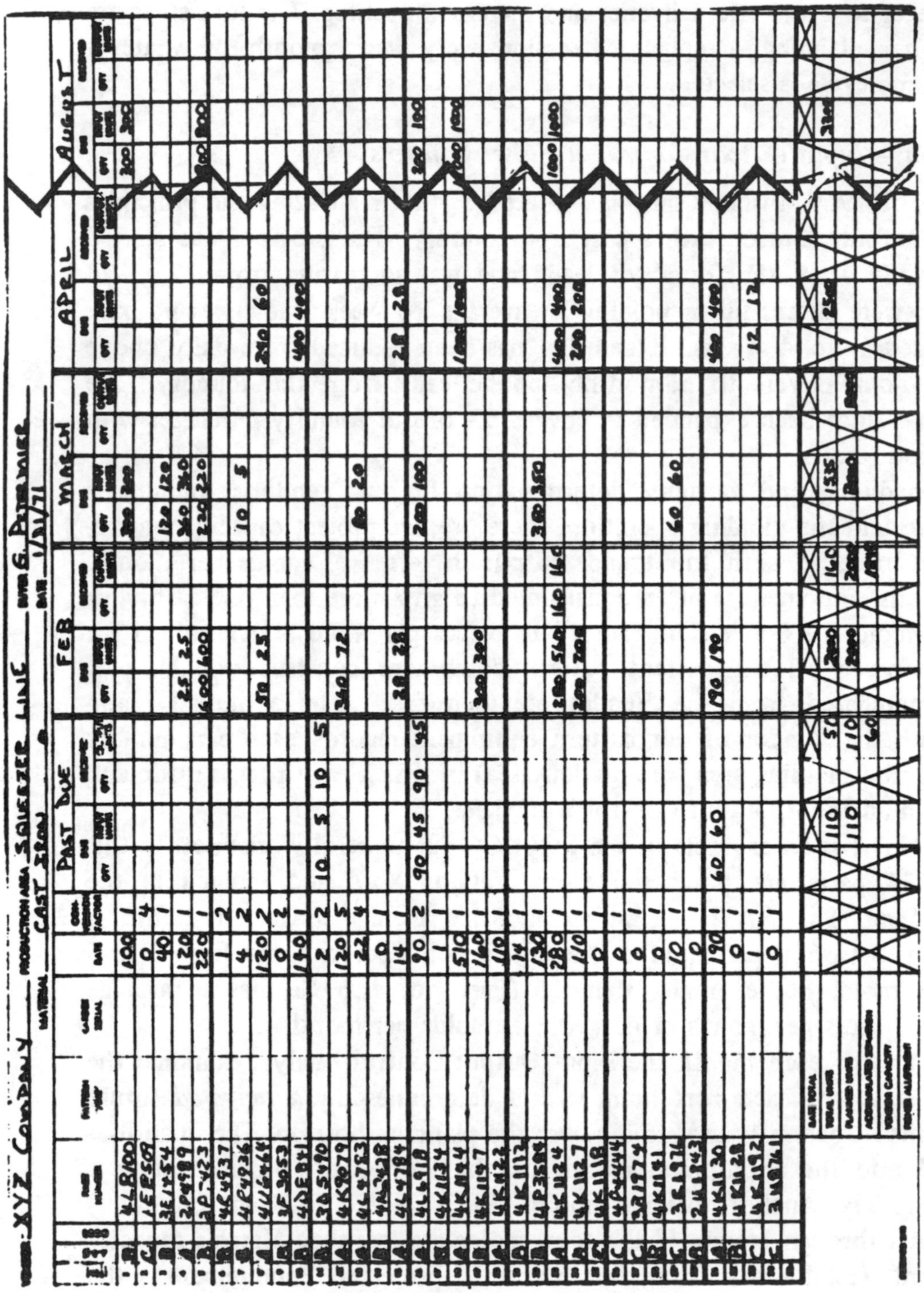

Figure 1. Input/Output Control Worksheet

1. He may select to order some of the parts required and notify the Inventory Planner of the parts which will not be ordered and have them make their future customer delivery commitments accordingly.
2. He may reduce the order quantity on some of the high volume parts, thus having some of all the parts as required and still not exceed his capacity commitment.
3. He may check with the Vendor and see if additional uncommitted capacity is available. In this case, it is the Vendor's choice to accept or reject the additional capacity request.
4. If alternate sources are available, he may shift his orders to the alternate source where committed but unused capacity is available.

After firm orders for specific parts are placed requesting delivery in March — a lead time of 4 to 8 weeks — the Analyst turns to *Planning April's capacity requirement*. April, May, June, July and August projected requirements are totalled and divided by 5. After weighing Marketing's general long range forecast and the average projected future requirements, the capacity commitment for April is established.

The historical results, current commitments and future plans are assembled in aggregate onto the Input/Output Control Summary — see Figure No. 2. After the Input/Output Control Analyst has placed purchase orders for delivery in March and established the capacity required for April, he tallies last month's receipts in molds and completes the accumulated deviation. The Analyst also forecasts but does not commit capacity for an additional six months. In Figure No. 2, the Vendor's required shipment (Output required for February) is 60 molds from past due orders plus 1840 molds due in February. The Input/Output Control Summary is signed by Fisher's Purchasing Buyer as official notification of capacity commitment and a copy forwarded to the Vendor along with purchase orders for parts requiring shipment in March. The Vendor examines the capacity required for April and confirms that he can meet our requirements by filling in 2000 under April on the Vendor Acknowledgment line. The Summary is signed by the Vendor Representative and a copy returned to Fisher acknowledging that the Vendor can meet our requirements. If the Vendor does not feel that he can meet our April capacity requirement, we negotiate with him until a mutually agreeable capacity commitment is reached.

During the current month (February) receipts from the Vendor are recorded by a Purchasing Clerk, converted to molds and totalled at the end of the month. During the last week of February the planning cycle repeats itself.

FISHER CONTROLS COMPANY

DATE __1-31-71__

PRODUCTION LINE __SQUEEZER LINE__   MATERIAL __CAST IRON__

PURSUANT TO THE INPUT/OUTPUT SCHEDULING AGREEMENT BETWEEN FISHER CONTROLS COMPANY AND __XYZ COMPANY__

THE FOLLOWING COMMITMENTS ARE IN EFFECT FOR THE MONTH OF __FEBRUARY__

PLANNING PERIOD	PAST DUE	PURCHASE ORDERS ISSUED		FIRM COMMITMENTS	FORECAST					
MONTH		FEB	MARCH	APRIL	MAY	JUNE	JULY	AUG	OCT	NOV
FISHER REQUIREMENTS		2000	2000	2000	2500	2500	3000	3000	3000	3000
VENDOR ACKNOWLEDGEMENT*		2000	2000	X						
ACCUMULATED DEVIATION		X	X	X						

	PAST DUE	FEB	MARCH	APRIL
ORDER PLACEMENTS	110	2000	2000	2000
MATERIAL RECEIPTS	50	160	0	
ACCUMULATED DEVIATION	60	1900		

←——— Next months anticipated placements

*Vendor to review Fisher requirements and reserve capacity for time periods and confirm their ability to fulfill requirements shown to Fisher within 5 days after receipt.

BUYER FISHER CONTROLS COMPANY

VENDOR COMMITMENT ACKNOWLEDGED BY

Figure 2. Input/Output Control Summary

A typical question is, "Why should I, the customer, smooth Input to my Vendor?" Examine Figure No. 3.

The numbers shown are the actual requirements to satisfy inventory needs for 65 different parts. Without

Month	May	June	July	Aug.	Sept.	Oct.	Total
Molds	260	680	0	460	200	800	2400

Figure 3. Projected Mold Requirements per Month

any Input Control, the inventory system would have required orders to be placed with requirements for 400 per month on the "average" but would have required receipts ranging from 0 to 800 in each month – all within the same lead time! Assume the lead time is 4 weeks. During May, purchase orders would have been placed which required a total of 680 molds. Assuming the Vendor had foresight to plan an average of 400 molds per month capacity, he would have reacted in June by producing 400 with the balance of 280 produced past due in July. In effect, he smoothed the Output by increasing the lead time on 280 molds to 8 weeks! The Input must be smoothed to control backlog and stabilize lead time by pulling load from the future peaks into current valleys.

A large family (65) of parts would intuitively indicate a random distribution of load; however, the production units (molds) per each part, are not randomly distributed over the 65 parts. Orders for some of the parts are in lot sizes of 10 molds, while others go as high as 200. Lot sizing causes the "lumps" in the load.

RESULTS: *Vendor's Viewpoint*

Vendors were initially reluctant to accept the Input/Output Control Program. The idea of a shorter lead time and less backlog is discomforting. It is diametrically opposed to a long-standing tradition – keep a 3 to 4 month backlog and get as much lead time as possible! However, after one or two months' experience with Input/Output Control, the Vendor becomes one of the system's biggest supporters. Look at the advantages for the Vendor. He doesn't need a short range forecast from his marketing department's crystal ball. He has a firm capacity commitment with zero deviation for three months into the future. He has a forecast beyond three months from the source of his future business – the customer's inventory system!

The Vendor isn't nearly as vulnerable to the unexpected surge of incoming orders demanding 150 to 200% of his capacity for delivery within the "standard" lead time. He isn't plagued with files upon files of open orders and the inevitable multiple reschedules which follow.

Most of our Vendors on the Input/Output Control program are now requesting their other customers to adopt the system and offer shorter lead times to entice them.

In Short – VENDORS LIKE IT!!

RESULTS: *Purchasing's Viewpoint*

The Buyer is relieved of the endless job of expediting hundreds of individual orders and gets an opportunity to BUY — negotiate better prices, better quality, develop new sources.

We have all read about and discussed vendor performance programs, but few have really developed any concise, impartial measure of Vendor delivery. Look at the special Note on Figure No. 4 indicating loss of sales due to past poor delivery performance.

Input/Output Control has added a new parameter to consider when sourcing parts — Capacity. Are your Vendor's facilities capable of meeting your required volumes? Now and in the future? What bargain do you *really* have if the Vendor can supply only 2/3 of your requirements? Before Input/Output Control it was nearly impossible to objectively evaluate this parameter. We usually resort to asking the salesman if he can meet our requirements. Did you ever meet a good salesman who turned down an order?

Gary Petermeier, Casting Buyer, stated the evaluation well, "I spend the same total time buying the same amount of castings, but now I get results. More time is spent planning and less reacting. In fact, before Input/Output Control, I called the foundries every day to expedite — now they call *me* twice a month. We are getting more *needed* material than ever before."

In Short — PURCHASING LIKES IT!!

RESULTS: *Inventory Control's Viewpoint*

Lead times are significantly *reduced*. When the inevitable forecast error is encountered, the Inventory Planner has a *faster recovery time* to restore inventory levels and meet customer requirements. He can react within the system. He does not have to resort to the "Hot List" and "Red Tag" emergency systems.

When an Inventory Planner examines his stock status record and sees castings due in 3 weeks, his confidence is much higher that he will get delivery as promised. If additional castings are needed to satisfy a new order, he doesn't allow the "extra" two to four weeks in his delivery promise to offset lead time fluctuations which he previously encountered.

Foundry vacation shutdowns are planned well in advance. The planned Input and Output are adjusted for the vacation period. Some of the parts required during the shutdown period are ordered for delivery in earlier months to avoid costly raw material shortages while the foundry is closed for vacation.

FISHER CONTROLS COMPANY

DATE __12-30-70__

PRODUCTION LINE __COPE AND DRAG__

PURSUANT TO THE INPUT/OUTPUT SCHEDULING AGREEMENT BETWEEN FISHER CONTROLS COMPANY AND __M and E COMPANY__

THE FOLLOWING COMMITMENTS ARE IN EFFECT FOR THE MONTH OF __JANUARY__

MATERIAL __STEEL - WCB__

PLANNING PERIOD	PAST DUE	PURCHASE ORDERS ISSUED		FIRM COMMITMENTS	FORECAST					
MONTH		JAN	FEB	MARCH	APRIL	MAY	JUNE	JULY	AUG	SEPT
FISHER REQUIREMENTS		800	800	300①	800	800	800	800	800	800
VENDOR ACKNOWLEDGEMENT*		800	800							
ACCUMULATED DEVIATION	✗	✗								

	PAST DUE	JAN	FEB	MARCH
ORDER PLACEMENTS	730	800	800	300
MATERIAL RECEIPTS	230	20		
ACCUMULATED DEVIATION	500	1280		

⟶ Next months anticipated placements

① December requirements have been reduced due to continued poor delivery performance. Increased reductions in the forecast period requirements should be anticipated until an acceptable level of performance is achieved.

*Vendor to review Fisher requirements and reserve capacity for time periods and confirm their ability to fulfill requirements shown to Fisher within 5 days after receipt.

BUYER, FISHER CONTROLS COMPANY

VENDOR COMMITMENT ACKNOWLEDGED BY

Figure 4. Summary – Delivery Performance

Merle Maiden, Inventory Control Manager, recently stated, "When the Sales Department calls and has an emergency order or wants short delivery for a special order, I can immediately determine what other purchase orders, if any, will be put in jeopardy. Input/Output Control has significantly reduced the guesswork in making delivery promises and given me better control to get what I need when I need it!"

In Short — INVENTORY CONTROL LIKES IT!!

I/O Control and YOU

Look for a production area in your Plant or with a Vendor where a family of items use a common capacity. Select a measure of capacity (production rate). Project the requirements into the future for the individual items and total the requirements in production units to determine the capacity required. Once the average capacity requirement is established, select the items most urgently needed to match the capacity (planned production rate). Measure the Output from this production area. If Output is less than Input, stop putting work in until the Output increases! The name of the game is to keep backlog down and wait as long as possible to commit orders for individual items.

Stabilize existing lead times and once under control, reduce them. Fisher Controls didn't immediately reduce their lead times to the minimum; in fact, they want them to go even lower than the current 4 to 8 weeks. However, they are reduced and under better control than ever before.

The example in this article illustrates the application of Input/Output Control in solving foundry lead time problems but the same principles apply to other manufacturing operations. Fisher applied the same principles in the assembly department with equally effective results.

The largest single obstacle in applying this technique to solve delivery problems in your business will be *getting started*. Too many of us see the merits of new ideas but try to anticipate all possible situations, make every measurement precise and consequently never implement the solution and attain the potential benefits. *Improvement* in operating the business better today than yesterday *is the objective — not precision* in the measurements and *perfection* in control.

Summary

Input/Output Control attacks the cause of late deliveries, not the effects. Inventory Control plans future capacity requirements which increases their confidence that capacity will be available when needed. The Inventory Planner who has the inventory records and can best decide what is most needed establishes priority within the capacity he planned. The Plant or Vendor is measured on his ability to fulfill his Output commitment. He is relieved from selecting which items are needed first and is allowed to concentrate on meeting the Output commitment.

If you have excessive lead times and delivery date integrity problems, take action now. Prepare yourself for the time when business picks up. The luxury of scheduling to excess capacity will soon be over. Avoid the unnecessary extension in lead times. Plan capacity and control Input and Output to achieve — Delivery as Promised!

About the Author—

R. DAVE GARWOOD *graduated from Purdue University in 1964 and joined Fisher Controls in Marshalltown, Iowa after graduation. He held various positions at Fisher including Design Engineer, Inventory Control Manager, and Materials Staff Specialist. Since January 1971, he has joined Mallinckrodt Chemical Works in St. Louis, as Assistant Manager of P.I.C.*

The preparation and accomplishments described in this article were performed while the author was with Fisher. Mr. Garwood wishes to express his appreciation for their publication approval.

HIDDEN HURDLES IN THE PATH OF SHOP FLOOR CONTROL

Jack Gips, President
Jack Gips, Inc.

. The MRP logic is sound.
. The computer equipment is the best money can buy.
. The reports are standard and proven.

But . . . Shop Floor Control is failing at Company X!

Why ? ? ? Because they are blocked by three basic requirements that must be met to make Shop Floor Control succeed:

1. Valid dates,
2. Valid data, and
3. Good management and measurement on the shop floor.

Although these requirements are basic, there are some aspects that are not readily visible during implementation. These should be considered carefully.

Hidden Hurdle No. 1 - Valid Dates

It is often said that the quality of a company's planning systems can best be measured on the shop floor. This has been proven many times over by those companies that have attempted to install shop floor controls without first having achieved a high degree of validity in the due dates emanating from their Master Scheduling and MRP operations.

It is not until the first dispatch list and the first capacity requirements plan are generated that a complete picture of the status of the planning systems comes into focus.

When this happens, the manufacturing organization often gets a reaffirmation of the impossible task they are faced with - trying to meet the due dates!

Then, to add insult to injury, an edict is passed down from the Top - "Now that we can see how far behind the shop is, you must begin to deliver the orders on schedule immediately!"

When the shop supervisors criticize the reports that show 10 weeks of past due capacity requirements and many orders due in stock 20 weeks ago, they are met with the comment - "The orders are in the right sequence. Work the oldest one first!"

The dispatch list shown below is indicative of the problem the supervisors face when the dates are not valid.

DISPATCH LIST

SHOP DATE 151   DEMO. CAP. 75 STD. HRS

WORK CENTER - 101

PART NO.	ORDER NO.	OPER. START	ORDER DUE	STD. HOURS
L1011	101	118	130	20
B0747	187	121	140	5
DC009	113	128	135	14
A0100	102	128	129	26
F0111	102	142	149	32
C0141	163	145	153	8
C005A	145	148	148	55
F0018	123	149	158	12
DC008	129	151	153	35
F0104	117	153	160	26
A0037	131	153	161	21
B0027	109	155	159	15
B0029	106	165	185	22
				291

The order for part L1011 is the oldest on the list and according to the rules should be given the highest priority. But no one has even approached the supervisor in work center 101 to ask about its progress!

The General Manager, the manufacturing manager, and two expediters have all asked about the status of F0018 because it is really needed for this month's shipments. Under these circumstances, the dispatch list does not reflect the true priorities, so the supervisors must resort to their own informal lists to determine the sequence of work.

The oldest order usually gets that distinction because no one really needs it. Many of the orders that have everyone's attention are also past due, but in the middle of the pack. Some are scheduled in the future. The supervisors must work on these first if the shipment goals are to be met. They know the dispatch list is wrong and soon ignore the list and the edict to use it in favor of the hot lists. Valid dates must be obtained <u>before</u> turning the dispatch lists loose on the shop.

Hidden Hurdle No. 2 - Valid Data

Lurking in the woodwork of all manufacturing companies are the "Easy Route" bugs. The goal of all "Easy Route" bugs is to find a short cut or more convenient way of doing things, often to the detriment of the original goals of the manufacturing systems. The "Easy Route" bug loves to work in the Valid Data area of a Shop Floor Control system. Let's see how he works . . .

. Keeping Dispatch Lists Current

A shop supervisor can use a dispatch list only if it tells him the truth. This means that the orders must actually be in the work centers where the list shows them. Yet, there are times when it is desirable for the supervisors to change the sequence of operations on an order, or to move the work to a different work center from the one specified on the original routing. When this occurs the computer must be told about the change. If not, it assumes the original routing is still correct and the dispatch lists will be created showing the work in the wrong work centers.

The "Easy Route" bug moves the parts or changes the sequence, but does not process the transaction because that is "paperwork" and not as important as "getting his job done."

Material movement transactions are required to notify the system when it is time to move an order from one work center's dispatch list to the next. Typically, this means a "material arrival" transaction must be processed in the receiving work center as soon as the material is physically moved there.

The "Easy Route" bug is determined to avoid this "extra" reporting, so he decides that it will be easier to let the computer "assume" that the material arrives when completion of the previous operation is reported. Thus, he moves the order from one dispatch list to another even though the material may not have moved. With this system installed, the supervisors need a hand-written list of the work available in the work center to tell them which of the "orders available" on the dispatch list are really available!

. Keeping the Dispatch List Complete

The "Easy Route" bug figures that routing rework operations and one-time special parts, and loading them into the system would require a lot of effort. So, he chooses to avoid this work. Therefore, they are not included on the dispatch lists. Since they are not on the priority list or in the supervisor's performance measurements, they sit in the work centers gathering dust and rust. Since they are low efficiency, low incentive pay parts with many opportunities for quality problems, no one wants to work on them anyway.

Sooner or later, however, they become crucial to shipments and must be expedited through the shop, breaking setups along the way. The net effect is that they cause lower efficiency, higher scrap, and require more effort than if they had been added to the formal system and treated like the standard parts in the first place.

. Keeping The List Accurate

As orders pass through the shop, scrap occurs, parts are lost or mis-placed, orders are split, etc. The "Easy Route" bug sees no reason to go to all the effort of notifying the computer when these things happen.

But the system assumes that all is fine unless it receives messages to the contrary. An order whose parts are scrapped or lost is assumed to be intact. MRP is not given an opportunity to expedite an order with parts missing until they turn up short in assembly. The second half of a split order is not rescheduled out to a lesser priority because the MRP system still assumes there is only one order.

So the "Easy Route" bug, who has saved so much effort by not reporting these occurences, must now expedite parts through the shop to cover the surprises in assembly if scrap or lost parts reporting has been ignored. He has utilized valuable capacity to make low priority parts if split orders have not been reported. But, he has successfully avoided the reporting!

Thorough understanding of the goals and philosophies of Shop Floor Control must be established early in the development of the system to prevent the "Easy Route" bugs from multiplying and diminishing the effectiveness of the system before it gets off the ground. Early education is the best prevention for the damage they can do.

Hidden Hurdle No. 3 -
Good Management and Measurement by the Shop Managers

Good management in the shop means that the supervisors are held accountable and measured on:

. Working on the right parts,

. Providing enough output and,

. Providing timely feedback.

It means that shop managers frequently visit work centers to review dispatch lists to assure that the highest priority orders are being worked on.

The dispatch list below is an example of what the shop manager might find if he were to make this review.

DISPATCH LIST

SHOP DATE 151   DEMO. CAP. 75 STD. HRS

WORK CENTER - 101

PART NO.	ORDER NO.	OPER. START	ORDER DUE	STATUS
L1012	123	148	151	
B0748	174	150	151	C
DC010	169	151	155	
A0101	163	151	163	
FO112	108	156	159	R
C0142	192	158	167	R
C006B	144	160	171	
FO019	156	166	172	
DC007	116	166	180	
FO105	120	175	183	
A0038	184	177	186	R
B0028	124	180	185	
B0030	122	188	196	

He must now ask the supervisor in this work center why he is working on orders near the bottom of the list, but not on some near the top. This measurement causes the supervisors to justify the priority of the orders they work on. Good management means that capacity meetings are held weekly to discuss out-of-tolerance work centers that are identified on input-output reports. Shop managers must

help their supervisors adjust their capacity to stay on schedule.

INPUT / OUTPUT REPORT

	8/25	9/1	9/8	9/15	9/22	9/29	10/6
INPUT PLAN	500	500	500	500	500	500	500
ACTUAL INPUT	490	530	510	480			
DEVIATION	-10	+20	+30	+10			

TOLERANCE ± 100

	8/25	9/1	9/8	9/15	9/22	9/29	10/6
OUTPUT PLAN	500	500	500	500	500	500	500
ACTUAL OUTPUT	470	440	480	460			
DEVIATION	-30	-90	-110	-150			

TOLERANCE ± 75   QUEUE 300   STD. QUEUE 150

The input-output report above shows a work center that has been out-of-tolerance on a cumulative basis for three weeks. This work center should have been discussed in the previous two capacity meetings and should be a major topic for the meeting this week. The actions taken so far to resolve the output problem have not worked, and the work center is rapidly becoming a bottleneck.

Good management means that shop managers review daily the anticipated delay reports they receive and take action on them. And it means that they question supervisors who are not providing this feedback to find out why.

The anticipated delay report shown below indicates that the supervisor in department 012 has identified these orders as unlikely to arrive in stores on schedule. He has identified these orders while the problem that is delaying them still exists, giving the shop manager the greatest leadtime to resolve the problem or have the schedules changed. The shop manager should assure that all the supervisors are providing this feedback.

Dept. 012
Date 2/12/81   ANTICIPATED DELAY REPORT

Part No.	Due Date	New Date	Problem	Action
12B1	2/14	2/21	Machine down	Move to slow mach.
32C5	2/21	2/28	Bad die	Resinking
15A2	2/21	3/7	Tool lost	Reordered

The job of the shop manager is to manage and measure the supervisors - not do their work for them. As shop managers shake-off the urge to expedite and carry parts around the shop on their mopeds and golf carts, more time becomes available to do the things that prevent the shortages from happening. And Shop Floor Control tools become more effective in helping manufacturing.

Any company can install the Shop Floor Control tools, but only those that recognize and address the hidden hurdles will reap the full benefits from them. Valid dates, valid data and good management are the keys to success in Shop Floor Control.

Jack Gips is President of Jack Gips, Inc., a firm that provides high quality education and consulting services to manufacturing companies. He has assisted many companies in the implementation and operation of successful material control and manufacturing systems.

Prior to this, he spent nine years as a practitioner with the Warner and Swasey Company where he was Materials Manager and Manufacturing Operations Manager. At Warner and Swasey, he was responsible for the design, implementation, and operation of systems for Master Scheduling, Capacity Planning, MRP, Shop Floor Control, and Purchasing in an on-line, real-time environment.

Mr. Gips has a B.S. and an M.B.A. degree from Case Western Reserve University. He is a member of the APICS Certification subcommittee for Production Activity Control. He is a frequent speaker at APICS and other professional society meetings and was Chairman of the 1977 APICS International Conference.

IMPLEMENTING STOCKLESS PRODUCTION IN THE UNITED STATES

Robert W. Hall
Indiana University

Much is made of the productivity gap in key industries between Japan and the United States. Early efforts to explain this focused on cultural differences and the work ethic. Then we turned to a few techniques, notably quality circles, just-in-time production and KANBAN, but usually without fitting the techniques into the context of their overall use.

It is time to take a broader view of Japanese productivity. What are they doing? How does it work? What can we do to match their performance?

Begin with goal of stockless production, for it explains the reasoning behind many of their practices: It is to obtain the effect of automating an entire industry at minimum cost.

If the imagination is left to run free, what kind of system would that call for? A system to make the products the customers want at the rate the customers want them, no more and no less. This simple goal is the guide to many actions great and small. Material should flow from raw stock to finished goods in the minimum time possible, meaning that inventories should be as close to zero as possible and lead times (actual throughput times) should be as short as possible. Low inventories means that there is little investment and that there is no slack to rework defects. Therefore quality must be high -- nearly perfect. Short lead times mean that there is no time during which to revise priorities or revise the orders. The customer should know what he wants because he will get it rapidly.

Furthermore, since we only want to produce units at the rate the customers want, the goal of automation is only to produce units at that rate, nor a faster rate. High-rate production means building ahead of the market, hence inventory. Therefore, automation means the conversion of equipment to run at the market rate with all processes feeding each other at the market rate.

Keeping the goal in mind allows one to make sense of the overall Japanese system of production. Interpreting what is done from the viewpoint of lot-size thinking only confuses.

HOW TO ACHIEVE THIS OBJECTIVE

It is easiest to see how to achieve the effect of automation by straight-through flow of material in the case where a few products are made almost continuously by repetitive manufacturing. The more irregular the specifications for the product and the more it must be made to customer order, the more difficult this becomes. Many products must be made in small quantities to order by job shop methods. The system to be described applies most to the case of repetitive manufacturing, but job shops can benefit greatly from application of the principles wherever possible.

To attain the goal of stockless production requires the achievement of the following steps in the approximate order in which they are given:

1. Get control of quality by improved training of the workforce so that they can control the production process itself. The number of defects produced must be very near zero to avoid stalling the material flows with rework or delays. This means programs of preventive maintenance, and practices which provide immediate feedback to floor workers on the quality status of their work.

2. Plan a level schedule in final assembly. In repetitive manufacturing, this means more than just leveling the workload. It means producing

a small amount of everything every day during 10-day to 30-day periods during which the final assembly schedule is planned to satisfy the market rate of demand for each model produced as closely as possible.

In job shops, leveling the schedule means to release orders so as to provide a level labor requirement and also stay within the capacity limits of each work center. (The Japanese system begins with the notion of capacity control and subcontracting the overages.)

3. Revise the plant layouts for repetitive manufacturing so as to get fixed routings and smooth flows of material through the plant. Two material stockpoints should be defined as specific locations next to each work center -- an inbound stockpoint, and an outbound stockpoint.

4. Establish a pull system of material control. Make the flows of material and the status of operations highly visible to everyone on the shop floor so that they have the means to coordinate themselves. Post the rates of assembly of different models so that everyone can see how their operation is directly linked with final assembly.

5. Drastically cut inventories to eliminate stockrooms for all work-in-process inventory. Manufacturing inventory should be kept in the stockpoints at floor work centers. Cutting the inventory means an intense program for:

> Drastically reducing set up times.
> Drastically reducing lot sizes.

The idea is to increase the flexibility in the use of each work center over the range of parts which it can produce. Those parts or products which cannot be made to fit the system may be given to suppliers to make. The objective here is to focus the plant's mission and actually make physical changes in the plant to make the system work, not compromise the system to make the plant work.

6. Continue to reduce inventories, using the system to pinpoint specific problems which must be corrected. The production control system is designed to do this. By reducing the inventories to the lowest levels possible, the plant moves, step-by-step, closer to the goal of stockless production and finally to full automation.

The objective of production control is not to make maximum use of capacity or to untangle the priority problems of the moment. In this system no work centers are worked to capacity unless it is necessary to catch up if they fall behind. When a daily schedule is complete, the extra time is used to "experiment": decreasing set up times, improving process control or simplifying the work. The plant floor becomes a production laboratory with workers experimenting themselves and with foremen as proejct leaders. Staff people are advisors. Their experimenting is not aimless. The work is done to attain step-by-step objectives set by the top management in plotting their course to stockless production.

7. Extend the system to suppliers. Only after an internal program of stockless production is well established will suppliers be invited to learn the system themselves. At the beginning of the program suppliers will only be asked to deliver in smaller quantities more frequently. As supplier companies become adept in stockless production themselves, they will eventually be regarded as another work center which happens to be outside the plant -- and shared with other companies.

8. Continue to full automation whenever possible, keeping in mind that automation requires only production at market rates, linking work

centers together so as to physically transfer workpieces between them. If this is done while retaining the ability to quickly set up for production of any model within the range of those possible on the equipment, eventually the goal is reached: Production of any one of a variety of models whenever wanted.

Not many plants will become totally automated. Common sense dictates that such a goal is for the 21st Century, not next year. However, a program to press as far toward stockless production and full automation as possible brings great improvement to every part of production, both in quality and in productivity.

MAKING PROBLEMS VISIBLE -- BY THE CARD SYSTEM -- AND OTHERWISE

The type of stockless production most often described is KANBAN, often considered as only a card system of production control. The card system, however, is only one of the methods of making problems visible. There are two primary functions of the cards:

1. To provide a method to control the WIP of each part number in each floor location. This allows systematic reduction of WIP at specific point in order to study the true nature of the resulting problems.

2. To provide the pull system of production control the means to coordinate modest deviations from the daily level planned schedules.

There are two types of cards:

1. A Move Card authorizes the movement of one standard container of one part number from the outbound stockpoint of the producing work center to the inbound stockpoint of a using work center. Sets of move cards are issued only for use of one part number between one pair of work centers.

2. A Production Card is used only for one part number at the work center which produces that part. It authorizes the production of one standard container of that part number to replace a container which was taken from that center's outbound stockpoint.

Note that one card goes on one standard container. Therefore the maximum of WIP authorized for any given part number is proportional to the total number of production cards plus move cards issued for that part number.

This card system will only work for either production control or problem visibility if the rules for their use are rigorously observed:

1. One of the two types of cards must always be attached to a standard container holding parts, and the correct number of parts must always be placed in each container.

2. The using work center always sends for a replacement standard container of parts using a move card. (The move card is removed from a standard container as soon as parts from it begin to be used.) This insures a pull system. Never "send" parts ahead to the next work center.

3. Only produce a standard container of parts when an unattached production card authorizes it. When a standard container is picked from an outbound stockpoint, the production card is removed and left behind as authorization to produce a replacement container. The move card is attached to the container as it begins its trip to the using work center.

If the rules are followed, a very simple pull system is established whereby the movement of material is synchronized to its rate of use at final assembly.

The actual lot size at the producing work center is as small as one container full if possible. If set up times cannot be reduced immediately to a level which permits this, several production cards may accumulate before a "run" is made to replace that part. However, the idea is to reduce lot sizes as much as possible, meaning the use of small standard containers and a minimum number of cards in circulation.

PARTS FLOW IN STOCKLESS PRODUCTION

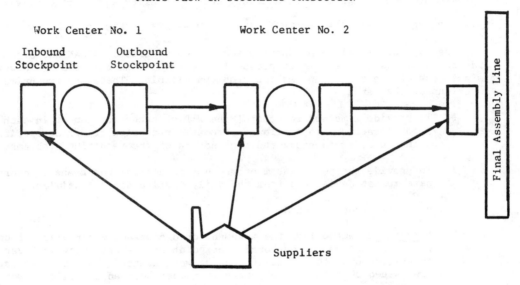

Card (Signal) Flow Paths in Stockless Production

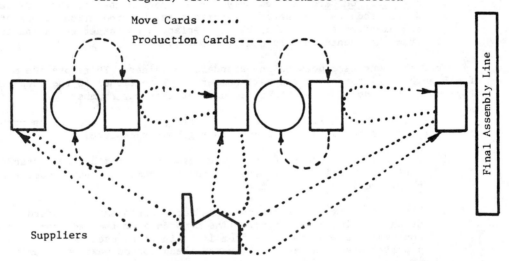

The most important role of the cards is in reducing inventory so as to make visible the problems which impede attainment of full automation. This procedure works as follows:

1. At the start of each new frozen, level period in the production schedule, issue the cards and start the flow moving. At each point on the floor supervisors should remove cards from the system which allow excess inventory. No work center should operate with a comfortable level of inventory.

2. At those points where particular problems need study, pull one or two more cards from the system. This means overtime, shortages, or both in the short run, but the purpose is to focus attention on the real physical reasons why the work center(s) cannot function with a lower level of inventory.

3. Make changes to allow operation at the new, lower level of inventory. The changes may be equipment changes, procedural changes or whatever is necessary to accomplish the purpose.

4. As soon as these improvements have been consolidated, remove one or two more cards from the same point in the system and repeat the process.

5. Repeat this again, and again, and again -- until finally, no cards are required at all. At that point, two or more work centers or machines have reached a state where it is possible to study how to transfer parts between them one-at-a-time, thus development of full automation.

More important, note that this method of study stimulates the development of automation by incremental improvements which should be accomplished at very low cost, using ingenuity to adapt existing equipment where possible, buying different equipment only when the same purpose cannot be achieved by simpler means. Automation does not mean the development of high-speed equipment to attain a false economy at only one step in production while piling up inventory. It means the development of the lowest cost way to produce units at the market rate, keeping in mind the goal of automating the entire production system.

If a level production schedule can actually be executed every day, then the use of the cards for production may not be so necessary. Some companies use only circulating containers with part number I.D.'s attached. Some use colored washers or other signalling methods to accomplish the role of the cards.

In addition to the cards, most Japanese companies on this system issue copies of the final assembly schedule to many work centers in the plant, post the production rate (cycle rates) of the various models in production, post hourly how actual final assembly compares with the schedule for the day, use a signboard to indicate which work centers are having trouble, and so on. All these methods allow each worker to see a great deal of information showing how his operation fits into the complete pattern of the plant at any time. Visibility throughout is the key.

REQUIREMENTS FOR IMPLEMENTING STOCKLESS PRODUCTION

The requirements of stockless production point to a number of problems in implementing it. It is a rigorous and difficult program. The method is not "natural" to Japanese either, and they report numerous cases in which the stockless production programs were miserable in the early going. Americans can learn from the Japanese experience. Our own experience with it is still mostly experimental, but some non-Japanese problems can be projected.

1. Quality by Process Control. If there is little inventory, the production of defective parts can easily plug the system. All the Japanese companies starting stockless production had quality programs preceding it. The best-known aspect of Japanese quality improvement practice is the quality circle, but the most important requirement is achieving control of the process so that defects are not made.

Process control means a program to discover the true sources of quality problems and to solve the problems, and this is how the Japanese use the quality circles. However Americans go about it, the parts made must be good ones.

The most promising ways to do this involve automatic measurement of

100% of the parts made with automatic stopping and correcting of the production process when it goes out of control. This methodology is obviously the only way to assure that inbound parts are always good ones. Accumulating parts for inspection only adds to inventory and lead time. It furthermore delays feedback to the operator or equipment at the source of the problems when they arise.

From the viewpoint of job shop production and trade-off logic, stopping the equipment at the first sign of faulty production may not make sense. However, when the ultimate objective is full automation, zero defects is the only way. The major problem here is the conversion of American thinking from concentrating on immediate production efficiency to attaining the ultimate goal.

2. <u>Leveling the Schedule.</u> Leveling the schedule does not have to be done for the entire company at once. A pilot project should start by organizing a final assembly area in which a level schedule is possible, and then work backwards into the processes which feed that final assembly.

Leveling the schedule to produce a little bit of everything every day sounds like an impossible dream at first. It cannot be attained overnight. It begins by cutting lot sizes and working on assembly set up times so as to attain the goal over time, several months or a year. It may also require the redistribution of products among several different assembly areas in order to get started.

The understanding of Marketing is needed. Freezing a schedule means that Production is no longer going to provide immediate response to a request to change the mix coming into finished goods tomorrow. However, when entering a difficult period in the program, Japanese companies have sometimes built a little finished goods ahead of time so as to preclude excessive customer complaints while the project is under way.

Leveling the schedule does not necessarily mean that the exact schedule planned is run every day. It does mean that deviations from schedule are not permitted to wreck the system. What Marketing must understand is that by greatly reducing lead times, the general response to the marketplace can be improved. Both planning lead times and actual lead times can be substantially cut.

3. <u>Reduce Lot Sizes.</u> How quickly lot sizes can be reduced depends on how quickly set up times can be reduced. However, reducing lot sizes is a major stimulus for set up time reduction. When people are asked to perform set ups frequently, they look for more efficient ways to do it.

4. <u>Reduce Set Up Times</u>. The initial problem for most Americans is to believe that set up times can be reduced drastically without major expenditure. It does take effort and ingenuity, but the Japanese have done this without spending huge sums for equipment revision. It is mostly done by small improvements over time using the in-house talent. Operators convert to doing the routine set ups while the set up personnel convert to developing better ways to reduce set up times, guided by the technical staff.

Learning how to do this involves several general "principles" for it, but in actual practice, it means getting started so as to acquire experience with the specific types of equipment involved.

Set up times cannot be greatly reduced for all types of equipment, so where this is true, set up time reduction may take longer. If possible, the company should select equipment which is very flexible. Where this cannot be done, use several small machines rather than one large one.

(Example: Several small polymer extruders constantly set up for one color rather than one large one which needs total cleaning for a color change.)

5. Balance Operations. Americans think of balancing an assembly line. Stockless production requires balancing all operations, all the way back to the suppliers. The hardest instinct to overcome is again the false measurements of efficiency. Machines should run at a balanced rate equal to the use rates of the parts they produce. High-speed equipment only creates inventory (and sometimes a layoff while the inventory is worked off.)

Those working with stockless production learn to see the problems of imbalance by living with them -- a sensitivity acquired over time. Workers and supervisors need to acquire this sense, and it is one of the reasons for all the methods for creating visible feedback in Japanese plants.

Another very difficult point for Americans is that stockless production requires multi-functional workers. If the schedule must balance the workload of many workers who will only do one job, a level schedule has more variables to consider than it can often handle. Therefore, in a stockless production program, workers must be measured and rewarded for being versatile and for making improvements, not for producing as fast as they can. The problems of adjusting thinking in many American plants are obvious.

6. Detailed Work With Suppliers. This should only be done after internal development has progressed to where the suppliers can be given a demonstration of what is wanted. Initially, the work with suppliers should only include getting material from them which has no defects and in reducing the delivery quantities as much as possible within the scope of their capabilities. If suppliers insist on shipping many days' or weeks' worth of parts at once, they should be kept in inventory at a distant warehouse and metered out as the using processes demand. No one in the plant should be allowed to have a comfortable inventory cushion.

Cutting the delivery quantities in Japan was easier than it will be in the United States because of the differences in the trucking systems. However, there are huge gains to be made in analyzing how to reduce shipment sizes where this can be done. If suppliers think their customers want them to carry their inventory for them, that is no problem. It really costs about the same to hold inventory no matter where it is stored. The major questions are transport cost and reliable quality.

Stockless production is a radical enough change for Americans that there are many pitfalls. A few of the early experiments have either failed or stalled for several reasons, some of which have also been problems in Japan.

Top management must totally support and direct the program. There is no way to execute the changes without that. Basic work relationships and performance measurements usually must be changed. Even after long coaching, only one manager in a critical spot can obstruct progress. Only top management can provide the resources and remove the obstacles.

Study the entire system and its implications carefully before starting. Americans are very impatient. We would like to have the project complete before we have begun. The understanding of a great many people is required to make stockless production a success, and it is necessary to build a base of support before beginning. There are also many implications for basic changes which must be thought though, and if people in the organization whose understanding of the objective is minimal get some unexpected surprises, support can be quickly lost.

Before jumping into a big project, study for months or perhaps a year, involve many people, and if possible, see stockless production in action.

The project is also a long-term effort. One of the hazards is that a project teram will experience so much personnel instablity that it can really never get started. This does not happen in Japan, but in the United States, talented people do not feel bound to one employer, or they may jump to a promotion in another division of a big company at a disastrous time for the project.

Morale is also important. Stockless production is a grueling experience. Most of the Japanese companies began a build-up of morale well before starting the proejct itself. Springing these ideas on the union a few days before they are to go into effect is a sure defeat. It is very important that they understand that stockless production is not a workpace speedup, but a program to work precisely.

It is also tempting to regard stockless production as the next great buzz-word, possibly as a way to be recognized for introduction of the next magic tool in production. It is not a magic tool, but very hard work. No Japanese say that going through the process is totally enjoyable.

Despite all the problems, stockless production is not Japanese culture. It is a method of production, elements of which have been seen in the United States. Because of the culture, the Japanese have been very persistent in developing it in their way. Americans must not do less than be very persistent in developing it in our way.

Reprinted from the APICS *1983* Conference Proceedings.

THE STANDARD COST ACCOUNTING INTERFACE

Stewart R. Hanson, CPIM*
The Torrington Company

FOREWORD

The purpose of this paper is to trace the flow of information from the shop floor through the standard cost accounting system and show the feedback available to management in the form of reports and variances. Special emphasis will be placed on the design of the standard cost accounting data base and its relationship with the shop floor and the bill of material. All standard variances will be explained, as well as the idle capacity variance. Indirect labor and overhead costs will be addressed with special emphasis on the fixed and variable portions of indirect labor.

The overall purpose of this paper is to show how the standard cost accounting system ties into the shop floor control system and into the overall MRP system.

THE STANDARD COST ACCOUNTING SYSTEM

The job of the standard cost accounting system is to take the information generated from the shop floor and distribute these costs to the products manufactured. It calculates actual performance and any variances from standard cost. The standard costs are arrived at by using industrial engineering time studies or historical performance based on records. The standard cost should be a reasonable expectation of performance.

Standard cost accounting accumulates the material, labor and overhead cost associated with each shop order as it is processed through the plant. As these costs are accumulated or built up, they can be compared with the standard cost and variances can be calculated. These variances can be used by management to take corrective action.

Figure 1 shows a diagram of the flow of information through the standard cost system. Raw material costs flow from the storehouse to the cost center or work center. Costs that flow from the work center include direct labor, indirect labor, indirect material, and other miscellaneous payroll information, such as shift premium or overtime. These costs flow into the standard cost accounting data base, which also uses other files, such as the routing file, bill of material, product structure, and open order file. As the costs are reported from the shop floor, they are accumulated and rolled up in the standard cost accounting data base to reflect the activity from the shop floor. The open order file will show the progress of the parts through the plant and using the standard cost associated with that stage in production will cost out the work in process available at any direct labor operation. Other files important to this data base are the forecasting file and the master schedule.

BASIC COST COMPONENTS

The basic parts of the standard cost accounting system include fixed costs, which are costs that cannot be changed in a short period of time and are associated with the general overhead or operation of the business. This type of cost would include taxes and insurance on the building, security systems, and a minimum amount of power. Other items that might be included in fixed cost would be a minimum staff. Fixed costs generally would be thought of as costs that could not be avoided in the short run.

Variable costs are costs that vary with the production of the product. These would include raw material, direct labor, and the variable portion of indirect labor. We would expect this type of cost to vary with the production of the product in a direct proportion to the rise and fall of the schedule.

Overhead costs are costs that cannot be directly tied to an item within a product and must be spread over the entire product or several products. An example of this would be a foreman's salary, which would be difficult to split up based on the attention he gave to each item or each product going through his department. We would consider his salary part of overhead and spread that cost on a proportional or percentage basis over all the products and items going through his department. Another example would be a person who washed or weighed parts and we would not want to take the time to account for every weighing or washing based on the item or product handled. We would spread his cost on a proportional or percentage basis over all the products going through that area or department.

It is possible that overhead costs will be distributed and redistributed by service departments until they reach an operating department producing product. For example, the data processing cost might be distributed on a pro rata basis to the machine shop. The machine shop may distribute its cost on a per hour basis to the operating departments. In this example the data processing cost will be distributed to the machine shop and further distributed by the machine shop to an operating department which produces product. Ultimately the data processing cost will be distributed to an item or product.

Figure 2 shows the relationship between fixed cost, variable cost, total cost and sales in an organization. This break-even point diagram explains how fixed costs are absorbed into production based on units produced until all fixed costs have been absorbed at the break-even point. This process is called full absorption accounting.

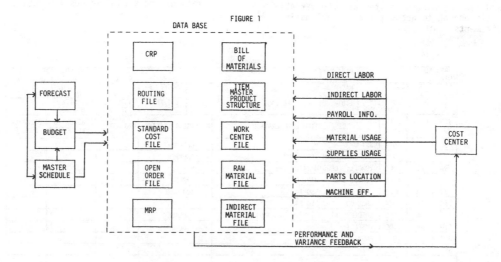

FIGURE 1

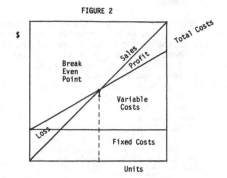

FIGURE 2

BUDGETS

The budgeting system is based on the expected production level in the plant in the coming months or years. The master production schedule is an excellent tool to use for budgeting purposes. This is especially true if the master production schedule contains 52 weeks of information. It is possible to design the master production schedule to include weekly schedules for a period of time up to six months and then show monthly master schedules from six months to one year. This design depends on the normal lead time of the individual business. The budget would be based on the normal production expected during the time period. This production would be calculated in direct labor hours or some other equitable base, such as machine hours. Most standard cost accounting system would use direct labor hours.

Based on the direct labor hours, fixed and indirect costs would be allocated based on the anticipated direct labor hours. For instance, assume that the grinding department has a schedule of 100,000 direct labor hours for the year and that the total overhead cost for the year is $500,000. By dividing the $500,000 by the 100,000 hours, we will arrive at a rate of $5 per hour for overhead. Overhead would be distributed to this department at the rate of $5 for every direct labor hour worked. If the department only worked 90,000 hours during the year, it would only earn or absorb $450,000 of the overhead and we would have an under absorbed or under applied overhead variance of $50,000. The normal procedure to dispose of this variance would be to apply or book it directly to the profit and loss statement as an unfavorable variance or loss for the period. This type of budget is actually a variable budget because as production increases or decreases from the budgeted level, more or less overhead will be earned, reflecting need for additional resources as production increases beyond the budgeted level.

We must recognize that some costs are neither fixed nor variable but are semi variable as production varies. For instance, we might not need another plant security guard as production increased, but we might need another fork truck driver.

The standard cost accounting system and the variable budget are flexible enough to account for variations in production requirements.

RELATIONSHIP WITH THE SHOP FLOOR

The shop traveler or operation sheet is the basis for the routing of the parts through the plant. The shop traveler or operation sheet is based on the routing file housed in the computer. The open order file listing of open orders in the plant would in most cases contain identical information to the routing file and to the operation sheet or traveler that moves with the parts. Figure 3 shows a typical operation sheet or traveler, which moves with the work and identifies each operation to be performed. Some of the pertinent information contained on the operation sheet would be part number; part name; computer code; order number; lot number; lot size; raw material required (both size and number of pounds per unit of production); the sequence of operations and the work centers or departments they are to be performed in as well as the computer operation code for that particular operation; a short description of the operation, including special information such as tolerances or dimensions; the machine to be used on the operation; and the number of units to be produced per hour or other time period. Operator sign-off of the completion of the operation and number of parts produced should be included. The production should be fed back to the computer and standard cost accounting system via (1) manual card, (2) CRTs, (3) bar coding, (4) magnetic strip readers, (5) other similar methods. The important thing is to feed back to the standard cost accounting system as well as the MRP system the information from the shop floor to be used to drive the systems outlined in Figure 1.

Integrity is very important at this point. The information being transmitted from the shop floor needs to have a high degree of accuracy, 98 percent or better, to insure the integrity of the MRP system.

This information will be used for parts location in the MRP system as well as capacity planning through the availabilities showing at all the work centers.

One factor that must be considered when designing the standard cost accounting system is the operations that are going to be considered direct labor operations and the operations that are going to be considered indirect labor operations. Here there is an opportunity for some value judgments and decisions to be made by the designer. The more operations that are designated direct labor operations will improve the accuracy of the standard cost accounting system. However, this also entails reporting of direct labor hours for each one of these operations. The more operations that are designated direct labor operations, the more shop floor reporting there will be. On the other hand, the more operations that are designated indirect labor operations will cause more cost to be put into overhead and spread to products and accuracy may decline. The more operations that are considered indirect will require less reporting from the shop floor. For instance, in a plant of 1,000 people, if 800 are working on direct labor operations reporting ten jobs per day, it would result in 8,000 transactions per day, or 40,000 transactions per week. If in the same plant 500 people were working on direct labor operations, it could result in 5,000 transactions per day, or 25,000 transactions per week. We must weigh the accuracy of the system versus the cost of obtaining and

FIGURE 3
OPERATION SHEET

PART NO. 012345		PART NAME SHAFT		DATE ISSUED 8-24-79	DATE REV. 9-12-83	REV. NO. 2	DRAWING NO. 100-00-000
PART COMP. CODE 70-00103170-20		MATERIAL 6442 WIRE, 50100		CHECKED BY	ISSUED BY EHW	SHEET NO. 1 OF 1	
ORDER NO. 13579	QUANTITY 4,000,000	.101+.001 CODE 160100		WGHT./M .98#	UNITS/PAN 600,000	LOT SIZE 4,000,000	
SEQ. NO.	DEPT. NO.	OPER. CODE	DESCRIPTION OF OPERATION	MACHINE & TOOLING	STANDARD PRODUCTION HOURS	REPORTED PRODUCTION	OPERATOR NUMBER
50	20	1094	SET UP	CHOPPER			
70	20	1004	CHOP: LENGTH .407-.403	CHOPPER			
90	20	3000	TUMBLE: LENGTH .416-.396	BARREL			
110	20	6000	TUMBLE END MIN. O.D.	BARREL			
130	20	0024	PLOT LENGTH SSQ 14	ADJ GAGE			
150	20	0024	GAGE OD SSQ 24	ADJ GAGE			
170	45	1002	HARDEN, WASH & TEMPER RC 60-64	FURNACE			
590	65	1000	INSPECT	VISUAL			
610	10	1000	PACK				
650	11	1000	SHIP				

processing the information. Some operations, such as inspection, can be considered direct or indirect. Normally, a direct labor operation is an operation that changes the configuration of the part, such as machine, grind, assemble, etc.

THE COST ACCOUNTING DATA BASE

The cost accounting data base serves the function of storing and keeping track of all the components produced and their related raw material types and costs; all the operations performed on the part in the different work centers, including setups and indirect labor; all the standard costs per item; and all the overhead values, including fixed, fringe and controllable. It is the job of the standard cost accounting data base to store all this information for each component produced and through the bill of material relate these components to their assemblies, where the costs are further rolled up into a total cost for the item. Also included are the scrap values or scrap allowance percentages for scrap or shrinkage at different points in the process if required. Figure 4 shows the relationship of components to assemblies through the bill of material. As components are assembled into assemblies, the costs from the lower level components are rolled up into the assembly.

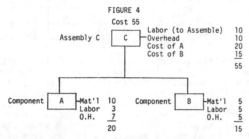

FIGURE 4

The advantage of this type data base is that any component can be costed out at any stage of manufacture. At the end of the month or accounting period, work in process can be priced out at last completed operation using availability figures from the open order file. The open order file run against the standard cost accounting data base will price out all work in process at last completed operation, which would be the most recent cost affected. This will give an accurate work in process inventory costing at any point in time, daily, weekly, etc. This cost can be compared to the cost accounting book value, which is a summation of all transations into and out of work in process. This includes raw material transactions into work in process, direct labor and overhead into work in process, and the transfer of product out of work in process to finished goods. It is important to constantly monitor the difference between the priced out work in process using open orders run against the cost accounting data base and the cost accounting book value maintained independently to make sure that the two are in sync. Any

large discrepancies between these two values should be investigated immediately to determine if there are errors in the book value or problems with the cost accounting data base. It is also useful to determine if there is poor floor reporting or undetected shrinkages on the shop floor.

Figure 5 shows the cost accounting data base. This data base is very similar to the traveler or operation sheet that moves with the work in the sense that it is an outline of the direct and indirect labor operations to be performed on the work. Also included are setup operations, if required. As shown in the exhibit, the standard cost for the operation is increased by the appropriate overhead amounts for controllable overhead, fringe overhead, and fixed overhead to get the total cost for a particular operation. The total cost for each operation is added to the cost of the previous operation and to the raw material required to get the total accumulated cost to that point to produce the part. Setup costs are prorated on the basis of the lot size to be produced. Also included are the labor grades of the operators performing particular operations so that labor costs can be calculated using the appropriate wage figure. As wages change, it is only necessary to change the value of the labor grade in the program.

The total cost for each component is broken down into setup costs and running costs with a total setup cost for the item. The total setup cost can be used in further calculations with the EOQ formula to reset the lot sizes as usage changes. It is important to separate the total setup cost for this purpose if any type of lot sizing is to be done automatically.

The important factor is that the standard cost accounting data base is a mirror image of the operation sheet or traveler and that the open order file is also a mirror image of the operation sheet and the standard cost accounting data base. As production is performed, the open order file reflects the position of the parts in the plant and the standard cost accounting data base reflects the accumulated cost roll up to that point.

VARIANCES

Variances from standard are normally expensed to the profit and loss statement on a monthly basis. An unfavorable variance would indicate that the department earned less than the standard cost allowed for a particular number of pieces and a favorable variance would indicate that the department earned more than the standard cost allowed for a particular operation. The time that the operator expended doing a particular lot of parts times his personal labor rate would indicate the actual amount of money spent on that lot. This would be compared to the allowed or standard housed in the cost accounting data base and the difference would be a variance.

FIGURE 5
STANDARD COST

ITEM 012345	PART CODE 70 0123450-20	PART NAME SHAFT	LOT SIZE 4,000,000									ACC. COST
MATERIAL 6642 WIRE	.101+.001	CODE 160100	.98LBS./M	COST/LB.	.678							.6640
SEQ. #	DEPT. #	OPERATION	DESCRIPTION	MAN HOURS	MACHINE HOURS	LABOR GRADE	LABOR COST/M	CONTROLLABLE COST/M	FRINGE COST/M	FIXED COST/M	SCRAP ALLOW.	TOTAL COST/M	
50	20	1094	SETUP	1.0000	1.0000	06	.0025	.0700	.0070	.0490		.1285	.7925
70	20	1004	SHOP	.0034	.0168/M	07	.0306	.0660	.0060	.0470		.1496	.9421
90	20	3000	TUMBLE	.0019	.0209/M	07	.0171	.0390	.0040	.0270		.0871	1.0292
110	20	6000	TUMBLE	.0013	.0146/M	07	.0117	.0270	.0030	.0190		.0607	1.0899
130	20	0024	PLOT	INDIRECT LABOR									
150	20	0024	GAGE	INDIRECT LABOR									
170	45	1002	HARDEN	.0015	.0051/M	07	.0135	.0016	.0040	.0260		.0451	1.1350
590	65	1000	INSPECT	.0047		10	.0282	.0060	.0080	.0150	.0227	.0799	1.2149
610	10	1000	PACK	.0014		09	.0098	.0110	.0030	.0070		.0308	1.2457
650	11	1000	SHIP	.0011		08	.0088	.0110	.0020	.0110		.0328	1.2785
										TOTAL COST/M		1.2785

TOTAL SETUP COST 514.00

Some typical variances are as follows:
1. Raw Material
   a. Price Variance - The standard price versus the actual price that the purchasing department pays.
   b. Usage Variance - The standard allowed raw material versus the actual amount the department used to make a given quantity of parts.
2. Direct Labor
   a. Price Variance - The standard cost per hour of the employee versus the actual rate per hour of the employee.
   b. Efficiency Variance - The number of standard units per hour that the employee should produce versus the actual number of pieces that the employee produced at the standard rate. We could use a higher priced employee on the job who could produce more than the standard number of pieces and have offsetting variances which would cancel out. We also might use a higher priced employee who would not produce the standard and we would have unfavorable price and efficiency variances.
3. Supplies
   a. Price Variance - The price paid for the supplies versus the standard cost allowed for the supplies.
   b. Efficiency Variance - The number of dollars of supplies allowed versus the actual dollar expenditure for supplies. The purchasing department may be able to purchase the supplies at a favorable price, but the using department might use more supplies than were allowed for the job.
4. Idle Capacity Variance
   The idle capacity variance, sometimes called the fixed variance, measures the cost of idle plant capacity. See Figure 6. In this example it was determined that the plant had capacity of 100,000 standard direct labor hours per month. Actual production for the month was only 80,000 standard direct labor hours; thus there was an idle plant capacity amounting to 20,000 direct labor hours. The 20,000 direct labor hours of idle plant capacity multiplied by the fixed component of the overhead rate, $1 per hour in this case, gives the variation of $20,000. This point may be further clarified by computing the variation as follows: 20,000 direct labor hours divided by 100,000 direct labor hours times $100,000 (monthly fixed cost) equals $20,000 variance. The idle capacity variance alerts management to the cost of running the factory at less than full capacity. This can be justification for plans to acquire more business to utilize the idle capacity.

FIGURE 6

Plant Capacity	100,000 DLH
Actual Production Earned	80,000 DLH
	20,000 DLH Lost
	X $1.00 Per Hour Fixed Overhead
	($20,000) Idle Capacity Variance

Indirect labor may have a fixed and variable portion. This is not always a smooth curve or a direct percentage of direct labor. For instance, a department with 20 operators per shift may have indirect labor of two crib attendants per shift. As production drops to the point of 12 operators per shift, the department may be able to operate with one crib attendant per shift. However, as production drops to seven operators per shift, the department would still need one crib attendant per shift. Indirect labor may be fixed at one crib attendant per shift down to a very low point in production and above 10 or 12 operators per shift indirect labor may vary in proportion to the number of direct labor operators. These types of situations will not give us a smooth cost curve or an absolute percentage that can be applied to the direct labor to absorb the indirect labor. In cases such as this there will be variances as production moves up and down.

FEEDBACK TO THE SHOP FLOOR

The purpose of the standard cost accounting system is to give feedback to management to show their historical performance. A more favorable term or approach to be used is "feed forward." What we are really trying to do is feed information to management that will help them assess what is going to happen before it happens so that corrective action can be made before the fact and not after the fact.

First, let's take a look at some of the traditional approaches of the standard cost accounting information. One of the most important is to feed to the first line supervision performance reports showing how they did against the direct labor standard, fixed standard, and controllable standards. Figure 7 shows a typical direct labor report showing actual hours and dollars expended versus standard dollars and hours earned. Performance is expressed in dollars and percentage of standard.

FIGURE 7

DEPARTMENT # 10
DIRECT LABOR ANALYSIS FOR PERIOD (DATE) TO (DATE)

PART #	PRODUCTION	STANDARD HOURS EARNED	ACTUAL HOURS	VARIANCE IN HRS.	VARIANCE IN $	% OVER (UNDER)
1256	10,000	500	550	(50)	(500)	(10)
1257	5,000	250	200	50	500	20
1258	50,000	200	180	20	200	10
1259	2,000	100	100	0	0	0
1260	1,000	150	125	25	250	17
TOTAL	68,000	1,200	1,155	45	450	4

Additional reports would be fed to the first line supervisor and his immediate manager showing raw material usage and variance and controllable usage and variance. These figures can be analyzed on a cost basis to determine why variances were favorable or unfavorable. Favorable variances should be analyzed with equal vigor because they can tell us that either the standard is wrong and the standard cost should be adjusted or some type of superior performance or method was used that could be applied to other areas.

FEEDBACK TO MANAGEMENT

Management is interested in the same figures as the first line supervision, including performance against budget for direct labor hours, controllables, and fixed earned; analysis of all variances from standard; and total profit and loss for the operation. Division management should be able to track backward from total division operation to total plant operation to individual department performance to product performance within the department and item performance within the department so that unusual variances can be traced from their source to the total or from the total back to the source. This type of audit trail allows all levels of management to analyze important cost figures.

FEED FORWARD REPORT

The great need in this area is for feed forward information that will alert management to potential problems or areas of concern. By integrating the MRP system and the standard cost accounting system, the master schedule can be priced out and this information can be fed forward to the operating departments, who can examine the direct labor hours that will be available to a department during the coming time period. Period staffing can then be adjusted to meet the pending production requirements. This type of analysis can help to prevent lack of or too much labor being available in the ensuing periods.

Controllable expenses can be calculated in advance based on the master schedule and operating departments can budget their expenditures based on expected overhead earnings during the coming weeks.

This type of feed forward information allows the department manager to better manage his resources of labor and material and avoid variances due to fluctuating production schedules.

A costed out master schedule and a costed out work in process inventory can provide valuable tools to materials management personnel to plan and achieve inventory goals and raw material expenditures. Using the costed out master schedule in relation to the sales forecast provides the necessary data to calaculate pro forma statements of finished goods inventory, work in process inventory, and raw material inventory for the ensuing time period.

CELL TECHNOLOGY

As we produce more and more items using cell technology, the question arises of how to interface the standard cost accounting system with the products produced on the cell. I will suggest two alternatives and discuss the pros and cons. Basically the cell takes a product through several manufacturing operations, in come cases from start to finish, of a component, or the cell may assemble several completed components and pack them for shipment. One method for accounting for the cost of the cell would be at a composite rate, or one cost for the entire operation of the cell. In other words, the entire cell would be treated as one operation. This is a very simple method and the production from the cell only has to be reported one time with all costs of the cell operation divided equally among the parts produced. This simplifies the cost accounting procedure and simplifies the production reporting, reduces work in process, and satisfies the needs of the MRP system. This is a very clean, easy approach.

Method number 2 would be to report each station of the cell, thereby having an individual cost and production reporting system for each individual operation. This might be useful as machine tools change within the cell and would save some time rebuilding costs as this occurred. It would also involve more reporting on the part of the cell operators, which would result in some redundancy.

FLEXIBLE CELLS

As we gravitate toward flexible cells, where machine tools are moved in and out of the cell on a weekly or monthly basis to satisfy production needs, additional problems arise. Costs may vary as one person runs two different machine tools one month and a different combination of three machine tools the following month. The standard cost system should be able to handle this problem by setting the standard cost based on the attention time needed by the employee to produce the item on that machine tool. As the employee splits his time between different machine tools, he should still be able to make the standard adjusted by the standard cost system. In other words, his efficiency should not change per se, only the amount of time he devotes to a particular operation. As cell manufacturing becomes flexible, our standard cost accounting system needs to be adaptable to this flexibility.

WORK CENTER LOADING

The allowed standard hours contained in the standard cost accounting data base should be able to be used for work center loading and unloading. Input-output control based on the standard hours should be accurate enough for capacity requirements planning. This gives us a dual functioning system which will calculate standard cost plus serve as a basis for the capacity requirements planning system.

The standard cost accounting system is an integral part of the MRP system and is directly related to all the important files found in the MRP system. The outputs from the standard cost accounting system serve as invaluable tools to assist managers at all levels in running the business. This part of the financial interface is an extremely important part in closing the management loop. This phase of the system is not extremely difficult to design or implement when other portions of the system, such as master scheduling, material requirements planning, and shop floor control are in place. The benefits of the financial interface outlined in this article will assist managers at all levels to control their operations with information fed forward to them from the standard cost accounting data base.

ABOUT THE AUTHOR
Bob Hanson, CPIM*

Bob is materials manager at the Clinton Bearings Plant of The Torrington Company, a division of Ingersoll-Rand.

He is a graduate of the University of Connecticut and holds an MBA and a master of accountancy degree from the University of South Carolina. He is an adjunct professor of business at Limestone College in Gaffney, South Carolina.

In addition to speaking frequently at APICS chapter meetings, he presented papers to the 1976, 1978, and 1980 APICS International Conferences.

Bob is certified at the fellow level by APICS and is a certified purchasing manager by the National Association of Purchasing Management.

ALTERNATE ROUTINGS: PANACEA OR PAIN?

Ed Heard, CPIM*
Plossl and Heard

FOREWORD

Alternate routings are frequently referred to in the Production Activity Control literature in a highly positive manner. Almost invariably, alternate routings are offered as one solution to short-term scheduling crises. They are also said to permit increased productivity through better utilization of available manpower and equipment. While these claims are true under certain conditions, positive results are neither automatic nor guaranteed. Inventory accounting, input/output control and machine assignment are all affected by alternate routings. This paper will show how each of these activities is affected by alternate routings, identify new problems thus created, and suggest straightforward, easily implementable procedures for problem resolution.

IMPORTANCE OF ALTERNATE ROUTINGS

Two production schedulers from Bigger is Better Machine Tool Company in Ohio once attended a Shop Floor Control seminar conducted by the author of this paper. After listening quietly for four or five hours they finally spoke up. Their problem, as they expressed it, was that they couldn't seem to keep all the machinists in department 12 busy. From that point, the dialogue between the schedulers and the author went something like this:

A - Do all the machines do the same thing?
S - Well--they can.
A - You mean they have similar functional capabilities.
S - Sure.
A - Then you've got too much capacity.
S - No, no, there's always work stacked up in front of department 12 and it never meets its deadlines.
A - You've got me. I'll have to think about it for awhile.
-------- Later --------
A - You're sure these machines can all do the same thing.
S - Hell, they're all the same brand and model number.
A - Are the same machinists idle over and over?
S - Pretty much--all but one of them.
A - Does he run the same machine all the time?
S - Yeah, sure.
A - And you're sure its just like the other ones?
S - Well--its newer. Three years as compared to 10-15.
A - Say, who decides which machine the work gets done on?
S - The department foreman.
A - Who is his boss and how does he evaluate the foreman?
S - Its the plant manager and I hear the foreman growling about labor variances all the time.
A - Say, remember those routings you mentioned. Do they distinguish between a primary routing and secondary ones?
S - Sure they do. Each part number has a primary routing and several secondary ones.
A - Is there any pattern to the primary routings for department 12?
S - What do you mean?
A - Does any one machine show up primary more often than the other?
S - No, not really. My buddy in IE says they try to balance the workload for all the machines.
A - That's interesting. With primary and secondary routings for machines that are just alike, I guess it doesn't make any difference which one they use to set the standards.
S - Oh, no. IE sets all the standards on the machine that's busy all the time. They say they have to do that to keep the operator from cheating. Otherwise, the operator of the fast machine would just run parts that list his machine as secondary so he could beat the standard.
A - And the foreman worries about labor variances more than idle time.
S - Well, he says the plant manager gripes about idle time but he really raises hell about labor variances.
A - I believe I see the problem.
    Still later at the same seminar, another scheduler spoke up.
S - I see how those other guys got in trouble. We don't do it that way. We have alternate standards to go with our alternate routings.
A - Great!

S - But we still have a problem. We have an input/output control system but we still can't manage our queues.
A - What do you mean?
S - Well the easiest way to say it is that although we keep our inputs and outputs in balance, our queues still grow. Every once in awhile, we have to ignore what the I/O report says and hold work back to keep from flooding the shop.
A - Do you mean your planned and actual inputs and outputs are in balance most of the time?
S - Both. We show standard hours of work to be done and standard hours that were done.
A - Let's just look at input. Can you tell me exactly how input is calculated?
S - Sure, we take the number of pieces on a work order and multiply it times the operation standard.
A - What about output, how do you measure that?
S - Same way we do input--pieces times the standard.
A - Primary or alternate?
S - What do you mean?
A - Do you use the primary routing standard or the alternate standard to compute output?
S - Why, we use the standard for the machine the order was run on of course.
A - What about input--primary or alternate?
S - We have to use primary for that because we don't know which machine it'll be run on for sure.
A - Now that's really interesting. The work can actually grow on the way through. You put 100 hours in, I run it on an alternate machine and get more than 100 hours out. Or maybe you put 100 in, I take half of it and run it on an alternate machine and still get 100 out.
S - But wouldn't that make the queue grow?
A - Give that man a cigar!
    Unfortunately, these comedies are all too common. In the first case, the IE attempt to balance workloads with primary routings is commendable. But, in a classic example of double think, they defend their right to set a single standard for a part using the machine that can run it fastest even though that machine may not be primary. From accounting's standpoint, a standard is a basis for variance calculation regardless of where it comes from. Often, accounting simply isn't aware that different machines can perform the same operation or that they can take different times to do so. The plant manager doesn't have time to do accounting's job. From his viewpoint, accounting is responsible for maintaining labor cost standards. It simply may never occur to him to question the standards being used to calculate labor variances.
    In the second case, IE has avoided the double think phenomenon by established alternate standards in conjunction with alternate routings. But there still appears to be some confusion about how standards are supposed to be used. The use of alternate standards to calculate incentive pay for the machine operator is correct. But, as the previous example illustrates, alternate routings can play havoc with input/output control if they are used incorrectly.

ACCOUNTING PROBLEMS

The presence of alternate routings seriously complicates the accounting process. Operation standards are inputs to incentive pay computation, management performance evaluation, pricing decisions and inventory accounting. Explanations of these functions are based invariably on the assumption of a single operation standard. But, when alternate routings exist, is such an assumption reasonable? Should a worker's incentive pay for performing an alternate operation be based on the time standard for the primary operation? Should plant management performance be evaluated relative to primary routing standards even though his capital investment requests continue to be denied? How can rational pricing decisions be made if operation standards are based only on primary routings? Does it make any sense to add to and relieve inventory based on fictitious primary routing standards? Since the answer to these questions is clearly no, some other way of dealing with these issues has to be found.

ACCOUNTING SOLUTIONS

Incentive pay--In many ways, this is the easiest problem to resolve. Alternate time standards corresponding to alternate operations can be adapted for this purpose.

The computational procedure does not change but the standard does. Suppose a worker spends 55 hours performing an alternate operation on 100 pieces. Then the two different computations of his efficiency would look like this:

WRONG

Primary Routing

Quantity	Std. Hours Per Piece	Hours Allowed	Efficiency
100	.5	50	91%

RIGHT

Alternate Routing

Quantity	Std. Hours Per Piece	Hours Allowed	Efficiency
100	.5	60	109%

Plant management evaluation--Evaluating plant management performance in an alternate routing environment is tricky. Such evaluations are usually based on direct labor variances. Consider the incentive pay example. Variances are designed to highlight not just differences between standard and actual but also the reasons for those differences. Analyzing the incentive pay example in variance terms leads to the corrective measures below. Assuming that labor costs are $10 per hour yields the following analysis:

WRONG

Labor Cost Allowed	-	Labor Cost Required	=	Total Variance
$500	-	$550	=	-$50

RIGHT

Labor Cost Allowed (primary)	-	Labor Cost Allowed (secondary)	=	Routing Variance
$500	-	$600	=	-$100

Labor Cost Allowed (secondary)	-	Labor Cost Required	=	Supervisory Performance Variance
$600	-	$550	=	$50

Routing Variance	+	Supervisory Performance Variance	=	Total Variance
-$100	+	$50	=	-$50

Clearly the usefulness of the right approach to management performance evaluation far exceeds that of the wrong approach. In the first case, management would be castigated for the $50 negative variance while, in the second case, the supervisor and worker responsible can be rewarded for superior labor performance. The second case also clearly reveals the existence of a routing problem. Further exploration would be necessary to determine if the routing variance was due to improper machine assignment or unbalanced primary routing workloads.

Pricing decisions--Pricing is usually based on careful analyses of manufacturing costs and market demand. The standard cost of a product is used as a basis for pricing. In many cases, standard material and standard labor costs are analyzed in detail. Suppose that standard labor costs are based solely on primary routings. Assuming that all operations are performed as indicated by their primary routings, there is no problem. Now suppose, more realistically, that 80 percent of the operations are executed primary and the other 20 percent are executed using alternate routings. The standard cost of the product will be clearly incorrect. But how can that be avoided? One easy way is based on the routing variance concept introduced in the previous section. For pricing purposes, composite standard labor cost can be developed based on the variance analyses from the most recent accounting period:

Total Routing Variance	÷	Total Labor Cost Allowed (primary)	=	Total Routing Variance Percentage
-$100,000	÷	$500,000	=	-20%

Standard Labor Cost Per Unit (primary)	x	$\left[1 - \begin{array}{c} \text{Total Routing} \\ \text{Variance} \\ \text{Percentage} \end{array} \right]$	=	Standard Labor Cost Per Unit (composite)
$10	x	[1 - (-.20)]	=	12

An even more precise composite standard labor cost per unit can be developed if routing variances are recorded by product. Most accounting systems lack the necessary precision to make this possible. In fact, the accumulation of routing variances will require a major step forward for most manufacturing accounting systems.

Inventory accounting--The presence of alternate routings and standards severely complicates inventory accounting. Completed products are transferred to finished goods inventory at cost and relieved from finished goods inventory when sold. Assuming that LIFO is in use, the question still remains as to which cost is to be used for transfer and inventory relief. The accountant's stock answer to this question is "the standard cost, of course." But which standard, primary or alternate? In an accounting sense, there is nothing wrong with using the primary standard for inventory transfers while accumulating variances due to routing and/or labor performance. The variances are usually closed to the inventory account at the end of each accounting period. This procedure can produce rather sudden and dramatic changes in a plant's fortunes as reflected by its financial statements. It should be apparent by now that an accounting standard cost based on a composite direct labor standard cost (see previous paragraph) can often lend stability to otherwise shaky financial performance.

INPUT/OUTPUT CONTROL PROBLEMS

Although input/output control is a relatively new concept, it is almost universally accepted as an attractive approach to queue management. Queue management using input/output control is usually described with a display like Figure 1.

FIGURE 1

		Periods		
		20	21	22
INPUT	Plan	350	350	350
	Actual	355	345	310
	Cum. Dev.	+5	0	-40
OUTPUT	Plan	380	380	380
	Actual	385	340	360
	Cum. Dev.	+5	-35	-55
QUEUE	Plan	350	420	390
	Actual	350	355	305

When alternate routings are used frequently, the main problem that arises is one of determining a consistent and reasonable approach to measurement for input, output and queue. On the one hand, it may appear to be unreasonable to measure input by primary routing standards when it is obvious that alternate routings are utilized frequently. But, on the other hand, it doesn't appear to be reasonable to measure input by alternate routing standards since machine/work order combinations are not fully determined until work actually commences. On the surface, output measurement appears straightforward. Once work has been done, it seems to make sense to measure it in terms of the standards for the routings actually used. But, as will be shown shortly, that can be a real mistake. Since the queue represents work waiting to be performed, choosing an appropriate measure for the queue is subject to the same considerations as choosing a measure for work center input.

Choosing apparently rational measures for these three items independently is not sufficient to assure success. In fact, inconsistent measures can lead to disastrous consequences. Consider the input/output report in Figure 2. After careful scrutiny, a single conclusion is inevitable. The numbers must be wrong. At the end of period 20, there were 350 hours in queue. During period 21, 345 hours of input occurred while only 340 hours of output were produced. Shouldn't the queue increase by five hours, not fifty? In light of the preceding discussion there is another possibility. Suppose input and queue are being measured by primary standards while output is being measured using standards for the machines on which the work was actually processed. After all, we have been advised repeatedly that labor reporting systems provide an ample basis for actual output computation. If that's the case here, the input/output report for period 21 has a different interpretation. During period 21, the input was 345 primary routing hours, but the output measured in primary routing hours was only 295. The 340 actual output hours achieved represented pieces times standard <u>for the machine actually used</u> whether <u>primary</u> or <u>alternate</u>.

FIGURE 2

| | | Periods | | |
		20	21	22
INPUT	Plan	350	350	350
	Actual	355	345	310
	Cum. Dev.	+5	0	-40
OUTPUT	Plan	380	380	380
	Actual	385	340	360
	Cum. Dev.	+5	-35	-55
QUEUE	Plan	350	420	390
	Actual	350	400	450

Suppose primary routing hours are used for all three measures. That should take care of most problems but not necessarily all of them. The planned output rate is not a measure of work to be done but is instead a measure of capacity to do work. If this concept is not well understood, some highly undesirable consequences can occur as illustrated by the augmented input/output report in Figure 3.

FIGURE 3

| | | Periods | | |
		20	21	22
INPUT	Plan	350	300	250
	Actual	355	295	210
	Cum. Dev.	+5	0	-40
OUTPUT	Plan	380	330	280
	Actual	385	290	260
	Cum. Dev.	+5	-35	-55
QUEUE	Plan	350	350	300
	Actual	350	355	305
INDIRECT LABOR		150	155	150

What has happened here is that demand has dropped off and consequently so has planned and actual input. The input/output planner correctly recognizes that less output will be required so he plans less. In this plant, output planning is <u>not</u> done in conjunction with manufacturing. Manufacturing's argument is that staffing is its prerogative and that it always picks up over or under staffing by watching indirect labor trends. But notice, at the bottom of the report, that indirect labor hours do not show the expected reduction. What has happened? The work center foreman is deathly afraid of two things--his queue getting too short and idle workers. So when he saw the work dropping off, he did what was in his mind the only reasonable thing to do. He started using a lot of alternate routings thus reducing his output as measured by primary routing standards and keeping his people busy.

INPUT/OUTPUT SOLUTIONS

Input/output problems can be resolved using several approaches. But all of the approaches have one thing in common. Both planned and actual input, output and queue must be measured on the same basis. If output is measured in apples, then input and queue cannot be measured in oranges. The principle to keep in mind is that measurement refers to some independent but consistent appraisal of work to be done versus capacity to do work versus work actually accomplished. The machine that was actually used to do some amount of work is irrelevant to the independent measure of how much work was done. Consider the work orders and work requirements in Figure 4.

FIGURE 4

Work Order	Primary Hours	1st Alternate Hours	2nd Alternate Hours
A	100	112	135
B	75	92	99
C	<u>120</u>	<u>130</u>	<u>143</u>
Totals	295	334	377

There are two simple ways to measure the amount of work to be done in these three work orders. In terms of their primary routings, there are 295 hours of work. Suppose we know from this work center's history that it usually produces 65 percent of its work on primary routing, 20 percent on the first alternate and 15 percent on the second alternate. Then we could compute a weighted average of the three totals above and conclude that the true measure of the work to be done is 315.1 standard weighted hours. Queue contents can be measured using this same approach but what about output?

In order to maintain consistency, the machines that work was actually done on must be ignored. The orders processed must be arrayed as in the previous example and a weighted measure of the work done must be calculated using the <u>same weights</u> used to measure input and queue contents. Once input and queue have been computed using a standard weighted hour approach, the only way that comparability can be maintained is to measure output the same way.

The second approach to measurement involves the use of primary routing standards for the input, output and queue. This approach offers several advantages. It is consistent in that input, output and queue are all measured in apples-- no oranges. It is simple and easy to understand. Finally the foreman's attempt to keep his people busy during slack periods by using alternate routings is immediately obvious in that actual output will drop below planned output by a significant amount.

One further qualification is needed. Planned capacity must be measured in the same terms as the items already mentioned. This implies that the productivity factor used to compute planned capacity must be based on demonstrated capacity in terms of primary standard hours of work accomplished during a given period. Long-run trends in this productivity factor for a work center should be watched carefully. A gradual degeneration over an extended period may imply growing primary routing workload imbalances. That is, already busy machines are being designated as primary for more and more work orders/parts. Consequently, the percentage of hours actually run on primary routing in the work center is decreasing relative to the percentage run on alternates. The result is the observed gradual decrease in the work center productivity factor.

MACHINE ASSIGNMENT PROBLEMS

Alternate routings increase the range of choices facing the individual with machine assignment responsibilities. Increasing the range of machine assignment choices further complicates an already complex situation. Basically, the machine assignment problem occurs when the foreman or dispatcher has a number of work orders with roughly equivalent priorities which must be run on a set of machines with roughly equivalent capabilities. The sequence of work orders that a dispatcher chooses for a particular machine controls the total amount of changeover time that machine experiences during a specific time period. Figure 5 shows how different sequences control total changeover time.

FIGURE 5

Changeover Hours

| From Work Order | To Work Order | | |
	A	B	C
A	X	.4	.7
B	.8	X	.2
C	.3	.5	X

Alternative Sequence Evaluation

	A B C	A C B	B A C	B C A	C A B	C B A
Total Changeover Hours	.6	1.2	1.5	.5	.7	1.3

When viewed this way the choice is clear. The preferred sequence is ABC because it results in the least total changeover time for the single machine. But this is a tremendously simplified problem. In the midst of ongoing operations involving numerous machines and work orders, such an analysis is virtually impossible since it requires total enumeration of all possibilities.

The assignment of work orders to individual machines also controls resource utilization since work order run time is machine-specific. That is, a work order may require differing amounts of run time for a given operation on different machines. In the example in Figure 6, the run times on different machines reflect the different standards associated with primary and alternate routings.

FIGURE 6

Run Hours

Work Order	Machine		
	1	2	3
X	40	50	60
Y	30	20	40
Z	40	30	50

Alternative Machine Assignment
Run Time Evaluation

Machines						
1	X	X	Y	Y	Z	Z
2	Y	Z	X	Z	X	Y
3	Z	Y	Z	X	Y	X
Total Hours Run Time	110	110	130	120	130	120

This example highlights the consequences of different machine assignments. If a different machine was primary on each of the three orders, the choice would be obvious. But that is not the case in this highly simplified example nor in reality. Because such problems can be extremely large in realistic situations, enumeration of all possibilities appears to be an unrealistic approach. Fortunately, shortcut approaches to problems of this particular type do exist. The real problem is to devise a set of decision aiding procedures that will allow work center dispatching/assignment personnel to arrive at consistently good machine assignment decisions in terms of both changeover times and run times.

MACHINE ASSIGNMENT SOLUTIONS

At this point, many plants have effective priority dispatching systems. Dispatch lists are prepared daily showing the relative priorities of those orders ready or almost ready to be run in the respective work centers. Most dispatch lists are not machine specific. Instead they are work center specific. Since work centers often consist of multiple machines, assignments have to be made. The succeeding discussion assumes the existence of an effective daily priority dispatching system.

Machine assignment in many plants is currently a highly unscientific process. Its earmarks are high setup costs and large negative labor variances. This is an unfortunate situation since rational practical approaches are readily available. But it is the intelligent combination of some of these techniques that produces practical implementable machine assignment procedures. The system suggested here operates on a daily basis. The dispatch list serves as an input to the assignment process. The first problem is to determine which work orders will be assigned to which machines based on their relative run time requirements. Naturally, this problem does not exist if each work order has only one permissible routing in the work center. The second problem is determination of the actual sequence to be used at each machine.

The machine assignment approach suggested here is illustrated by Figure 7. The work orders in the lefthand column are taken from today's dispatch list. They represent work ready to run in this work center. The daily capacities of the three machines in this work center are shown below the second horizontal line of the figure as are the hours previously assigned and the hours which can be assigned today. The bottom row (Hours Assigned) would not be filled in until machine assignments have been determined. The numbers

FIGURE 7

Run Hours

Work Order	Machine		
	1	2	3
u	10✓	15	12.5
v	20	10✓	22
x	2.5	5	2✓
y	4✓	3	--
z	6	5	7✓
Daily Capacity	24	16	16
Hours Previously Assigned	8	5	6
Hours Available	16	11	10
Hours Assigned	14	10	9

in the body of the figure represent run hours for each work order on each machine with one exception. Machine three is not a permissible routing for work order y. Assignments are made sequentially by reviewing one row of the table at a time starting with the top one. Notice that work order u requires only 10 hours on machine one and substantially more on the other two machines. Since the run time (10 hours) does not exceed the 16 hours available, work order u is assigned to machine one. In the second row, machine two offers the minimum run time (10) and it does not exceed the unassigned machine time (11). So work order v is assigned to machine two. In row three, work order x can be processed fastest on machine three and the two hours required are substantially less than the unassigned available time. Work order x is assigned to machine three. In the fourth row, it is clearly advantageous to process work order y on machine 2 but there is not enough unassigned time available. So work order y is assigned to machine one which does have enough time. In the fifth row work order z is assigned to machine three, the most inefficient alternate operation, because it has enough available capacity and machine one and two do not.

Implementing this procedure is fairly easy because it is not hard to understand. It can be taught to virtually anyone in a few minutes. In an actual implementation, the work order list might be longer than the one shown. The stopping point for the assignment procedure occurs whenever one runs out of capacity or work orders, whichever comes first. Any leftover work orders will show up on tomorrow's list. Does the procedure produce optimal results? Not necessarily, but results should be close to optimal and they are consistent. Since the procedure is so straightforward, it can be implemented on the shop floor. Standard forms with machines and work orders labeled but unidentified can be provided. The foreman or dispatcher can fill in the primary and alternate routing run times. Subjective inputs such as operator/machine capabilities or deficiencies can even be incorporated. This can be done by adjusting or in some cases eliminating the official expected run times. The idea is to provide easy to use tools to help make consistent decisions systematically--not to second guess or circumvent experienced intuition.

Once machine assignments have been determined, the actual sequence of work orders to process on each machine needs to be established. In the top half of Figure 8, the work orders to be run on a machine are shown across the top and down the left side. The numbers in the table represent the fraction of hours required to change over from each work order to every other work order. Work order A is the last work order in the sequence determined yesterday. Given that a particular work order is running, there is always some other work order that can be changed-over to more efficiently than the others. This work order can be found in each case by looking for the minimum value in each row. If any other work order is chosen instead of the one with minimum changeover time, an opportunity cost is incurred. In the bottom half of Figure 8, the row minimums have been subtracted from the remaining elements in each row. What remains is an opportunity cost matrix.

The changeover sequence is determined as follows. Draw a horizontal line from the AA element to the first zero element. Then, draw a vertical line from the zero element to the first x. Next, draw a horizontal line to a zero element. If a vertical line has already been drawn in the column where the zero is located, draw a horizontal line to the smallest non-zero number in the row in which the zero is located. Continue until all work orders have been accounted for.

FIGURE 8

Changeover Hours

From Work Order	To Work Order				
	A	B	C	D	E
A	X	.2	.6	.8	.4
B	X	X	.3	.5	.7
C	X	.9	X	.7	.4
D	X	.6	.5	X	.9
E	X	.9	.3	.4	X

Changeover Opportunity Cost
(Hours)

From Work Order	To Work Order				
	A	B	C	D	E
A	X	0	.4	.6	.2
B	X	X	0	.2	.4
C	X	.5	X	.3	0
D	X	.1	0	X	.1
E	X	.6	0	.1	X

Recommended Sequence:

A B C E D

As in the previous case this procedure does not guarantee optimal solutions but it will continually produce very good solutions. It must be repeated daily for each machine in each work center. It, too, can be facilitated by standard forms. The foreman is probably in the best position to estimate changeover times. This approach can help him to do systematically what he's probably doing haphazardly at present. The procedure can be taught in a few minutes. It does take several run-throughs to fully grasp its significance.

SUMMARY

In the production activity control and capacity planning literature, alternate routings are offered as solutions to temporary capacity imbalances and schedule crunches. Problems that may be created by the too prevalent uses of alternate routings are not addressed. This paper has examined the interaction of alternate routings with manufacturing accounting, input/output control and machine assignment. When alternate routings are used indiscriminately in the absence of understanding of their consequences, some rather strange side effects occur. There are practical tools to solve the problems that alternate routings create and to prevent undesirable alternate routing side effects. Some of these ways were described and illustrated in this paper.

ABOUT THE AUTHOR

Ed Heard is a principal in Plossl and Heard and in Ed Heard and Associates, management services companies engaged in manufacturing control systems education, counseling, use and development. Ed is a frequent speaker at professional society meetings, conferences and seminars. His background includes a combination of hands-on practical experience and academic know-how. He has been consulting, publishing and teaching for a dozen years and currently serves on the faculty of the University of South Carolina College of Business. Ed is certified at the fellow level by APICS and is active in both APICS and AIIE.

Reprinted from the APICS 1986 Conference Proceedings.

JIT APPLICATIONS IN THE JOB SHOP ENVIRONMENT

James P. Kelleher, CFPIM
Westinghouse Electric Corporation

OBJECTIVE OF PRESENTATION

When "Just-In-Time" was first presented in North America, the main focus was on Repetitive Manufacturing. It was in this segment of industry that foreign competitors, employing "Just-In-Time" methods were, having the most extensive and visible impact on Western Manufacturers. It was also in this segment that most Americans perceived our manufacturers as being the world leaders. Finally, it just seemed more natural that the JIT approach blended well in a Repetitive Manufacturing Environment.

We have since learned that "Zero Inventories" has much to offer in the Job Shop environment as well. The objectives certainly apply as does many of the techniques. Certainly, the typical Job Shop treated Inventory as the safety net for circumventing problems rather than solving them. This presentation will address the application of Zero Inventories in the Job Shop environment.

ZERO INVENTORIES

The objective of Zero Inventories is to lead a consistent program to eliminate waste within our industries that will ensure continuing worldwide manufacturing leadership. Our industries are non-competitive unless they recognize that waste is anything that does not add value to the product. Our major problem is simply waste. This applies not only to the "hands-on" production worker, but to our staff and support personnel as well.

The waste that exists is not readily identified in our accounting statements. It is manifested in:

    Inventory - Too High
    Quality - Too Low
    Lead Time - Too Long
    Material Movement - Too Far and Too Often

Many companies point with pride to their computerized, multilevel Automatic Storage and Retrieval System (AS/RS). Many of these are justifiable. However, some are examples of "solving the wrong problem". The question to be answered is why is the inventory so high; not how to use sophisticated hardware and software to store and retrieve it.

Poor quality increases costs for rework and replacement, disrupts manufacturing operations, and causes deliveries to be rescheduled. It also increases Inventory as we apply "yield factors", "safety stock" and "attrition allowances".

Long lead times increase Work-In-Process Inventories and forces companies who produce for stock to manufacture goods based on forecasts that extend over long horizons. This increases forecast error as the accuracy deteriorates as the horizon is extended. The result is excessive finished goods inventory, lost sales, or both.

Many companies have inventories that equal 1/3 to 1/2 of their assets. While serious, this is only part of the problem. Inventories are kept high to avoid solving problems. We need to lower the inventory so as to expose the problems, and apply the resources and techniques to solve them. We hold the Production & Inventory Control Manager responsible for Inventory Investment. This is analogous to holding the accountant responsible for costs. It is the Process that determines Inventory levels. If we are to achieve Zero Inventories results, we need to concentrate on the Process --- not on Inventory.

CONCEPTS UNIVERSALLY APPLICABLE

In a Job Shop environment, the Zero Inventory Elements that require our attention are:

    Housekeeping
    Quality through Process Capability
    Reduced Set-Up Times
    Small Lot Sizes -- Down To "Lot-Size = 1"
    Preventive Maintenance
    Reduced Inventories (To uncover problems).

    Reduced Space (Shorter Material Travel).
    Capacity Control
    Multi-functional Workers
    Excellent Pre-Production Preparation

The Zero Inventory elements listed above are similar in both principle and application to both Repetitive and Job Shop environments. A program of continuous improvement must be applied to these elements. Zero Inventories is not a goal --- it is an unending journey.

MODIFICATIONS FOR JOB SHOP APPLICATIONS

Some characteristics of Job Shops require that the application of Zero Inventories be modified. These are shown in Table I.

COMPARISON OF JOB SHOP & REPETITIVE MANUFACTURING

ELEMENT	JOB SHOP	REPETITIVE
Plant Layout	Manufacturing Process	Product Flow
Work Authorization	Work Order	Flow Rate
Process Routings	Variable by Part	Fixed
Cost Accounting	Job Cost	Process Cost
Load Leveling Factor	Labor	Material
Operation Balancing	Limited	High
Material Handling	Irregular	Standardized
Plan & Control	Lots	Rate

TABLE I

These characteristics result from the following conditions of the typical Job Shop:

    Irregular/Low Volume Product Demand Mix
    High Variety
    Queues
    Frequent Engineering Change

The volume and mix of product demand in a Job Shop is highly variable from time period to time period. There is no consistent pattern of demand. Thus, the Job Shop cannot develop a level final assembly schedule with a repetitive sequence of product mix.

As Job Shops utilize Work Orders and lots move from one manufacturing process to another in a sequence specified on a routing that varies according to the product design, one Zero Inventory technique applied in repetitive manufacturing that is not practical in a conventional job shop is a "pull" system for triggering component replenishment. A "pull" system has two requirements:

    Fixed Volume Upper Limit
    Signal For Replenishment

As we indicated earlier, Job Shops usually have an irregular, low volume product demand mix. Also, without a uniformly sequenced final assembly schedule, there is no consumption of an individual component at the next higher assembly level to signal the need for a replenishment. In view of this, a "push" system is more practical for most Job Shops. A "push" system implies that component replenishments will be driven by a requirements planning schedule.

Material Requirements Planning (MRP) is a computerized system for determining schedule requirements. There has been some criticism that using MRP does not reduce lead times and Work-In-Process Inventories to the extent achievable with a "pull" system. There may be some truth to this. Most of the problem is, however, more the result of perception than reality. If an MRP - driven Production Control System uses long lead times, and large lot-sizes, then long cycle times and high Work-In-Process Inventories will result. The same effect can occur from a loose "pull" system. Thus, the problem is more related to application than technique selection.

In any Job Shop, lead time consists of five components:

    Set-Up Time
    Run Time
    Move Time
    Wait Time
    Queue Time

It is not unusual for queue time to account for 80 - 90% of the lead time. The advantage of repetitive manufacturing is that a product flow plant layout reduces or eliminates queue time. As a result, if a Job Shop can change some or all of its operations to a product flow layout, significant reductions in lead time (and Work-In-Process) will result. Where this is not possible, changes that move in the direction of flow manufacturing or even automation can be extremely beneficial.

Job Shops can emulate Flow Manufacturing by applying Group Technology and Flexible Manufacturing Systems. While there may be great variety in the design of the end products, there frequently is considerable commonality in the components. Group Technology is a technique that allows parts to be classified according to the operational sequence in which they are manufactured. A classification and coding system that concentrates on part geometry and material is required. Getting Engineering to standardize component design can greatly facilitate this effort. Manufacturing cells can then be designed for each of the classifications into which the majority of components have been identified. Work stations are then located according to the sequence in which operations are performed for each classification. The layout can be in a straight flow or a U-line as illustrated in Figure 1.

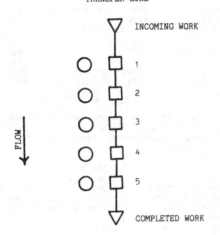

TRANSFER LINE

INCOMING WORK

∇ STORAGE

☐ WORK STATION

◯ OPERATOR

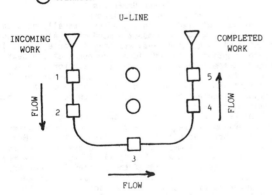

U-LINE

FIGURE 1

As a lot-sized release is made, it is kept in incoming inventory at the cell, until it is ready to be put in work. The first piece from the lot is put in work in Operation 1. When finished, it is moved into Operation 2 and the second piece is started in Operation 1. This continues until all the pieces in the lot are completed through Operation 5. Once the lot is completed, it is located in the Outgoing Storage area. This eliminates queues between operations and allows operations to be "overlapped". Once a piece is put in Operation 1, it is never laid down again until it is finished.

Naturally, there is a need to keep the operations balanced (synchronized) to avoid queues between operations. Also, machine utilization can be less than

achievable in a process layout, as when there is no requirement for parts produced by a cell, the cell is idle.

Transfer of parts between work stations can be mechanized, as can the loading and unloading of parts in the work station. The advantage of the U-line is that, with a low volume, one operator can run more than one machine.

Flexible Manufacturing Systems (FMS) are available that allow a part to be completely machined in one set-up. These machines, which are computer controlled, can select and load a wide variety of tooling in the proper sequence while adjusting the work table so as to properly orient the part.

It may not be possible to justify producing all parts in Group Technology Cells or on Flexible Manufacturing Systems. This can result in process-oriented Job Shop "islands". Again, the focus should be on reducing queues. Good Priority and Input/Output Controls are required. A good schedule-driven priority system should determine the sequence in which jobs are put in work. The release of work to a Work Center or Cell should be balanced with the Output. This is necessary to maintain a minimum backlog and thus control the queue (the major component of lead time in a manufacturing facility).

SET-UP REDUCTION

One factor that extends queues (and lead time) is large lot sizes. However, lot-sizes cannot be arbitrarily reduced. If we were to reduce lot-sizes, the result would be to increase the number of set-ups. If the time required for set-ups remained the same, we would actually increase waste. No value is added to the product by the set-up. Also, the time spent in making set-ups reduces the available capacity for producing products. It follows that we can produce in small lot-sizes only after we conduct a vigorous program of set-up reduction.

A careful methods analysis of each set-up is required to accomplish this. The fastest payoff can be realized by studying the set-ups that require the longest set-ups first. The first step is to document the current methods. In many cases at the present time, the method is not documented, but left to the judgment of whoever does the set-up. This lack of standardization can result in poor quality and high cost.

In accordance with good Industrial Engineering practice, the set-up should be divided into three elements:

External - Tasks that can be performed while the previous operation is still running. These could include getting special tools and gauges, jigs and fixtures, etc. Arrangements can be made to have all items needed for a set-up delivered to the Work Station before the set-up is changed. This would include hand tools.

Internal - Tasks that must be performed with the machine idle. The methods should be studied so as to reduce the time necessary for the exchange to a minimum. The design of the tooling to be used can include features that will reduce this time (This includes match plates, locating pins, carts with rollers, etc.). It may be necessary to have other operators assist the operator running the machine on which the set-up is being changed.

Eliminate - This can be accomplished through good tool
Adjustments   design and standardization and modularization of tooling. As an example, on punch presses, a standard die height will reduce the need for adjusting the length of the ram stroke. Also, modular "desk drawer" tooling will eliminate some adjustments on machine tools.

Some dramatic reductions in set-up time have been accomplished. General Motors Buick Division was able to reduce set-up on 500-1000 Ton Danly Presses in 3 months as shown below:

	Before	After	Percent Reduction
Downtime	6 Hours	18 Minutes	95%
Labor Time	46 hours	4 Hours	91%

SMALL LOT SIZES

Reducing the Lot-sizes will reduce queues and result in getting a small quantity of several part numbers, rather than a large quantity of a few. This generally results in improved schedule performance.

Set-up time reduction will reduce the average set-up time. It is also advisable to reduce the variance in set-up times among jobs so as to avoid the tendency to select jobs in a sequence that optimizes set-up change over, thus improving efficiency measurement results. What is important is running the right job. The sequence (priority) should be based on satisfying schedule requirements, not efficiency or machine utilization. Releasing jobs that are not yet required in order to improve efficiency or utilization adds to queues and increases throughput times.

There are advantages and disadvantages to this approach. As there are more orders to process there are more transactions, which increase the data processing load. Also, there are more work orders on the floor to be controlled. On the other hand, work caused by reworking defective components, cancelling work orders no longer required, rescheduling, and "splitting" lots is reduced. Improving shop performance reduces the need to adjust the system.

CAPACITY REQUIREMENTS PLANNING & CONTROL

As discussed earlier, most Job Shops cannot develop a level Final Assembly schedule, due to the fluctuations in product demand and the variety of product mix. The only parameter that can be leveled is labor hours. We need a system for determining Capacity Requirements and comparing the result with available capacity. Integrated Manufacturing Information Systems frequently include Master Production Scheduling (MPS) modules that have "Rough Cut Capacity" capability that can be used for measuring the "fit" of new business. They also include Capacity Requirements Planning modules that calculate time-phased load by work station for more detailed planning. Decisions must then be made concerning alternatives for matching available capacity with requirements. The Master Schedule should always be realistic and doable.

Even though the Capacity Requirements may match the Capacity available in aggregate, there can be overloads and underloads in specific work centers. It is here that another Zero Inventories principle needs to be applied – namely; a multi-functional work force. Operators trained and qualified to perform several jobs provide flexibility to satisfy needs created when this situation arises.

ENGINEERING

Frequent Engineering Change is another condition frequently found in Job Shops. This is especially true of Manufacturers who produce products designed for a specific application that are made to order. There is no Engineering Breadboard or Prototype Development Units. The first unit built to the Engineering design is shipped to the customer. The impact of Engineering Change can have a serious effect on both cost and delivery performance.

Product design should involve participation by not only Engineering, but Manufacturing and Quality as well. Engineering should have a "Design-to-Cost" procedure that includes Value Engineering. Producibility and Reliability depend heavily on product design. Engineering changes should only be generated after a complete review with Manufacturing and Quality personnel. This review must include an evaluation of the effect on cost and delivery.

Finally, the Manufacturing organization must have flexibility in incorporating the change promptly and efficiently, without a deterioration in product quality. This requires careful, accurate and complete information on the Engineering Change, that is in terminology that is clear and not ambiguous to those employees that will implement it.

IMPACT ON THE ORGANIZATION

Without the entire company being committed to Zero Inventories, the full benefits cannot be achieved. In many Job Shops, especially those that manufacture to order, it is not unusual for a large portion of the lead time to be used for order entry and defining the product. Top Management must participate in Zero Inventories and make sure that all parts of the organization supports it.

Manufacturing must have the following items on schedule and of high quality:

- An accurate and complete order that defines their task (quantity, part number, schedule, etc.).
- Engineering Drawings.
- Quality specifications.
- Process specifications.
- Routings with time standards.
- Product structure and data for the Bill of Material.
- Purchased material lead times.
- Tooling.
- Software for computer-controlled processes.
- Test Equipment.
- Packing and Shipping Instructions.

SUMMARY

Zero Inventory Philosophy and Practices offer many opportunities to improve productivity and quality in Job Shops as well as in Repetitive Manufacturing. Due to the characteristics of Job Shops, some of the applications may require modification or even a different approach. This paper offers some suggestions that address Job Shop conditions. However, whether being applied to Repetitive Manufacturing or Job Shops, the objective of Zero Inventory is still the elimination of waste.

BIOGRAPHY

J. P. "Spike" Kelleher was the 1982 International President of The American Production and Inventory Control Society. He has a B.S. in Industrial Engineering and an M.S. in Business Administration. He is Certified by APICS at the Fellow Level. He has been employed by Westinghouse Electric Corporation for 34 years. He currently is the Commodity Planning Manager at the Defense & Electronic Center in Baltimore.

He was the Team Director for two APICS-Sponsored Study Missions to Japan. He has been an Adjunct Faculty Member at three Baltimore-Area Colleges. He currently is the President of the APICS Educational & Research Foundation and the Chairman of the Aerospace & Defense Special Interest Group.

Reprinted from the APICS 1982 Conference Proceedings.

JOB-SHOP SCHEDULING: A CASE STUDY

Ray Lankford - Plossl & Lankford
Tom Moore - Remmele Engineering, Inc.

Even though Remmele Engineering, Inc. had virtually no prior experience with computer-based manufacturing systems, they recognized that better management of capacity could help them achieve a significant competitive advantage. In this case study, the Vice President of Operations of Remmele describes their implementation of a capacity management system with exceptional capabilities, and he assesses the performance improvements they achieved. To provide a perspective on capacity management systems, the consultant on the Remmele project evaluates developments of the last decade in an effort to define what is the "state-of-the-art" today.

CAPACITY SYSTEMS IN PERSPECTIVE (Ray Lankford)

Ten years ago, in the early 1970's, the revolution in systems of manufacturing planning and control had just begun. Not only did the innovators of those years bring to the attention of the world the power of MRP and the importance of master scheduling, but they also stimulated thought and development in major aspects of capacity management. The formative paper on Input/Output Control appeared in 1970 (1); a redefinition of what was thereafter called Capacity Requirements Planning occurred at APICS Conference of 1971 (2); and at the Conference of 1973, I spoke about the feasibility of what we now call Operation Sequencing (3).

Interestingly enough those three papers are still in the reprints offered by APICS for study for the certification examination. They represent pioneering thought and are still useful for the study of basic concepts, but they come from an early period in the "systems revolution" of the 1970's and 1980's. As chairman of the APICS Certification Committee on Capacity Management, I am involved now in the search for and examination of new papers which will replace the earlier ones for our study - new works which portray what we have learned and what we have developed in the intervening decade.

There have been significant developments in recent years, which I will describe and evaluate. At the same time, there is a tremendous gap today between what we <u>know</u> about capacity management and how we <u>apply</u> the techniques available to us. This "proficiency gap" between what we know and what we accomplish in capacity management is one of the most serious problems of manufacturing control today. It is the root of failure of many firms to derive benefits from their installation of MRP. It is a major impediment to increasing productivity in countless manufacturing companies. Without a doubt, improving the management of capacity offers for most companies the greatest single opportunity for improving performance of any sector of manufacturing planning and control. And because of this common "proficiency gap", the fact that a company relatively inexperienced with systems implemented and is successfully using an advanced capacity management system makes the Remmele story interesting and significant.

Remmele's capacity management system consists of Capacity Requirements Planning and Operation Sequencing. They elected not to use Input/Output Control because of characteristics of the production environment which Tom Moore will explain. In this perspective on capacity management, I will not focus on Input/Output Control, since that was done in a paper at the 1980 Conference (4). We will look, however, at the "state-of-the-art" today in CRP and Operation Sequencing.

In 1971, George Plossl and Oliver Wight wisely proposed the term "Capacity Requirements Planning" to replace what was previously called "infinite loading" or "loading to infinite capacity". They pointed to two weaknesses of traditional machine loading:
1. a typically high past-due load; and
2. a misleading decay of load derived from released orders only.
A solution was proposed for each of these defects:
1. improve priority planning with MRP, so as to reschedule late but unneeded jobs to their time of actual need; and
2. use planned orders from MRP to portray future loads over the entire CRP horizon.

Thus Capacity Requirements Planning took its place as a major module of the integrated manufacturing system.

Despite the demonstrated effectiveness of the technique, however, a "proficiency gap" still exists today. A minority of companies are using CRP effectively - not unlike the situation ten years ago when a relatively few companies had mastered MRP. Moreover, the capacity planning modules of commercial software are usually the weakest part of the packages, making CRP unnecessarily difficult to use effectively. Finally there are some extraordinary misconceptions regarding CRP which may cause confusion to potential users. One such misconception is that CRP is expensive. One consultant has written, "It probably consumes more computer capacity than any other single step within MRP". Leaving aside the semantic confusion of this reference to MRP, this commentator is simply misinformed.

In a plant handling 6,420 manufacturing jobs using the same software as Remmele, total processing time for MRP, CRP, and Operation Sequencing (with networking) is about four hours, with CRP requiring about 60% of the time of MRP. In terms of actual CPU time, excluding file manipulation and printing time, CRP loading requires about one minute.

Certainly, when compared to the benefits of having advance visibility of capacity overloads and underloads, the cost of CRP is acceptable and should not deter anyone from using it.

Some other misconceptions about CRP will be dispelled in a later section.

When the manufacturing people at Remmele Engineering decided to improve their ability to schedule their shop, the specific technique they wanted was Operation Sequencing. As Tom will explain later, they arrived at this conclusion independently, without the advice of any so-called "expert" advisor. This was probably fortunate, because no technique in manufacturing control is more misunderstood by consultants and practitioners alike than Operation Sequencing.

Operation Sequencing is sometimes thought of as "finite loading" because it loads work centers only to their known capacity - i.e., to "finite" capacity. Just, however, as the term "infinite" loading was a disservice to the perfectly valid technique we now call Capacity Requirements Planning, so the term "finite loading" bestows confusion and even animosity on what is really an extremely powerful and useful technique of capacity control.

Correctly understood, Operation Sequencing is a technique of <u>simulation</u>. It simulates in advance, inside the computer, the sequence in which manufacturing jobs will flow through the various work centers of the plant. Unlike some of the more complex mathematical methods sometimes applied to real-world problems, computer simulation has proven effective in many applications. In their classic book of 1967, Plossl and Wight devoted a section to Job Shop Simulation, which concluded, "Simulation will undoubtedly become one of the most important tools for controlling shop operations efficiently."(5) Indeed, at that time a number of companies, especially in Europe, were already using simulation successfully. One of my clients in Scandinavia has had the technique in continual use with good results since 1968.

The development of manufacturing systems in Europe has been very different from that in the United States. Because of the damage sustained by manufacturing plants during World War II, European industry in the post-war years concentrated on the management of critical capacity. In the United States, by contrast, capacity was plentiful and readily expandable, but materials were frequently critical in a booming economy. It is not surprising that the thrust of systems development was toward materials planning and inventory control. Of course, the eventual development of MRP improved priority planning for both purchased and manufactured items. Nevertheless, capacity management received far less emphasis in the United States than in Europe.

Recently, a group of manufacturing system specialists came from Europe to review several major U.S. software packages for potential purchase. Their conclusions were that the U.S. uses bills of materials far more expertly than they do, and that Master Scheduling and MRP software are highly developed here. They were, however, appalled at the crudity of the capacity management modules which they examined and, in particular, they were shocked at the infrequent use of Operation Sequencing, which they regard as commonplace.

That Operation Sequencing became both misunderstood and controversial in the United States is one of the major misfortunes of the generally productive past decade of system evolution. Several factors contributed to the confusion:

1. the "infinite" versus "finite" debate carried over from prior years tended to polarize opinions before real analysis could begin;

2. the development of MRP concentrated thought and effort, and rightly so, on priority planning methodology;

3. companies implementing MRP were so totally occupied with the demands of data integrity, master scheduling, rough-cut capacity planning, and MRP utilization that they were slow to develop beyond MRP to capacity management; and

4. some of the major opinionmakers in the field, for a variety of reasons, quickly denounced Operation Sequencing as unworkable.

It is both interesting and useful to examine this last factor and ask whether some of these early denunciations were valid then or remain valid now. Certainly Remmele Engineering went into their implementation of Operation Sequencing fully aware of the reasons given by some "experts" as to why the technique will not work. Remmele simply concluded that the objections of a decade ago are no longer valid today.

Criticism of Operation Sequencing derives from that fundamental misconception referred to earlier, that it is the same as finite loading. Let's look at the facts.

Oliver Wight has described finite loading in this way: "It automatically revises the need priorities - that is, the priorities developed by MRP, for example, in order to level the load." (6)

Does Operation Sequencing do this? Absolutely not! It uses the required dates developed by MRP to prioritize all jobs and does not revise them.

The definition of Operation Sequencing is: "...a simulation of what is likely to happen on the shop floor, given the current production plan and existing man power and machine availability." (7)(Underlining emphasis was added by the author.)

By "current production plan" is meant the Master Schedule converted into manufacturing jobs with required dates developed by MRP. As will be seen later, Operation Sequencing at Remmele uses the required date of each job to state its priority and always endeavors to schedule to that date.

Although Operation Sequencing loads work centers to finite capacity, it clearly is something different from "finite loading".

As a result of the confusion over finite loading, some of the defects of that limited technique have been linked to Operation Sequencing.

In the early 1970's, four specific problems were attributed to any system using "finite" loading:

o Assumes predictable job arrival.
This alleged defect of simulation is ironic, in that the prediction of job arrivals by simulation is far more accurate than it is with backward planning, upon which CRP and conventional Dispatch Lists are based. Some early ultra-sophisticated simulators pretended to predict events to fractions of an hour, which deserved the ridicule of practical manufacturing people. The objective of Remmele's system is to do better - much better - than backward planning which uses "planned" queue allowances, which frequently do not prevail in the plant. This will be illustrated in the section on the mechanics of Operation Sequencing.

o Component priorities are usually dependent.
Here the objection was that getting all components of an assembly scheduled to complete at the same time required endless reiterations of the loading process. This is really a "paper tiger" in that the purpose of simulation is not to schedule all components equally late, but rather to identify those which will probably be late so that early action can be taken to solve the problem.

o Automatic master scheduling is risky.
Nothing could be more true! However, no practical proponent of simulation ever advocated letting the computer have the final say in determining the schedule. All simulation purports to do is to make a reasonable estimate of completion dates, to highlight potential problems in advance, and to allow production controllers and master schedulers to decide if problems can be solved or if the Master Schedule must be revised. Again, this will be demonstrated in a later section.

o There are easier, better ways to do the job.
In some production environments, this is unquestionably true. But for the complex network of thousands of manufacturing jobs competing for capacity at hundreds of work centers in a job shop with non-uniform routings, the alternatives of CRP, Input/Output Control, and conventional MRP pegging are grossly inefficient in the solution of the enormous number of daily problems confronting the production controller.

In addition to these alleged problems, there are two other misconceptions which often perplex critics of Operation Sequencing:

o One must use either Capacity Requirements Planning or Operation Sequencing.
In reality, of course, these techniques are used together, as was recognized by Plossl and Wight fifteen years ago when they advised, "Orders are first...loaded to infinite capacity to see where overloads will occur, then orders are rescheduled ...based on available capacity after corrective actions have been taken..." (5)

o It requires enormous amounts of computer time.
Here, two things have happened in the last ten years: simulators have become simpler and computer power has become cheaper. Tom Moore will address this issue in his remarks.

Where, then, does the "state-of-the-art" stand today? On this matter Oliver Wight has proposed: "Since we've abolished infinite loading, if we're going to continue with our progress, in my opinion, we should abolish finite loading, and if necessary replace it with some kind of a shop simulator that tells the planner what he might want to do in order to do some load leveling on the vital few, rather than having the computer automatically do the load leveling on everything." (6)

This is sound advice. "Finite loading" is a dead issue. But what about simulation? Wight goes on: "I would have no objection to somebody using the basic logic of finite loading in simulation mode, where they showed the planner what would happen if jobs flowed through different work centers at the current production rate." (6)

Remmele Engineering is doing exactly that. They call it Operation Sequencing, and Tom Moore is here to tell you how they got started.

THE MANUFACTURING ENVIRONMENT (Tom Moore)

Remmele is in three basic businesses: 1. contract machining, 2. fabrication, and 3. designing and building special machines. Manufacturing operations are located in five plants comprising a total of 271,000 square feet. Each plant is individually designed and equipped to offer a specialized type of precision machining or machine building and fabrication service.

Each of these basic businesses presents a somewhat different manufacturing environment.

Contract machining - Remmele's contract machining or general machining activities encompass a broad spectrum of part sizes and lot quantities. At the top end of the size range are a number of large boring mills. The largest is capable of machining a work piece 100 feet long by 14 feet high and weighing up to 75 tons. At the lower end, equipment such as small jig bores handles very small precision work to tolerances of .0001" on a production basis. Lot sizes vary from single piece parts to quantities of 1,000 per week in continuous runs.

Fabrication - Fabrication activities are targeted at jobs requiring both machining and fabrication. These jobs have ranged from the complete fabrication of large paper-making machinery on a one-of-a-kind basis to producing pumps used in the oil fields in quantities of several a month.

Special machinery - The special machines activity consists of designing and building special purpose equipment ranging from individual units to complete production lines. Applications have included the automation of: assembly, fabrication, packaging, testing, processing, machining, and web-handling functions. Although these machines are primarily one-of-a-kind, there are occasional repeat orders for a previously-built machine. In addition to designing machines, this activity also includes building machines to a customer's design.

It should be evident from the above description that the manufacturing process in all three product areas meets a number of the criteria of a classic job shop. These criteria can be grouped generally into demand and processing characteristics as follows:

Demand characteristics - Production is initiated with a customer's order. There is no production to a forecast and no inventory is kept at any level.

Demand is predominantly independent demand. Because of the non-repetitive nature of the special-machine business, the bill of materials is approached as a simple, minimum-level bill without emphasizing assemblies and subassemblies and their relationships. Further, since materials and purchased components are bought to order, there is no need to net against inventory levels to determine required production quantities. These demand characteristics led to the conclusion that Materials Requirements Planning was not essential at the present time.

Unexpected demands and the rapidly changing nature of the product mix require frequent and rapid rescheduling.

The one-of-a-kind or low-volume, nonrepetitive production may result in more frequent changes to the process and to estimated run times than would be the case with repeat production.

Repair orders, which may be time-and-materials, and other types of emergencies are part of the business.

Process characteristics - Batch-mode processing with complex routings across a variety of general purpose machine tools characterizes the small lot or one-of-a-kind production. Overlapping operations are the rule in high-volume parts production.

Machine assembly operations, such as mechanical, hydraulic, and electrical, are seldom sequential but tend to be in parallel.

The plant load at the outset of the project consisted of 3,000 manufacturing jobs requiring 15,000 operations. This load was spread over approximately 150 work centers, including outside processes.

In the contract machining and fabrication business, there are three major features of the service that are being sold: 1. quality or conformity to the customer's specifications; 2. the timeliness and predictability of deliveries; and 3. the cost. In the special- machine design business, the added dimensions of engineering and a solution to the customer's problem are present. However, timely production of machine parts, which are competing with all other parts in the shop, is also essential to satisfactory performance.

With all of the above characteristics of the manufacturing process to deal with, two primary business objectives need to be accomplished:

1. improve the ability to set accurate delivery dates; and

2. once these delivery dates are set, improve the on-time delivery performance.

To accomplish these objectives, it was imperative to deal with capacity as a finite resource. Infinite loading did not seem to be a complete solution.

What was needed was the ability to simulate the manufacturing process on each of the jobs to give a realistic delivery estimate. This simulation needed to deal with the complexities of the routings and the diversity of the work centers. It also needed to recognize the finite capacity that existed in all the work centers. This led us to Operation Sequencing.

CAPACITY REQUIREMENTS PLANNING (Ray Lankford)

The five segments of an integrated manufacturing system are:

o Demand Management
o Priority Planning
o Capacity Management
o Production Activity Control
o Inventory Management

These correspond to the five subdivisions of the body of knowledge defined by APICS. An idea of the relationship among these segments may be gained by reference to Figure 1.

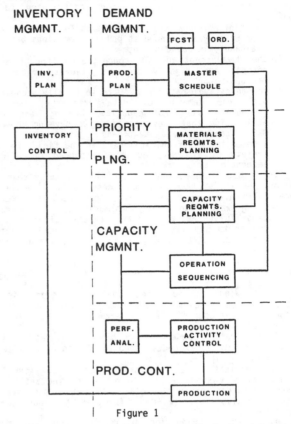

Figure 1

The software installed by Remmele is designed to do all the necessary functions of the Capacity Management segment of the integrated system. In addition, it provides some of the most important outputs needed for Production Activity Control, the most notable of which is the prioritized Dispatch List.

The purpose of Capacity Requirements Planning is to disclose the amount of work which must be performed by each work center in each time period in order to produce the products in the Master Schedule.

Master Scheduled items are normally exploded through MRP into time-phased requirements for subassemblies and components. The need for future capacity is then derived from two sources:

1. released manufacturing jobs resident in the open job file; and
2. jobs planned by MRP, but not yet released.

Because the great majority of Remmele's work consists of single piece parts, with customer stipulated required dates, they do not use MRP; because they do not forecast, their Master Schedule is their backlog of customer orders. Thus, there are no "planned jobs", and the only constituent of future load is the open job file.

The process of CRP has been described in the literature (8), but will be summarized here to illustrate technical features of the Remmele system.

The first step in CRP is backward planning, in which each job has operation start and finish dates calculated using planned values for move and queue times. Remmele utilizes a Move Time Matrix to specify transit time. Planned values of queue are specified for each work center in the Work Center Master file.

The second step in CRP is infinite loading, in which each future demand for capacity is registered on each work center for each future time period. These demands are totaled and a report is produced showing the overloads and underloads. Let's examine the information contained in a CRP report and be certain we understand the significance of the numbers.

An extremely useful feature of the Remmele CRP report is that it shows the action plan from which the work center's output will be derived. This action plan, which portrays how we intend to operate the work center in the weeks ahead, consists of two parts:

1. the Work Schedule in shifts per day, days per week, and hours per shift; and

2. the number of productive units (machines or people) which will be operational each shift.

The CRP report can thus be used as a working document to plan adjustments to schedules or to staffing and at all times shows the planner such things as planned overtime, personnel shifts, and scheduled holidays. It is apparent to the planner _where_ the capacity is coming from to meet the requirements of the Master Schedule.

It is sometimes said that the "capacity" to be used for CRP must be "demonstrated" capacity. This is provided in the case of Remmele by using the demonstrated productivity of the work center during the recent past. The reason for calculating capacity from the productivity ratio, instead of using some "normal" capacity in standard hours, is so that planned outputs for different operating schedules can be readily obtained. For example, there is a capacity of 809 standard hours in a week when six days are scheduled, but only 675 standard hours in a five-day week.

It is important to recognize this fact that capacity is not static, but rather adjustable. What is contained in the "Capacity" field of a CRP report is the planned output based on a demonstrated capability from actual output tracking in the recent past.

The "Load", on the other hand, is the required output, which must be achieved if the Master Schedule is to be accomplished.

When "output needed" is compared to "output planned", it may be necessary to adjust the capacity plan. Remmele's software will accept this adjustment to the Work Schedule and/or the Units in any period and will calculate and display the expected capacity.

Another important, but poorly understood, fact is that the required output in any period will, in fact, be required only if the jobs comprising it arrive in time to be worked on that period. That will occur only if these jobs wait in queues in various preceding work centers a total time equal to the planned queues at those work centers. If queues are longer or shorter than planned, the timing of required capacity may be quite different from that shown by CRP.

A CRP load profile by itself is of limited usefulness. Also required is a Detailed Load Report listing the jobs which comprise the load in each period. With this information, jobs may be routed to alternate work centers, shifted to other time periods, or pegged to end items which are to be rescheduled in the Master Schedule.

When Remmele first implemented CRP, they found some surprising maldistributions of load. Separate salespeople had sold the same machine time, causing unsuspected problems with promised delivery dates. Changes to personnel assignments would clearly be required in the future, but had not been foreseen. And perhaps most important of all, the amount of unsold capacity on each machine could be quantified for focusing the sales engineer's efforts on machine time that could be converted to revenues.

Tom Moore will tell you about how they applied the system, but first he will review how they got the company prepared for a new way of operating.

PREPARATIONS FOR CAPACITY MANAGEMENT (Tom Moore)

Focusing on operation sequencing as the major system feature, an extensive software search was undertaken including:
o Visits to a number of companies around the country
o Contacts with all major computer vendors either for references or their own software
o Independent software firms
o Custom development programs were discussed with several systems consultants and software firms

The overriding conclusion was that Operation Sequencing applications were relatively few in number and none were found in a business similar to Remmele's.

Most manufacturing systems were MRP oriented and involved a master schedule. One commercially-available system that was found was judged to be too complex. A "black box" solution complete with dedicated stand-alone hardware was discarded because we couldn't find out, to our satisfaction, the logical basis of the programs and how they worked. We were unwilling to turn our manufacturing process over to this type of systems solution.

With the findings above and the lack of alternatives, a program to develop in-house software was begun. Working with two mathematics professors from the University of Minnesota, the development of a prioritizing algorithm for use in operation sequencing was started. Although a workable program was ultimately completed and tested, the question arose as to whether Remmele had the experience or

the resources to design or even manage the design of a total system by ourselves.

An article on job shop scheduling, written by Ray Lankford when he was responsible for production control for an oil-field equipment manufacturer, ultimately led us to our consultant.

At the time we discovered the article, Ray was in the consulting business. Contact with him led to a visit by Remmele's top management group to the company featured in his article. In addition, the management group attended a Plossl and Lankford seminar on top management's role in manufacturing.

Seeing the complexities of an actual systems application and drawing on this seminar for background, we concluded that the assistance of a consultant would be very valuable, even necessary to implement a system in a reasonable period of time.

After a visit by Ray and a review of Remmele's operations, we agreed to work together on the implementation of a capacity management system.

Although the search for software had not produced any solutions considered acceptable, we continued our efforts, and ultimately became aware of a new capacity management package that had been successfully implemented, but was not, as yet, commercially released. This package, developed by Manufacturing Management Systems, Inc., incorporated both Capacity Requirements Planning and Operation Sequencing. We judged it to be suitable to our needs.

During implementation, the final documentation was completed and we had the opportunity to incorporate some features that were required to suit our operation.

The software, as it had been developed, did not operate on the computer we had selected. However, the vendor agreed to make the required conversion.

At the time this project began, the Data Processing Department consisted of a manager and two data entry people. Remmele had outgrown its small, punched card batch-processing computer and faced the need to expand due to needs for improved financial and general management systems, as well as manufacturing systems requirements.

No major manufacturing systems existed, except for a job-status reporting system that was driven by time cards. In the financial area, payroll and cost accounting were the major systems in place.

The first objective in the selection process was to select a computer that would meet the company's needs for the next five years. There were a number of key issues that emerged in this selection process:
o The computational requirements of the scheduling system required a certain minimum capability.
o As we examined the upper end of computing capability that we thought we might need, the cost and perceived complexity of large main frames pushed us in the direction of large mini-computers with 32-bit architecture.
o Except for the question of our scheduling requirements, other system needs could have been met by a comfortable, more evolutionary step to an interactive 16-bit mini-computer.
o Substantial differences of opinion existed within our management group over which course to take since there was no commercially-available software to benchmark; however, some tests run on the Operation Sequencing programs developed by the university professors led to a decision in favor of the larger computer.
o As it turned out, the purchased software was more computer efficient than we anticipated, but initially it had not been converted to the type of computer under consideration.

The conversion process was accomplished via a remote terminal tied into the new computer. The process went very smoothly and approximated the following timetable:

New computer fully operational	January, 1981
Software conversion completed	May, 1981
CRP in production	July, 1981
Operation Sequencing in production	August, 1981

A project team was established with the Plant Manager of the largest plant designated as the project manager. Also assigned to this team were the Plant Superintendents from two other plants, the Production Control people from each of the plants, the Data Processing Manager, and a representative from the Sales Department. As Vice President of Operations, I worked in a dual capacity: working with the consultant and the project manager, and also working on individual tasks as a team member.

To get the initial direction for the project and to bring the tasks into focus, we concentrated on the major files that we needed to build to get the scheduling system working.

Work center master file - This file contains all the capacity and schedule data for each work center.

Open job file - This consists of both the job master file (information about the job) and the job detail file (specific routing information).

Job chaining file - This file links the bill of materials of an assembly by job numbers.

For each of these files, it was necessary to determine the who, when, and how for all the pieces of information that were required. Certain general task groupings emerged:

Numbering system - After considering a change to a non-significant six-digit job number, we decided to retain our significant job numbering system. In retrospect, this was a good decision because the added complications of introducing this change along with the new system implementation would have outweighed the benefits. It was necessary, however, to establish a common definition of terms for the complete numbering system including sales orders, manufacturing jobs, part numbers, and detail numbers.

Purchasing system interface - Reliable material availability dates are essential to effective scheduling. In our situation, this meant the availability dates of raw materials, purchased components, or customer-supplied materials, such as castings or forgings, are necessary. Some consideration was given to finding a commercially-available purchasing system, but the idea was dismissed when a quick solution was not available. Instead, Remmele developed its own material-control system, which focused narrowly on meeting the needs of the scheduling process and left the implementation of an expanded purchasing system for a future date.

Labor reporting - The existing procedures for labor reporting had to be expanded substantially and formalized to support the requirements of the scheduling system. This was a lengthy process as the requirements of the system led to the development of new procedures to permit accurate execution on the shop floor. The approach we selected involved the use of three individual time cards: on-line operations, off-line operations, and attendance. Although we expect to streamline this process in the future, it was functional and met the necessary requirements of our scheduling and cost accounting systems.

Routings - When the system was first implemented, the quality and thoroughness of the routings varied widely, dependent largely upon the individual writing them. To meet the needs of an accurate scheduling system, it was necessary to include more detail in many cases. The existing route sheets were essentially complete, but it was necessary to make revisions to include additional information. Although the changes were not substantial, this represented a major educational effort given the large number of people involved in writing route sheets.

Networking - This task consisted of developing simple procedures for linking the bill of materials together at the time a special machine or any form of assembly was released to the shop. The goal here was to collect and present in meaningful form all the relevant scheduling information on a project, as well as to take advantage of the feature in the system that relates priorities to the relationship of jobs in the network.

Data integrity - The initial task was to measure the accuracy of the information collected off the shop floor. The target was set at a 95% accuracy level; Remmele was initially confident that it would be close to this figure. The issue was interpreted too narrowly, however, and the initial results were much worse than expected. The more detailed information requirements of the scheduler, the lack of consistent procedures, and poor file maintenance were major problems. With the aid of some very comprehensive audit programs generating time-card error messages, the target level has been achieved for information going into the system. Work is continuing on the reduction of errors and the resulting time-card rejections. Substantial improvement, primarily through education, has been made.

Data processing operating routine - The new computer, followed shortly by this new scheduling system, necessitated a dramatic change in data processing operations. The change in hardware from the batch-processed punched cards to a more interactive environment with the new system changed the whole data processing mentality. Before the scheduling system implementation, a job status run was made on Wednesdays with the previous Friday's time cards. Now, the new system is run at night with the day shift's time cards, and the foremen's work lists are ready at 6:30 AM the following morning.

Interface programming - This task consisted of formatting the data files which the Capacity Management System needed from our work-in-process master files. This was done on a part-time basis over a period of two months by the Data Processing Manager. In addition, a number of custom reports were created that would integrate the Capacity Management System results with the work-in-process data. On-line access has also been provided to display results generated by the system.

System documentation - Our response to this task was slow in spite of the consultant's continual stressing of the need to fully document policies and procedures. In addition to the uncertainties of feeling our way, our team, almost to the man, did not like to write nor had we much experience at it. After solving a couple of the same problems twice, however, we did begin to write down our conclusions with the objective of developing a Production Control Manual. With the focus on procedures, policy issues emerged for resolution, and this manual evolved into what would more appropriately be called a "business guide".

Project planning - As the project began, the breadth of these tasks was not apparent in all cases, nor was the interdependence of these tasks. The plan started using a simple, milestone-planning technique. As progress was made and learning occurred, the milestone chart was updated. This proved to be a very valuable tool to help manage the project.

Education - Implementation of systems of this magnitude are difficult because they introduce new concepts, and they involve almost everyone in the organization. A substantial amount was invested in education and communication to help overcome these difficulties. The major efforts were:

o Company newsletter - Even before a system was found to implement, the President of the company began to talk about the need for a system and its importance to the company. He continued to comment at various points throughout the implementation process and left no question as to his commitment to the project.

o Top management briefing - All members of the top management group attended an appropriate seminar.

o Capacity management seminar - After the project team was selected, all team members attended.

o System newsletter - The project team wrote a series of newsletters to all employees on different aspects of the system and its impact on them.

o Consultant - Ray Lankford conducted a number of educational sessions for the top management group, foremen, sales engineers, design engineers, and office people. In addition, his periodic visits during the implementation process provided necessary education and problem-solving aids for the project team.

o Production control meetings - Ray Lankford also attended these in all of the plants after the system was running. Focus then began on the effective utilization of the system output - actual on-the-job training.

o Employee meetings - Departmental meetings for all employees were conducted by the project team to explain portions of the system and introduce new procedures.

In addition to the above, there has been a lot of one-on-one training and small group sessions with all users and project team members.

OPERATION SEQUENCING (Ray Lankford)

Let's review the capacity planning process which has taken place before Operation Sequencing:

o The Master Schedule has been tested against a rough-cut capacity plan on critical work centers, so there are no gross errors in Master Schedule content.

o MRP has planned the quantity and timing of manufacturing jobs; some jobs have been released, while others are still at the "planned" stage.

o Capacity Requirements Planning has, for all work centers, displayed the "output needed" in each time period to accomplish the Master Schedule.

o An aggressive and resourceful Production Control Department has taken a myriad of actions to match the "output planned" for each work center to the "output needed", overtime has been scheduled, subcontracting has been arranged, personnel have been shifted, and jobs have been re-routed.

At this point, one thing is certain: A lot of problems still remain!

o Some work centers are still overloaded in some time periods and underloaded in others.

o Because each job takes a different route through the plant, it is impossible to predict the size of queues at all work centers in the future; hence, lead times are uncertain.

o Since queues at some work centers will undoubtedly differ from the "planned" levels assumed by CRP, the load profiles may contain significant errors.

o We are working to averages, but specifics are killing us!

o As each "problem" work center is recognized, the planners start trying to work their way up through the pegs to the end items to communicate with Master Scheduling. But there are hundreds of problems and several thousand jobs to deal with.

o The changes keep coming!

In short, as one knowledgeable realist recently observed, "No matter how carefully Master Scheduling has been executed (rough-cut cycles included), the planner cannot possibly foresee all manufactured-part shortages generated by standard lead time offsets." (9)

Before we conclude that the quality of life in Production Control is not likely to improve, let's look at what we have to work with.

The action plans for altering capacity devised by our energetic planner have been entered into the computer, so as to portray planned output for comparison with required output. In actuality, this data, derived from practical planning work, constitutes a mathematical model of the factory.

Moreover, we have a file of all current and future jobs with their priorities expressed by their required dates.

We also know from production labor reporting those jobs currently working in the plan, with their status of completion.

Common sense might tell us that we could see how our jobs, sequenced according to priority, might fit the capacity produced by our action plans. However, conventional wisdom in this body of knowledge says, "Don't do it! Ignore what you know about capacity and priorities."

The common-sense approach of simulating the processing of jobs in order of priority using replanned capacity is, of course, Operation Sequencing. This is what Remmele uses to schedule their shop.

The particular software at Remmele is significantly different from other simulation-mode scheduling routines. While it has some very powerful capabilities, it is much simpler and, hence, more practical than some of the elegant, highly-sophisticated simulators which have been used in the past. For example:

1. Time resolution is a half-shift, not a fraction of an hour.

2. It does not try to solve problems automatically. Instead, it reports problems to the human scheduler so that judgement and experience may be applied to the solution.

Because of these and other simplifications, the simulation program requires only a modest amount of computer time, meaning it can be run frequently enough to recognize changed conditions.

The second of the simplifications cited is quite significant! The point was made emphatically in an earlier section that the computer does not "automatically reschedule". What Operation Sequencing does is to produce a manufacturing job schedule which shows for each job the following information:

1. Required Date - from MRP or MPS

2. Planned Start and Finish Date - the standard lead time using planned move and queue times

3. Scheduled Start and Finish Dates - the probable, actual lead time, recognizing available capacity and the job's relative priority

Thus, the planner can see these jobs which will probably be late. From detailed operation dating, bottleneck operations are evident. Using this information, the planner can go to work solving the problems. The computer did not change the required date, nor did it automatically change the plan. It merely reported the degree to which reality will probably deviate from the plan. It is entirely up to the planner whether to solve the problem or to re-promise.

In cases of dependent demand in which a number of components are required at the same time for assembly, the software used by Remmele will simulate component job completion and the subsequent start and completion of subassembly and assembly jobs. This process is called "networking". It identifies any component jobs which will not be completed in time to support the Master Schedule, but it does not automatically reschedule all other component jobs equally late. It allows the planner to solve the problems causing lateness or to decide that rescheduling is, indeed, required.

Most make-to-order plants like Remmele require the ability to identify the manufacturing jobs which are providing components to the final assembly. Unfortunately, much MRP software provides only single-level pegging, whereby a demand for an item is linked to the next higher level part causing that demand. This linking is part number to part number. When a component job is going to be late, it is necessary to trace upwards through the pegs to identify all other jobs at all levels which will be affected. This is a time-consuming and laborious process.

The networking option in Remmele's software utilizes "job chaining", a form of multi-level pegging, which links requirements to sources by job number. Thus, for every sales order, Remmele can, at any time, see each job which is producing parts, subassemblies, and assemblies for that specific sales order; this is an enormously useful capability when answering customer inquiries or considering revision of the Master Schedule.

Since a simulation-mode scheduling system utilizes priorities to sequence operations at work centers, the manner in which priorities are designated is of some interest. Remmele's software offers a choice of two alternatives, each based on slack time: Critical Ratio and Index Number. The former is well-known, and the latter is described elsewhere in the literature. (3)

Tom Moore will now discuss this point and some other special requirements of Remmele's scheduling system.

APPLYING THE SYSTEM (Tom Moore)

Given the nature of Remmele's organization and it's business, we recognized a number of special problems that would require us to evolve our own particular solutions.

Remmele's decentralized organization had implications in two areas. First, there were three separate plants, each with an individual Plant Manager. The plants differed in size and somewhat in mission. The need for a "better" way was recognized in the largest plant, but was less apparent in the two smaller plants. We resisted the temptation to implement in the larger plant first and, instead, brought everyone through the process together. The result was a smoother implementation and broader acceptance in all plants when the switch was turned.

A second concern centered on the widely dispersed responsibilities for process engineering and production control. The routings for many of the jobs are the responsibility of the Sales Engineers, as is the responsibility for establishing required dates with the customers. These Sales Engineers, as well as the Design Engineers, function as project managers for their jobs, and in doing so, performed much of the production control function, working closely with the foremen. This "decentralization" or dispersion of responsibility required the involvement of many people in the process of changing our procedures and, to some degree, even the changing of key roles as a more concentrated production control function evolved.

In addition to the dynamic characteristic of demands, the one-of-a-kind or non-repetitive nature of much of the manufacturing means a minimum of up-front investment in process, design, and standard setting. While striving to constantly improve this, estimates and processes that change when the job reaches the shop floor are always present. Added operations and revised routings and estimates are a way of life on many of our jobs, and we had to find a convenient way of making these changes as well as getting the people involved to recognize the need to change our computer files.

We promoted the adage "You don't have to do things differently because of the system, just tell someone when you make a change." Most of the changes involved the route sheet file, so on-line file maintenance procedures were developed for use by the Production Control Department to make this task easier.

Operation overlapping - or as we call it "flowing" - was not in the software as we purchased it initially, but we knew this to be a requirement for effectively scheduling any of the volume-production jobs. This practice was also found useful with our small-lot production to reduce lead times in emergencies or to get work to open downstream work centers. Working with the consultant and software vendor, this capability was brought on-line six months after the initial implementation.

Two options for expressing job priorities are available in the software: Critical Ratio and Index Number. Index Number was chosen. Based on the required date, a number between "0" and "999" is derived from the time remaining and the work remaining. An external priority or management factor can also be applied to intensify the priority in an emergency.

Initially, the idea of structuring or formalizing the decision of which job to work on first was a difficult concept to become comfortable with. However, experience has shown that it has a sound basis in logic and, while not perfection, it does satisfactorily handle the vast majority of jobs.

The quantity and quality of information received from this system far exceeded what existed in the past. Initially there was more information than we could digest, and we had to learn how to efficiently use the system output to pinpoint problems and take the necessary actions.

Lacking the ability to accurately "benchmark" the system in advance, estimates of the computer resources required were made. Processing time remained a concern until the actual operation began, however, the results turned out to be fairly close to the estimates.

At shop workload peaks, the CRP and Operation Sequencing phases were both run within an hour. Report printing was a large time-consumer, but we are printing less and using the CRT's more. Currently our total cycle from building the work files to printing the reports takes less than three hours at night.

THE USER'S APPRAISAL (Tom Moore)

The value of this system to Remmele and the primary results achieved to date can be summarized as follows:
1. In terms of the primary objective of improving on-time deliveries, steady progress has been made. The system has contributed to this, but it can't take sole credit. With the impact of the recession and the resulting reduced work load, contention for scarce capacity hasn't been as pronounced as in normal times. It is expected, however, that when the demand for absolutely full capacity resumes, the system will make possible much more reliable delivery promising.
2. We have achieved the required level of accuracy in work-in-process reporting. Jobs don't get lost and the information as to their status is realistic. In addition to benefiting the scheduling process, this has paid dividends in cost accounting as well.
3. Capacity bottlenecks are visible, and the response to them is more timely.

The system has proven to be very well designed and a highly-effective tool. It has contributed substantially to Remmele's ability to manage its capacity.

IMPLICATIONS OF THIS CASE STUDY (Ray Lankford)

Ten years ago, the type of capacity management system being used today by Remmele was considered very sophisticated. Simulation-mode scheduling, what we now call Operation Sequencing, was regarded as extremely complex. Software was of limited availability, computer requirements were large and expensive, and applications were confined to relatively large companies.

Today, Tom Moore has described how his company, a relatively small firm with limited systems experience, is successfully using Operation Sequencing. Software, while not abundant, is more readily available; computer power is no longer the obstacle it once was. There are a number of other companies of various sizes using similar systems. Two examples are especially interesting. One large, aircraft-equipment manufacturer has been so impressed by the results of Operation Sequencing that for some years after its installation in 1973, no publicity about the system was permitted because management regarded it as a major competitive advantage. Only recently one of my clients, smaller than Remmele, programmed in-house for a mini-computer a simulator which is producing schedules enthusiastically endorsed by shop foremen, production controllers, and salespeople alike.

Another major improvement of the past ten years is the increase in knowledge about capacity management systems. And with knowledge has come understanding that some of the controversies of the formative years are behind us. Infinite loading and finite loading are obsolete concepts. True to the prediction of Plossl and Wight in 1967, simulation has developed into a technique of genuine usefulness. Today, it is the "sleeping giant" of manufacturing control.

Using simulation - Operation Sequencing, as we now call it - companies like Remmele are closing the "proficiency gap", applying with skill and enthusiasm the "state-of-the-art" in capacity management.

REFERENCES

(1) Wight, Oliver, "Input/Output Control: A Real Handle On Lead Time", Production & Inventory Management, Volume II, Number 3, Third Quarter, 1970

(2) Plossl, George W. and Oliver W. Wight, "Capacity Planning and Control", Proceedings of the Fourteenth Annual Conference of the American Production and Inventory Control Society, 1971

(3) Lankford, Ray, "Scheduling the Job Shop", Proceedings of the Sixteenth Annual Conference of the American Production and Inventory Control Society, 1973

(4) Lankford, Ray, "Input/Output Control: Making It Work", Proceedings of the Twenty-third Annual Conference of the American Production and Inventory Control Society, 1980

(5) Plossl, George W. and Oliver W. Wight, Production and Inventory Control, Prentice-Hall, Inc., Englewood Cliffs, New Jersey, 1967

(6) Wight, Oliver, "Finite Loading", Managing Inventories and Production, Oliver Wight Video Productions, Inc., Audio Tape Number 9, Copyright 1976 ASI

(7) Communications Oriented Production Information and Control System, Volume V, IBM Corporation, White Plains, New York, 1972

(8) Lankford, Ray, "Short-Term Planning of Manufacturing Capacity", Proceedings of the Twenty-first Annual Conference of the American Production and Inventory Control Society, 1978

(9) Thomas, Gene, "Real-Time, Behind Schedule Replanning", Production & Inventory Management Review, April, 1982

RAY LANKFORD

Ray Lankford is a principal in Plossl & Lankford, a firm engaged in management counseling and education. He has over twenty years of experience in manufacturing management. He was Vice President of Operations for McEvoy Oilfield Equipment Company, with responsibility for four plants around the world. Prior to that, he was Vice President of Manufacturing for Reed Tool Company. His experience includes management of production control, systems design, and plant supervision. He holds a Bachelor of Arts and a Bachelor of Science Degree in mechanical engineering from Rice University. He has served as Chairman of the APICS Certification Committee on Master Scheduling and Capacity Planning, and he has written several major articles on plant scheduling and capacity planning.

TOM MOORE

Tom Moore is Vice President of Operations for Remmele Engineering, Inc., a manufacturer specializing in contract machining and the designing and building of special machines. In addition to heading all manufacturing operations, he has responsibility for Remmele's financial, personnel, and data processing functions. Prior to joining Remmele in early 1979, his experience was primarily in the areas of general management, sales, and marketing. He began his career in international sales for Graco Inc., a major manufacturer of fluid-handling equipment. He progressed to general management positions in Japan and in Europe before becoming Vice President of International Operations. He has a Bachelor of Science Degree in Civil Engineering and a Master of Business Administration, both from the University of Minnesota.

PRODUCTION ACTIVITY CONTROL IN A JIT ENVIRONMENT

Robert A. Leavey, CFPIM
IBM Corporation

In todays changing production environment it is necessary to understand how Just-in-Time philosophies modify our traditional approaches to Production Activity Control(PAC). Elimination of waste through reductions in cycle times, setup times, overall lead time, and inventory are but a few of the changes that impact our traditional approaches. These approaches embrace the functional areas of Production Activity Control as seen in figure 1. These functions will be discussed with emphasis on how each is impacted by JIT. Before this detailed discussion, a few comments are necessary on the traditional PAC environment vs. the JIT environment.

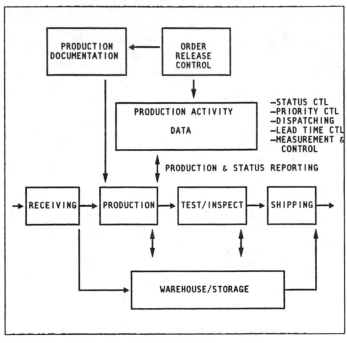

Figure 1. PRODUCTION ACTIVITY CONTROL

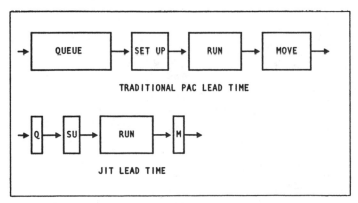

Figure 2. TRADITIONAL VS JIT LEAD TIME

Impact of JIT

In a Just-in-Time environment the objective is the shrink the lead time as much as possible. Figure 2 shows the impact on lead of a JIT implementation.
Implementing smaller lot sizes, reduced set up times, balancing work flow and producing only when needed contribute to shorter lead times and reduced work-in-process.
The adoption of Just in Time requires reduction in setups. Although traditional (non JIT) planning systems can accommodate these reduced setups physical organization and the tooling must be altered to actually accommodate such changes. Set up of machines must be looked at in such a way to reduce the actual time a machine is non-productive due to setups. Off-machine positioning of tools must be employed and quick changeovers a must.
In JIT production should be planned in lot sizes approaching one. EOQ's give way to lot-for-lot production quantities. As lot sizes are reduced, bottlenecks surface, indicating a need to further reduce machine setup time, or change the material flow for better material handling.
The calculation of the planned lead time is much simpler and probably more accurate due to the elimination of many factors mentioned above.

PRODUCTION ENVIRONMENT

Traditional Production Activity Control approaches have evolved over the years primarily in the job shop environment. In job shops discrete parts are routed through numerous work centers or departments each performing one or more operations on that part. The parts are controlled by lots or shop orders throughout the plant. These orders pass through the control of a number of supervisors, machine operators, material handlers and inspectors, with no single group having continued responsibility for the completion of the specific part.
The organization of traditional Production Activity Control is centered around work centers and the control of shop orders from Work Center to Work Center. These Work Centers are organized by similar type of operations and interchangeable machines, eg. the milling work center.

JIT

The philosophy of Just-in-Time is leading companies toward changing the flow of production from job shop and work center orientation to repetitive manufacturing and work cells. Group Technology techniques are emerging where similar parts can be grouped for manufacturing flow purposes, usually called a cell. A cell could be a single machine, a group of machines, or even an assembly line. Within a cell, parts flow through a series of operations.

The remainder of this paper will contrast the traditional PAC approaches and the impact on those approaches when adopting JIT. The JIT philosophies are almost universally adaptable to job shop or repetitive manufacturing.

PAC DATA REQUIREMENTS

In traditional PAC systems the basic data are oriented by production orders and work centers. A control data base is established for operations to be reported from the production floor. Material allocation data is built when orders are released to the plant.

In Just-in-Time systems, production is generally not controlled by orders, but rather by schedules. Because orders are not released, material allocation data cannot be established. The flow and cell orientation changes the data requirements from work centers and operations. This influences basic PAC data, the method of production authorization and certainly the way production is reported from the plant floor.

PRODUCTION AUTHORIZATION

Production Authorization includes all the activities before a production order is released to the plant. In traditional systems this process begins with the notification, usually from a material planning system, that a production order is ready for release. The timing of this notification is based on the normal standard lead time of what is to be produced. This notification includes the quantity required and the the due date.

The production authorization process includes checking availability of component inventory, tools, and key machines and people. Once it has been determined that these resources are available shop packet information is produced. This includes the shop order with routing information, engineering drawings, and other documentation necessary to produce the product in the shop.

In a JIT environment, production authorization is a signal to a workstation from a subsequent workstation that the product is needed. Inventory is delivered to the point of production and replenished when needed, allocation of components and pick lists are not necessary. Work is pulled through the plant as needed from the final workstation.

PRODUCTION AND STATUS REPORTING

A major function of Production Activity Control is to report and maintain data about production activity. This data is used for production status and costing, payroll and for feedback to planning systems.

In a job shop typical activities reported are starting and ending of operations, both set up and run; movement of work from one Work Center to another; arrival and departure from work; material receipts and issues; and Scrap reporting, to name a few. This large amount of operational data many times necessitates the use of automated data collection equipment.

Impact of JIT

There is still a need for feedback to monitor the plans and control the production process as JIT manufacturing is practiced. Changes are required due to reduced lead times resulting in a reduced need to report all activity. Also simplified production flow and the implementation of a 'pull' production system changes the production reporting requirements.

First production is controlled by schedules. Production quantities are generally reported by part number and compared on a cumulative basis to the schedule. Milestone operation reporting replaces individual operation reporting. Milestone operations or count points should be chosen to minimize reporting while still maintaining control. For example, if the cycle time through a manufacturing cell of six operations is 10 minutes, it may only be necessary to report the quantity complete as a part exits the cell.

Another change that milestone operation reporting requires is the need to use backflushing (post-deduct inventory processing) techniques to relieve inventory. This means that component inventory is reduced by the quantity completed at the reported operation. Scrap must be reported separately.

In addition a high level of quality must be maintained. This indicates a need for better control of maintenance, and quality control at the source, ie. the production operations. Quality must be monitored and reported as production is taking place.

The emphasis today on automating production operations and material handling makes PAC reporting easier. Robots, AGV's, AS/RS, Bar Code readers allow parts to flow with minimal interruption throughout the plant. Many companies have adopted Bar Code identification that requires no human intervention when reporting. The totes carrying the product or even the product itself has the bar code on it. This is read by scanners in the plant that route the material to its destination.

Many aspects of JIT impact production status and reporting. Short cycle times and the reduction of lot sizes result in a reduced need to report production until a part or assembly is finished. Inventory is relieved when manufacturing is completed for the part or assembly. Since queues and lead times are reduced, reporting of production approaches immediate feedback of production problems and scrap. Corrective action can be taken very quickly.

LEAD TIME DETERMINATION AND CONTROL

Production Activity Control is concerned with actual and calculated lead times. The actual lead time through the plant is determined by a variety of factors including level of work-in-process and priority. In a job shop 80 - 90% of lead time is typically made up of queue time or wait time.

Much time can be spent calculating lead times considering such factors as: lot sizes, lot splitting, parallel scheduling and alternate routings. Calculated lead time are at best an approximation of of the actual lead time.

SHORT TERM CAPACITY CONTROL

Short term capacity is typically monitored through Input/Output Control techniques. These help balance the input and output of individual work centers and the entire plant. Input/output flow in a job shop can be seen in figure 3. In job shops completely balanced flows are not possible, but Just in Time approaches can still have a large impact.

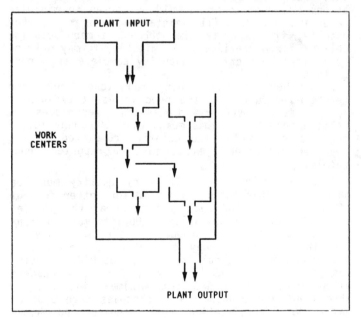

Figure 3. JOB SHOP INPUT/OUTPUT

Impact of JIT

Having plant layouts that have continuous flow of production, by definition have input and output for cells that are balanced. Other JIT techniques, such as 'pull' production makes the work flow smoothly in the plant. Therefore the emphasis in a JIT environment is away from the Input/Output

Control technique. Taking its place is the need to do line (or cell) balancing.

Standardization of parts, the leveling of the production schedule, and reduced set up time contribute heavily to achieving a balanced flow of work between operations and cells. Operations and workstations that have a layout that is conducive to repetitive manufacturing make the balancing problem easier to solve.

PRIORITY CONTROL AND DISPATCHING

The objective of Priority Control and Dispatching is to ensure that all work is completed on time at every work center.

Priority Control function is the sequencing the work at a work center so that the most important work is done first and that priorities for commonly required components are synchronized. Priority rules vary from the simple operation or order due dates to critical ratio. The technique used will be determined by the way management wants to run the business.

Work is usually scheduled before being prioritized. Operation or detailed scheduling is the activity of determining start and completion dates for each operation in an order. There are a variety of techniques used for scheduling whose use depending heavily on the production environment. Generally the approach is schedule backward from the order due date or forward from today's date. By considering setup and run times, and standard move and queue times, start and end dates can be applied to each operation in a routing. Many priority techniques use these dates in their calculations.

Dispatching is the means of communicating the priorities of work to the people on the shop floor. Dispatch lists are generated on a timely basis so that an accurate picture of the work in plant can be seen. For a variety of reasons, usually because the 'system' isn't working correctly, many companies have hot lists which really tell the workers which jobs to work on next. In addition, anticipated delay reports indicate which orders will not be on time, why, and when they will be completed based on the schedule.

Impact of JIT

In a Just-in-Time environment the priority of the work in the plant is set by the final assembly schedule and ultimately by the customer order. In an ideal JIT situation work is not started till a customer order is in hand. As previously stated once the need has been determined work is pulled through the plant to the final assembly operation. Hot lists and delay reports are virtually eliminated.

Since the focus of priority control is significantly changed, operation scheduling techniques have reduced use in flow manufacturing environment. Scheduling is made easier, since queues at work stations are reduced or eliminated through simplified work flows and reduced lot sizes. The sequence of operations is built into the layout. Thus material movement is significantly reduced and scheduling becomes merely sequencing the work at the entry point of the cell or line. More appropriate techniques such as line balancing and simulation are used to address this manufacturing process.

PRODUCTION MEASUREMENT AND CONTROL

Data captured in the PAC system allows comparison with historical data, preset standards, and with objectives. The key measurements of traditional systems have been costs, efficiency, utilization and individual performance (eg. piece work) and performance. There are two obvious differences between traditional and JIT systems: 1) The same data is not collected or available and 2) The JIT goals and philosophies make the traditional measurements obsolete.

Impact of JIT

First, production is not reported operation to operation. JIT production is generally reported at the time a component or product is finished. Actual production time can only be determined for a group of operations in the flow. Individual performance is impossible to measure.

Second, JIT means 'only work on what's needed'. There are times when nothing is needed. Workers clean their work areas or perform maintenance on machines. Utilization measurements will not work in this environment.

Traditional job costing methods have little applicability in JIT. Process costing or variations of it make more sense in this environment. Process costing is a method by which costs are accumulated by period and subsequently allocated to all the units produced during the period. Additionally, methods of applying overhead need to reflect the much lower labor content in today's manufacturing world.

It is possible to put meaningful measurements in place for the Just-in-Time PAC system. For example, meeting the customer delivery date, reduced work-in-process, and quality of products are but a few measurements that tell us how well our JIT system is working.

PEOPLE MAKE IT HAPPEN

The impact on the employees in the shop is one of the keys to success. Just in Time requires considerable team work and coordination between employees. Objectives of JIT, such as cleanliness of the work space, high availability of machines, and moving workers to the work, all require significant involvement of employees and the backing of management.

Another premise of JIT, not to produce something that is not needed (to be shipped out the door) is key to the accomplishment of these objectives. It is these times when an employee finds they have no direct work to perform. This is the time when employees must have the incentive to clean up the work area, perform maintenance on equipment, and learn other jobs in the plant.

Everyone in the plant must adhere to the basic JIT tenet of continually improving all areas of the business. Quality control circles are one approach that companies have found successful in uncovering and solving problems. The accomplishment of JIT is made possible by management's desire and direction to allow the employees to make this happen.

PAC/JIT IMPLEMENTATION

Where to start....

One school of thought says pick your most troublesome (costly) area - apply JIT philosophies and work from there. This is certainly a plausible approach.

But there are some basic table stakes that any company must do when trying to implement JIT. First is the management commitment and participation in guiding a JIT implementation. Since JIT is a philosophy, management must portray that philosophy in its direction and actions. If production workers see management heading in one direction, they will more readily adopt that same direction.

Next is the dedication and commitment of management and employees alike to continual improvement in the operation. JIT is like a long journey... many times we must endure hardships and setbacks on the way to the destination. Continual improvement of all facets of the operation is the key to sustained excellence and high productivity in production.

You can't play the game without putting up the table stakes. It is only after these table stakes have been accepted and are being permeated throughout the company that changes in the traditional systems should be undertaken.

After satisfying the table stakes, the next step then is one of simplification. All implementations of JIT require that the process or function be simplified as the first step, eg. it is unthinkable to try to put in a Pull (Kanban) system directly into a job shop. Likewise supplier JIT deliveries do little (and may even slow production) if the producing and receiving systems cannot accommodate this type of delivery.

Elimination of queues at workstations without high quality, and reduced lot sizes without reducing setup time can be expensive and disastrous.

The destination is clear, the journey is long -- the plan for the journey will determine how quickly and successfully you will get there.

CONCLUSION

The execution of production planning (PAC) is where JIT happens...the elimination of waste, working on only what's needed. Allowing JIT to happen is managements responsibility..adapting JIT management philosophies and striving for continual improvement.

There is no magic in JIT. It is like a high performance race car that is meant to be driven on a well kept track with high performance fuel. Driving it around the city with ordinary fuel, stopping and starting ,etc., will not yield excellent performance. Like wise JIT was not meant to be practiced without fixing the environment first. Simplify.. Streamline... Provide management commitment and direction that will enable Just-in-Time to be a reality in your company.

ABOUT THE AUTHOR

Robert A. Leavey is a consultant in Computer Integrated Manufacturing for IBM's Information Systems Software Development business unit. He has held many positions in both Development and Marketing for both COPICS and MAPICS, including Product Manager for the Far East operations. Over the past 25 years in IBM, some of his key responsibilities included IBM's COPICS Manuals and MAST Education for MAPICS.

In APICS he is currently serving on the Certification and Curriculum Council as Chairman of the Production Activity Control certification committee. He has been a speaker at APICS International Conferences, seminars and numerous chapter meetings.

Reprinted from the 1986 *APICS Conference Proceedings.*

FLAT BILLS OF MATERIAL WITH PRODUCTION ACTIVITY CONTROL

Terry Lunn
Terry Lunn Enterprises

Our objective is to describe the method one company uses to flatten their bills of material. We shall describe their analysis and the resulting methods of coding the bill of material such that multiple levels can be processed at one time. The emphasis will be on how they control the shop floor activities using these flattened bills of material.

CLASSICAL MRP

The classical MRP logic for processing a bill of material is very cumbersome. We enter bills of material into a computerized system level by level for the best control of the engineering and routing functions. And indeed that is the best way to maintain and update a bill of material processor.

However when it comes time to release work orders to the shop, we find this method very labor intensive. The standard MRP gross-to-net logic establishes a series of planned order releases. These releases are suggested to be released according to the lead time required to bring the components into stock in time to be used on the next higher level.

We release orders for the lowest level components first. As these components go into stock, they become available for the next level assembly. We then release an order for the assembly level. When it is complete and credited into stock; it becomes available for the next level assembly. And so this process continues all the way up the bill of material until we reach the Master Schedule Item.

CASE STUDY

The company in this case study implemented a MRP system with a bill of material processor that works just like the standard logic outlined above. They produce a wide range of steel fabricated products used in the material handling industry. These products are made from raw materials and purchased parts that come together in the classical components, subassembly and final assembly bill of material structure.

This shop would be classified as a high volume repetitive manufacturing with many common components that are often assembled with one or two make-to-order parts. The common items go in and out of stock, as the normal MRP logic would suggest. These items are so popular that it is inefficient to process issue transactions for the same component part for every assembly order. To solve this problem a system of bulk issuing with a back-flush explosion was implemented. However this did not address the problem of how to handle the items that were being produced only for the order.

In manufacturing, we recognized that some component parts are not really expected to go in and out of stock at each level. Many components, even if they are used on several different assembly bills are in fact made only "on-order". The item should indeed be a level on the bill of material processor. We can then control routings, and implement engineering changes all at one place. However the lot size is lot-for-lot and we expect to produce the components only when there is an order for the next higher level in the bill. Such parts are routed through the shop in so as to reach the assembly station just in time for the assembly operation to begin.

This approach is very popular with the current thinking towards Just-in-Time methods of controlling inventory and shop floor practices. Many items are not kept in stock. As setups are reduced, shop floor layouts are designed to flow parts directly into assembly without the move to and form the storerooms. The standard MRP logic does not fit this view of the manufacturing floor. Even though an item may be common and used on several different assemblies; we may not want to stock the part in the storeroom. As setups are reduced, lot sizes are reduced to lot-for-lot and production is planned so that parts can meet out on the shop floor.

TRICKING BILL OF MATERIAL LEVELS

What we needed was a way to trick the standard MRP bill of material processor into processing an order just as the shop was going to flow the product. At the same time keep the flexibility of handling all the levels the engineering departments had designed. This means that some items would be made lot-for-lot and produced only when a higher level assembly called for them. This is usually handled with a bill of material type called phantom.

A phantom or transient bill of material is defined as a non-stocked item with lead time set to zero and ordered lot-for-lot. The MRP logic will then drive requirements straight through to its components. This works well in planning. However to use a phantom item on the shop floor means that the item is expected to have zero lead time, hence no routing. Most software systems expect us to put any routing up on the heading item level. Also as shop orders are released to the shop, most system "blow though" the item and do not list the engineered part number. This can cause confusion as to which drawings are to be used to produce the part.

Our case study company defined an item having a logic similar to phantom but with two major differences:

    1. The part <u>does</u> appear as an item
       on the assembly bill
       along with its components
    2. Routings are used
       for shop paper
       and lead time offset

These items were given the name "make item".

A make item is defined as a component that is produced only when there is an order for the next higher level assembly. The shop order release should be for the highest level required to go into stock. Most often this is the MPS level. The MRP logic will go down through the bill normally and make the appropriate suggested planned order releases.

However when the time comes to release orders, the gateway operation plans are decided using the MPS level. As a shop order is released for this highest level assembly: each component code was reviewed and implemented as follows:

    Make item
       List the item on the shop order
       Detail out the routing
       Release a replenishment order
         Use the same order number
         Load the work centers normally
       List the component items
    Repeat this process for all make components

Bulk-issue items
   Do not print on the pick list

Stock items
   Print on the picking list
   Prepare stock issue transactions

To effectively implement this logic, each item had to be coded according to how it was to be controlled in the shop. Standard engineering codes were used for the regular bill of material, accounting and engineering logic. However special coding was used to control the shop order logic according to the above plan. (See Figure 1)

BILL OF MATERIAL
================

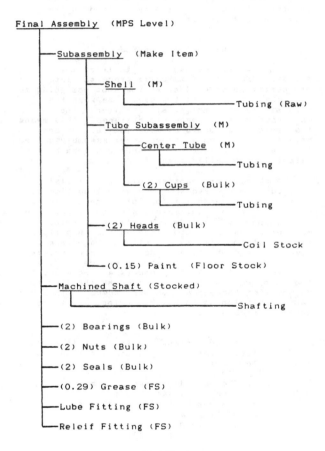

Final Assembly (MPS Level)

└─Subassembly (Make Item)

   └─Shell (M)

      └─Tubing (Raw)

   └─Tube Subassembly (M)

      └─Center Tube (M)

         └─Tubing

      └─(2) Cups (Bulk)

         └─Tubing

   └─(2) Heads (Bulk)

      └─Coil Stock

   └─(0.15) Paint (Floor Stock)

└─Machined Shaft (Stocked)

   └─Shafting

└─(2) Bearings (Bulk)

└─(2) Nuts (Bulk)

└─(2) Seals (Bulk)

└─(0.29) Grease (FS)

└─Lube Fitting (FS)

└─Releif Fitting (FS)

** FIGURE 1 **

One area overlapped. As work orders are closed for the highest level assembly; a back-flush or explosion was implemented. The credited quantity explodes through the bill of material and bulk issue items relieved from Work in Process inventory locations. Make items are costed to the assembly order and all the lower level work orders closed. This company accumulates all the cost to the highest level assembly order.

PRODUCTION ACTIVITY CONTROL

The main point of control in this repetitive production shop was the control of the work released to the gateway operations at the head of the assembly line. As the work was planned for the long-lead-time-item other flow lines were also planned so that the component parts would

arrive as required to meet the main assembly. (See Figure 2.)

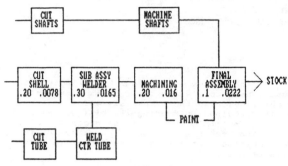

** Figure 2 **

Bulk issue components were expected to be available just like floor stock. Sufficient working stock is delivered to work-in-process locations for the production people to work independently of the order flowing down the production line. Regular stock items are issued form stores to the production line for each individual order. Make components flow through the shop and meet the assemblies at the proper machines independent of any stock room transactions.

So when the long-lead-time item was started; other production lines have to start at the proper time for the components to effectively meet. Such controls have to be carried out on the shop floor Production Activity Control office. All the items printed on one shop order contribute to this coordinated thinking. This main document is used to plan and control the assembly order (See Figure 3). The people involved - Production control, foreman, and shop operators all begin to think in terms of making assembly orders for customers, not building a series of component parts for stock.

The actual shop order paper and required documents go into a plastic envelope that is released to the gateway operation. In this case the shell cutting operation. This order packet is the main control document and flows with the first skid of material. A ticket called a Job Card (See Figure 4) is used to show that other make components are expected to be released to other operations and flow into the main line. This company uses these tickets to report completed labor operations to the office. However a good closed loop MRP system should be able to plan the feeding operations by the required dates on the dispatch plan.

** Figure 4 **

All of this requires considerably more knowledge on the part of the operators and the people working on the shop floor. These people must know how to read a shop order bill of material and how their operation fits into the overall picture of producing assemblies for the customer. This approach is consistent with the just-in-time philosophies of worker involvement and keeping waste out of the system.

We want the paper to work like the flow in the shop and eliminate the waste of multiple transactions. This company experienced one fifth the number of issue and credit transactions going in and out of stores by implementing this system. The shop feels this system exactly mirrors the way they make the product and hence most of the operators understand the interface between the order papers and the parts on the shop floor.

FLAT BILLS of MATERIAL

ADVANTAGES

    Release Orders
        Plan the MPS level
        Release Final Assembly Level
        Automatic release Lower Levels

    Flow in the Shop
        Make Items do NOT go to stock
        Components meet on the shop floor
        Use standard routings

    Transactions
        Reduce Stock IN/OUT transactions
        Back Flush floor stock items

DISADVANTAGES

    People must know more about
        Products
        Flow through the shop

    WIP is controlled on the shop floor
        Bulk stock stored at point of use
        Component parts must meet

** Figure 5 **

ADVANTAGES

Several advantages were realized by implementing this system. (See Figure 5). The standard MRP logic expects us to release orders one at a time going up the bill of material. We artificially flattened the bill by coding some parts as make items. Releasing a shop order for the highest level assembly automatically releases lower levels for the same order. This reduced the number of orders for the most common products form eight to four.

The actual flow of work in the shop dictated that many items should not be moved in and back out of stock. The parts should be made and mated with other parts right out on the shop floor. This company was able to code about four out of five possible items to process this way. The

standard routing was still visible to the shop people.

The number of transactions was greatly reduced. For every item that did _not_ go in and our of stock two main transactions (credit and issue) were eliminated. A whole host of move and transfer transactions were also omitted. This also relieved us of the transactions required to open and close work orders at all the lower levels.

Most of the other stock items were commonly used and could be handled as floor stock. But should be costed directly to the order. So the back-flush explosion process was used. Items coded as "bulk issue" were issued and costed to an order when the assembly was finished to stock. This further reduced the number of transactions on each order.

DISADVANTAGES

However there are also some disadvantage that we must overcome. This type of process requires the people know more about their products and the flow of how the product is produced. The make items meet at the main assembly line and the shop floor people must know where and how. The people must all know their operations and how it fits into the overall picture painted by the shop bill of material.

Controlling orders and parts through the system requires a fast method of seeing the state of the operations on the shop floor. It is more difficult for Production Control personnel to see the potential shortages and possible problems. No more "Pull the stock to make sure we have everything we need." The control of the process must be done using a lot of input form the shop floor; either inperson or via good data collection.

The level of work-in-process out on the floor is controlled by the shop foreman and his people as parts move around and are staged for the final assembly operations. This company also lets the foreman decide his own level of stock for the bulk issue type floor stock. So good management must be exercised; such as restricting floor space and good shop disciplines in place to control component parts movement to feed assembly.

CONCLUSIONS

The obvious advantage of this system is in reducing the paperwork required to convert MRP plans into shop floor implementation. This is accomplished by releasing multiple levels of the bill of material at one time for all the items coded as make items. This has the effect of flattening the bill of material without destroying the engineering controls at the part level.

The control of the parts out on the shop floor is designed to implement the bill exactly the way we produce the product. Those parts that are common to all orders are issued and moved in bulk lots. They are relieved from inventory and costed by computer back-flush explosion without all the paper transactions.

The disadvantages are all centered around the requirement that our people are more knowledgeable of the product and the flow of how the product is made. I would say that all of us want to improve the level of involvement of our people in how we produce the product. More than just reduced paperwork will result.

The total affect of this system was to reduce the overall paperwork by some 80% and still produce the same products. This was

accomplished by flattening the bill of material.
Then getting the people involved to develop
paperwork that reflects how the parts flow
through the shop.

BIOGRAPHY

Terry Lunn has a B.S. degree in Economics
from the Illinois Institute of Technology. Post
graduate work includes business courses at IIT
plus Industrial Engineering at Northwestern.
During college he was elected President of
Triangle Fraternity and a member of Who's Who
Among American Colleges and Universities.

He has over twenty years experience in
industry including industrial engineer,
production control and shop foreman. He has held
several managerial positions in manufacturing and
production control. He has managed the
installation of MRP systems and has extensive
experience in designing and installing
manufacturing control systems.

Mr. Lunn now has his own company serving as
an independent consultant. The main business
effort is to help clients use computer systems
more effectively. This includes a high degree of
emphasis on APICS style closed loop manufacturing
control systems right on through to program
design and modification to assist in better
control of manufacturing and accounting systems.

He is a member of APICS and certified at the
Fellow Level. He has taught hundreds of hours of
Production and Inventory Management for both
public institutions and private companies. He
conducts all the certification review courses for
the Memphis Chapter and has extensive public
speaking experience before groups including
APICS, IMMS, ABWA, DPMA, and others.

Reprinted from the 1984 *APICS Conference Proceedings.*

ATTACK YOUR P:D RATIO
Hal Mather, CPIM*
Hal Mather, Inc.

INTRODUCTION

The P:D ratio for a product is a key measure that defines the amount of speculation inherent in a product's procurement and production cycle. The objective is to reduce the ratio to reduce the speculation. The two choices are to reduce the "P" time (the preferable approach) or increase the "D" time. Constant pressure on this ratio will reap excellent and lasting benefits.

THE P:D RATIO DEFINED

I first came across this term, "P:D ratio", in Shigeo Shingo's book, "Study of the Toyota Production System". He called it the D:P ratio but I have switched the terms to avoid confusion with Data Processing.

The "P" time is the length of time it takes from placing a purchase order to procure materials and components until these are received and produced into a specific finished product. This is variously called the aggregate, stacked, critical path or cumulative lead time.

The "D" time is the length of time customers expect or want from the time they place an order for a product until they receive it. These two are shown schematically in Figure 1.

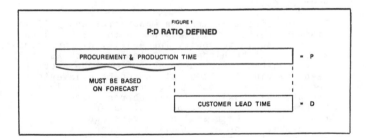

FIGURE 1
P:D RATIO DEFINED

PROCUREMENT & PRODUCTION TIME = P

MUST BE BASED ON FORECAST

CUSTOMER LEAD TIME = D

Any time the ratio is greater than 1, then procurement and/or manufacturing commitments must be made based on forecast input. We all know the first rule of forecasts - they are always wrong to some degree. Methods to cover this forecast error, for example safety stocks, are all costly and have limited effectiveness.

It's obvious the objective should be to make the P:D ratio equal to or less than 1. All commitments to buy materials and produce products can now be based on customers' orders, in most cases with less risk than basing plans on forecasts.

This will not always be possible, especially for consumer products. But in this case, the D period for the manufacturer is not the end consumer D time but the distributor ordering lead time. As it's not unusual for distributors to expect several weeks delivery time from a manufacturer, even in this case it's possible for a manufacturer to have an objective of P:D = 1.

Much of our historical attention to this problem of P being longer than D has been how to cope. We have developed ingenious methods of forecasting, such as planning bills of material, we have separated master production schedules from finishing schedules, developed "overplanning" as a technique of contingency planning, and had designers put variability into the product at the last minute. All these help us bridge the speculative gap between P & D.

We haven't put as much attention into the ratio itself, how to reduce it. Several companies who have attacked the ratio effectively have converted from make-to-stock based on a forecast to make-to-order only. The resultant increase in flexibility to customer needs, the reduction in contingency stocks and the stability of factory schedules have paid for the effort several times over.

For true make-to-order companies, the customer has to order at least as far out as your P time. In this case, the D time is the time between when the customer stops making specification changes and when you deliver the product. The reduction in the P:D ratio now enables you to build the product with less disruption and changes, always costly things to handle.

How do you do it? The first thing to attack is the P element. Reducing this should be the primary objective. But the P time is too big and complex to attack as one subject, so we need to break it into its constituent parts and address each one separately.

MANUFACTURING - QUEUES.

We all know that 95% of lead time is queue time. But few of us are doing anything about it. The causes of this phenomenon are clear and must be removed or reduced significantly.

If you want a short "P" period, materials must move quickly from the receiving dock to the shipping dock, being transformed along the way. Few manufacturing processes have this objective. Layouts are often in functional groupings with like machines all under one supervisor. This groups technical competence but at the cost of long process times. Breaking these functional groups apart and creating process lines can reduce the production lead times by a factor of 10 or more.

A good analogy is a road system. If you want to move quickly from point A to point B by automobile, the best choice is to use an Interstate. Little in the way of a "system" is needed to control your movement and that of the others around you.

The worst choice would be to use a city's streets. Traffic moves in every direction, you need a complex system of one-way streets, traffic lights, and police to control the flow, but it still moves slowly. Do you have Interstates in your plant or a downtown city center?

But even Interstates can get blocked. The morning and evening rush hour traffic effectively overloads the capacity temporarily, delaying us all from reaching our destination, even though the rest of the day there is excess capacity not being used.

Product often flows through a company in an erratic manner, similar to the highway analogy. If you could smooth out the flow, fewer stoppages and delays would occur.

One of the primary causes of erratic flow is large batch sizes. A large batch of product moving across several pieces of equipment temporarily causes a traffic jam so all other products now wait in queue. If the batch sizes could all be reduced, then products would flow in a smoother manner.

The big culprit with batch sizes is changeover or set-up times. The longer these are, the bigger the batch to amortize the changeover times. I am sure you have heard or read about the attack by some Japanese firms on changeover times. Some of their reductions have been outstanding, simply by engineering the changeover process better. A similar attack in your company could reward you in the same way, with lower batch inventories, smaller work-in-process, smoother flows, and a shorter P time.

The Master Production Schedule (MPS) also needs

improvement. Many companies promise in the MPS more than they can make or their vendors can supply. This is just like rush hour traffic on a highway except now you have consistently overloaded the road's carrying capacity. Slow lines of traffic are inevitable, as is slow movement of products through your factory.

The MPS must also be better balanced. An unbalanced MPS is another reason for erratic flow in a plant. By better balanced I mean the products and quantities must be balanced and levelled to the capacities of all workcenters. For example, this month our task is to produce 200 product A, 100 product B, and 100 product C. Our capacity is 100 of any of these products per week. Most MPS's would show 100 product A in week 1, another 100 product A in week 2, 100 product B in week 3 and 100 product C in week 4. This batching would be for efficiency reasons, learning curve effects, etc. But these different products have different components, hence different processes and times required on the various workcenters. And hence this MPS would put differing (erratic) requirements on the plant workcenters.

A better balanced MPS would be 50 product A, 25 product B and 25 product C each week. But this will only be possible if changeover times are reduced so this plan is still efficient. The ultimate of course is a schedule of one A, one B, one A, one C, one A, one B, etc. This would be a perfectly balanced MPS. If economic lot sizes for components were also reduced, a level load would now result on all workcenters.

PROCUREMENT.

We often put the blame for our problems on vendors. But bad vendors almost always service bad customers. Hence the place to start improvements is with our ordering methodology.

A vendor's factory is subject to the same limitations and needs as your own. Vendor's cannot put 2lbs in a 1lb bag any more than you can, neither can they handle erratic demands on their facilities without creating queues of orders. Both these problems show up as extended lead times.

So the changes necessary to improve your vendor lead times are the same as are needed to improve production lead times. A close relationship must exist between your demands for product and the amount of the vendor's capacity he can send you. If your demands exceed your allocation of his capacity, longer lead times are inevitable. Similarly, if you order in an erratic manner, the vendor will quote long lead times to smooth out the work to suit his capacity. Levelling your demands to match your share of the vendor's capacity is your first step to shorter lead times.

It's a well known fact that the larger the base of data, the more stable the results. This is obviously true in forecasting but is also true in most other statistical populations. Hence a large number of vendors means a small population of orders and unstable requirements for each. A few vendors means more stability. Reducing the number of vendors and buying more from each can help level out the demands you place on them. Of course, you must make sure each vendor can now allocate you the increased capacity otherwise this is useless.

The location of vendors is also critical. It has been said that communications problems increase as the square of the distance. Anyone who has had dealings with overseas affiliates will attest to this statement! On top of this, transportation times are longer the further distant the vendors. Cultivating close vendors who can meet your specifications and match close enough the remote vendor's prices can result in significant lead time reductions.

With fewer close vendors and a stable demand on

them that matches their allocation of capacity to you, it's now time to start conversing in different terms. You must start defining the flow rates of product needed to be shipped into your plant from the vendors. These flow rates should be defined long term and based on your aggregate business plan, employment plan, or some similar stable overall set of numbers.

The specific quantities of specific parts needed by the customer can now be determined and communicated to the vendor short range. This technique is often called capacity buying but has largely been a failure in the past. The reasons for the failure are unstable demands, lack of confidence and openness by both parties and a failure of customers to see the role they play in the success of this relationship. With an enlightened view by both managements plus the changes mentioned above, this failure rate can be completely reversed.

INFORMATION.

One of the key elements of P time is information transfer and decision making time. Sometimes it takes longer to come to a decision than make the product!

One of the reasons is the quality of information. It's a truism that the faster you want to travel, the more accurate data must be. Compare the navigational tolerances of a single engine private plane to a commercial jet, then to the Concorde and finally to the space shuttle. When things are happening slowly, errors can be corrected without serious consequences. As speed picks up, even small course errors result in huge deviations from your objective.

The same effect is true in manufacturing. If you wish or are forced to respond to the marketplace faster than in the past, the quality of operational data must be higher. Statements such as, "95% of the on-hand inventory records must be accurate" need changing to, "100% of the on-hand inventory records must be close enough to successfully operate this business in its current mode". Other records, such as bills of materials, routings, purchase and shop orders, work-in-process inventories and all the other data necessary to operate a business need the same levels of accuracy, that is, high enough to operate the business successfully.

We all know that our data should be accurate and that it's silly to try and operate with poor data. But we persist in our efforts to design and implement ever more complex systems and do little to improve the data.

The methodology required is known to all quality control people. You don't inspect quality into products, neither do you inspect quality into data. The process of creating and recording information must be attacked to remove all causes of error. Constant vigilance to keep the process under control will ensure quality data, a prerequisite to fast reliable reaction.

The next reason for slow information transfer is bureaucracy. As data moves across more and more people's desks, information transfer slows down.

It's necessary to have many people and functions involved in long and intermediate range planning. But here time is not a sensitive factor. Get people out of the way in the short range execution phase.

Streamline the information flow from order entry to production to procurement to the vendor. Time is of the essence when there is a market shift. Get this revised information into the hands of all affected people as quickly as possible to pick up valuable response time.

My last problem with information is capacity - of those people who handle data. We often talk about direct labor or machine capacity but rarely about indirect or administrative people capacity. But these groups have a capacity limitation just as surely as direct labor or machinery. Exceed the available capacity and information will slow down.

This means treating these functional groups just like any other workcenter. Rough cut capacity plans, and detailed plans if necessary, are needed to relate their work loads and capacities to the order booking volume. Aggressive management of these indirect capacities will now be possible to ensure a fast flow of information. This is especially necessary in make- or assemble-to-order businesses with many technical specifications or much engineering content related to each order.

As an example, one of my clients makes heavily custom engineered products. They traced their major bottleneck, and the reason for poor delivery performance, to the technical specifications people. They didn't have the capacity to develop the specifications for all the products they were selling. It wasn't until this bottleneck was removed that the information lead time, and hence their P time, was reduced significantly.

EXTENDING D TIMES.

The other way to get the P:D ratio equal to 1 is to extend the D period. This is a risky solution, as delivery times often have competitive influences, so this approach must be handled carefully.

But many times customers will tell you they would prefer a stable, reliable lead time to an unstable short lead time. They are often willing to accept some increase in their ordering lead time if it provides them stability and reliability. This should be tested for your products and customers to see if it is feasible and won't be viewed negatively.

The thing you mustn't do is transfer the speculation problem from you to your customer. Customers cannot predict their needs any better long term than you can. Frequently, because of the idea that purchase orders can always be cancelled, they pay less attention to what they are ordering than you would take over forecasting their business.

Every order placed is three wrong forecasts. The order states a certain item (wrong!) and a certain quantity (wrong again!) for delivery on a certain date (even more wrong!) What makes the error large is lead time, as shown in Figure 2. The further out the prediction the more wrong the information. Don't push the D time too far down this trumpet or you'll be receiving lots of false information.

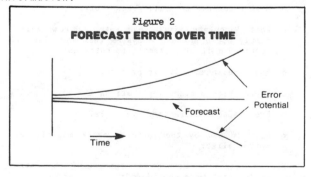

Figure 2
FORECAST ERROR OVER TIME

This is happening today in many industries where the D time far exceeds the P time, for example with integrated circuits. Some delivery lead times are over 52 weeks! You tell me how much false information is being passed back and forth between customer and vendor.

One way of avoiding the transfer of forecasting to your customer is similar to the suggestion of how you should work with vendors. Get customers to predict the volume of product they need long term, leaving specifics till later. If their products have common materials and use common resources, this would allow you to complete the time difference between P & D with a great degree of certainty. The forecast error problem is now minimized for both parties.

CONCLUSION.

The P:D ratio for a product is a critical measure of the efficacy of the operations management process. All companies should measure this ratio and have active programs to reduce it.

The ultimate is 1 or less. Benefits are higher the smaller the ratio. Ratios less than 1 mean a much firmer planning horizon, provided the D time doesn't extend beyond the accurate forecasting period.

The key element to attack is P. Break it down into its constituent parts and reduce each piece aggressively. Be careful of extending D because of competitive influences and the triple forecast error problem.

Companies who have achieved improvements in this ratio are reaping tremendous benefits. Some have even converted from make-to-stock based on a forecast to make-to-order. I'll leave you to calculate the inventory reductions, speculation removal, and increased flexibility to the market-place this change has made.

BIOGRAPHICAL SKETCH - HAL MATHER

Mr. Mather is President of HAL MATHER, INC., ATLANTA, GA., an International Management Consulting and Education company. Since 1973 he has been working with all types of industrial concerns on ways to improve their Business Planning and Control. Recent assignments have taken him throughout NORTH AMERICA, EUROPE, the FAR EAST, AUSTRALASIA and SOUTH AFRICA.

Mr. Mather is renowned for his personal consulting. He has worked with both large and small companies and has stimulated many successful projects with enormous paybacks.

Mr. Mather is a prolific author. His many articles have appeared in a number of magazines, among them the HARVARD BUSINESS REVIEW, and he has been quoted in FORTUNE MAGAZINE. His two books, "BILLS OF MATERIALS, RECIPES AND FORMULATIONS" and "HOW TO REALLY MANAGE INVENTORIES", are classics in the field.

Reprinted from the 1983 *APICS Conference Proceedings.*

BAR CODING: IT'S FOR SHOP FLOOR REPORTING, TOO
Bill D. Parker, CPIM
Schlumberger Well Services

INTRODUCTION

The use of bar codes for material identification has become somewhat commonplace in all phases of American life. It is used on products found in the supermarket, in the corner drug store, in the auto parts store, in the warehouse or distribution center--almost any place where there is a need to identify and count items. But, as widespread as these applications are, they are only a drop in the bucket compared to the full potential of bar coding. At least that's what the Schlumberger Well Services Manufacturing group believes. We believe it's for shop floor reporting too, and we've backed that belief by actually integrating it into daily shop floor reporting for work order scheduling and control as well as for labor reporting. This paper will describe the specific application implemented and will explore the future role that bar coding will play in the manufacturing cycle of this company.

In order to fully understand what was done, it is first necessary to understand the company, the manufacturing environment, and the problems being addressed by bar coding.

THE COMPANY

Schlumberger Well Services - Wireline is a major division of Schlumberger Limited (pronounced Shlum-ber-zhay). It conducts business anywhere that oil is found --currently over 75 countries--for the purpose of locating and defining oil and gas reservoirs and to assist in the completion, development, and production phases of oil wells. Wireline's only product is service--acquiring, transmitting, processing, analyzing, and interpreting data gathered by lowering various measuring instruments to the bottom of a drill hole by means of an armored electrical cable called a wireline. Manufacturing's objectives are to provide the measuring devices (tools) required to provide these services to wireline's customers. Wireline is Manufacturing's only customer--we do not produce to sell outside the Schlumberger Wireline organization.

MANUFACTURING ENVIRONMENT

The basic product manufactured is a highly technical mobile laboratory. Except for a small number of assemblies, individual electronic components, raw material, wire and cable, and a truck chassis, all major items are manufactured in house.

Schlumberger can be characterized as having some of the characteristics of both a job shop and a repetitive manufacturing plant. For most standard production items, the schedule is firmed quite far in advance. Lot sizes, on the other hand, are usually small. Due to the role that technology plays in the wireline business, there are also a large number of engineering prototypes and pilot series products produced.

The factory consists of a machine shop which operates on three shifts, a welding shop which operates on two shifts, a mechanical assembly shop which operates two shifts, and an electronic assembly shop that operates one shift only. At the time the project was initiated, there were just over 400 direct hourly employees in the factory.

While there are a large number of numerically controlled machines in the Machine Shop, factory automation had not proceeded beyond that prior to the time the project was begun. There has been a major shift towards more automation since then.

Procedurely, direct hourly workers in the factory manually recorded their time on time cards which were processed nightly. These labor transactions were used to update work order status. Material moves were not recorded.

THE PROBLEM

In early 1982, as the result of a major program to "modernize" manufacturing, a project team was established to define the requirements for implementing Shop Floor Control (SFC).

Among the problems being addressed by the Shop Floor Control project were:

o Data integrity - Since labor reporting was manual, information recorded was often incorrect, the correct information was sometimes misread when it was keypunched. First time rejects averaged just under 18%, of those, another 20% were rejected on the second input. It was not unusual to have unresolved labor record problems 60 days after the work order closed.

o Excess Work in Process - Work-in-process levels were excessive for our type of operation. We had almost $3 of work-in-process each month for each $1 shipped, or in other words, we had a three month backlog of work-in-process.

o Timing problems - Due to the lag between the time a work order operation was complete and the time the labor record (and therefore the work order status) was correctly entered, it was difficult to track a work order with any accuracy.

o Deliveries missed - As a result of the lack of accurate work order status, missed deliveries were frequent.

o Unresponsiveness to change - Once work was released to the shop floor, it was very difficult to respond to any changes that might affect the work order, such as implementation of Engineering Change Notices (ECNs).

After evaluating several commercially available packages and looking at the "roll your own" option, the Shop Floor Control project team chose Hewlett-Packard's PM3000 as the package that fit its requirements best.

It was the project team's belief that to obtain the full benefits of SFC, it was necessary to automate the data collection function in the shops. Not only would this eliminate a major source of error, it would speed data collection and would represent a significant milestone towards achieving the "paperless factory."

CHOOSING BAR CODES

In order to be an acceptable solution for the data collection problem, the choice had to meet the following criteria:

o High level of reliability. We were going to depend upon it.

o Unaffected by magnetic or electrical currents due to the large number of induction motors in the machine shop.

o High tolerance to dirt, grease, oil.

o Fast, accurate first read rate. Our workers simply would not use a system that was slow and required multiple attempts to enter data.

o Easy and inexpensive to produce.

o Expandable to other applications.

o Eye readable characters available.

o Easy to use by the factory worker and office worker alike.

Four alternative methods of automating the data collection function were considered:

o Punched cards

o Optical Characters

o Magnetically encoded strips

o Bar Codes.

Punched cards and optical characters were very quickly eliminated from contention--punched cards because it's really outdated technology, optical characters because of the difficulty in obtaining acceptable first read rates.

After a further evaluation, bar coding was chosen over magnetics because it offered these advantages:

o Not affected by magnetic or electrical currents as magnetics are.

o Integratable with planned warehousing, shipping, and receiving applications where bar codes are the de facto standard.

o Equipment to produce and read it are less expensive than for magnetics. Our survey indicated as much as 25% less.

o Reader contact with the code not required. This was important for future applications anticipated in the warehouse. It also meant that it could be encased in plastic up to 4 mils thick for use on employee badges.

o Portable readers were available.

Even though magnetics had the advantage of higher character density, this was not sufficient reason to offset the bar code advantages.

Once bar codes were selected for this application, the selection of the bar code symbology was quite easy. Code 39 was chosen because of its:

o Wide acceptance in manufacturing and warehousing.

o Alphanumeric capabilities.

o Adoption as the standard by the U.S. Department of Defense.

THE APPLICATION

Shop floor data terminals were strategically placed throughout the factory so that there was roughly one Hewlett-Packard 2624B CRT for every eight shop employees. The CRTs were to be used both for data entry and for inquiry purposes. To aid in data entry, a Hewlett-Packard 92911A bar code reader was attached to each CRT. These bar code readers simply translate the bar coded symbols into characters that can be read by the CRT.

Each CRT work station is provided with table of bar coded log-on and other related non-productive codes (figure 1) for use in time and attendance as well as work order functions. Each direct employee, each quality control supervisor and each shop supervisor have been provided with a bar coded identification badge. This was accomplished by sealing the bar coded identification number under the clear plastic badge cover. The badge cover is about 2 mils thick in order to provide maximum protection without inhibiting bar code readability. It is important to note that only the bar code symbols are printed.

The shop supervisors have been provided with a list of their employees and the corresponding bar coded identification numbers for use when it is necessary to perform employee related functions.

Work order paper is bar coded, too. Each work order released to the shop has a control card which stays with the work order throughout its life. Both the work order number and the part number are bar coded as well as eye readable. For each work order routing operation, there is a corresponding operation which has the work order number, route sequence number and operation number bar coded and eye readable.

Bar codes are used for two primary functions in the factory--labor reporting and work order reporting.

LABOR REPORTING

At shift change, the employee reports to the assigned work station. First, the "Start Shift" or the "End Shift" code (whichever is applicable) is read from the bar code table. Next, the employee identification number is read from the employee ID badge. The transaction then is automatically time stamped and updates a file that is batch processed at night for payroll purposes.

Since the reader emits a "beep" when a good read is made, the employee immediately knows that the transaction has been accepted.

Non-productive work is recorded as follows:

1. A non-productive transaction is called up on the CRT screen by pressing an appropriate terminal function key.

2. The employee identification number is recorded by "wanding" the employee ID badge.

3. The appropriate order related non-productive code is read by the wand and the Enter key is depressed.

4. The transaction is automatically time stamped by the computer. The clock will continue to run until the employee enters another transaction.

5. The transactions are entered into a file that is immediately accessible from the CRT. It is batch processed overnight to update the labor records for payroll and costing purposes.

WORK ORDER REPORTING

Work order status updates are accomplished by means of direct labor transactions entered from the shop floor by the worker.

1. When a job is received, the appropriate transaction screen is called up on the CRT by pressing a terminal function key.

2. The employee ID is entered from the employee ID badge and the bar coded transaction type is read from the bar coded log-on table. Transaction types are: start set up, start run and step complete.

3. The work order number, route sequence number and operation number are read from the Routing Operation Card.

4. The computer time stamps the transaction and updates the appropriate work order and work center files.

5. When the transaction is completed, the worker goes through the same sequence of events as above. The only exception is that the quantities completed, scrapped and bonused must be keyed in.

6. The step completion transaction automatically assigns the work order to an in transit or in queue status.

7. Labor and cost accounting are updated nightly with batch transactions.

At Schlumberger, quality control is an in-line operation with its own operation on the work order routing. Currently, reject reason codes are keyed in, they are not yet bar coded.

RESULTS

This rather small application has had some large results:

1. Employee time records are immediately in machine readable form--keypunching is no longer required.

2. First pass rejects have been practically eliminated due to front end edits employed and the elimination of manual data transcription.

3. Cost data accuracy, and therefore data integrity, has been vastly improved because the computer watches the clock, not the employee.

4. The three o'clock rush to the time clock has been virtually eliminated since there are only eight employees per station on the average.

5. Work order status is more timely and more accurate. Bar coding insures that the correct work order number and operation number have been entered.

IMPLEMENTATION DIFFICULTIES

Bar coding was surprisingly simple to implement in our shops. We anticipated some employee resistance so we went to great lengths to prepare our employees for the coming change. We used internal company publications and information meetings to provide general information. Then, each shop supervisor trained his employees in group and individual sessions. A demonstration unit was set up so that employees could practice on their own. When this was completed, implementation was accomplished without a hitch.

The most perplexing problem encountered was the selection of the proper bar code printer. We initially tried a dot matrix printer with mixed results. After much manipulation with bar code densities and alternate vendors, we stayed with our original Hewlett-Packard model but are continuing to search the market for a more appropriate printer. Our most satisfactory results to date have been with a laser printer, however, its cost makes it prohibitive for this single purpose application.

FUTURE PLANS

Immediate future plans for bar coding at Schlumberger include bar coding the most common quality reject codes so that they can be read with a wand rather than keyed. There are also plans for utilizing bar coding in the receiving, shipping and warehousing functions. We will also bar code all of our field equipment for tracking purposes. This is particularly important since some of the equipment contains radioactive sources for which the U.S. government requires extensive records on their past uses and locations.

SCHLUMBERGER WELL SERVICES
SFC BAR-CODE TABLET

Figure 1

ABOUT THE AUTHOR

Bill D. Parker is the Manufacturing Systems Manager for the Manufacturing Division of Schlumberger Well Services. He has 15 years experience in materials management, manufacturing and manufacturing systems at both the plant and corporate levels. His experience covers the electronics, chemical and oil tool industries. Prior to joining Schlumberger, Bill was the Corporate Manager of Manufacturing Systems for the Hooker Chemical Corporation.

Bill earned his bachelors degree from the University of Texas and an M.B.A. degree from Southern Methodist University. He is a member of the Houston chapter of APICS, certified, and is a Senior Member of the Institute of Industrial Engineers.

SHOP FLOOR CONTROL FOR PRODUCTIVITY AND PROFIT
William E. Pendleton, CPIM*
Productivity Group

The Master Production Schedule represents the game plan of the company whereas the shop floor is the execution arm. One cannot be successful without the other. The shop floor has been described as the graveyard of American manufacturing with its large work-in-process(WIP) inventories, low productivity and chaos. Yet, it represents a virtually untapped source of productivity and profit improvement.

The press in recent years has been enamored by the visions of Star Wars and the technical revolution. We have read about robotics, lasers, microelectronics and computerization of everything in sight. These advances are of great importance but few companies can afford to immediately replace their existing plant and equipment. Are they left out of the potential productivity boom? Of course not. There is vast potential for improvement with their existing facilities by implementing a formal shop floor control system.

The focus of this paper is threefold:

1. Identify areas of potential productivity and profit improvement within the factory.

2. Provide an overview of the prerequisites and functions of an effective shop floor control system.

3. Discuss the human aspects of productivity improvement.

A good shop floor control system will allow the shop to manage the resources inorder to accomplish its major goals, namely:

o Provide a high level of customer service.
o Produce a quality produce.
o Maintain high productivity and utilization.

When the factory seems to be operating at full capacity, a formal shop floor control system can increase throughput from 10-30 percent. Thus, sales can rise without the need for addtional facilities.

POTENTIAL AREAS OF PRODUCTIVITY AND PROFIT IMPROVEMENT

The objective of this section is to outline areas of improvement and suggest specfic items that can be quantified.

1. LOWER WIP INVENTORIES thru reduction of:
   - Staging of kits in advance of manufacturing
   - Overloading the floor because of inadequate order release control
   - Work center queues
   - Obsolescence and inventory shrink
   - Lost orders and materials
   - Incomplete or inactive orders
   - Orders awaiting QC dispostion

2. IMPROVED DIRECT LABOR PRODUCTIVITY thru reduction of:
   - Idle time caused by material or tool shortages
   - Idle time caused by excessive machine breakdowns
   - Set-up time
   - Rework due to ineffective engineering change control
   - Overtime premiums
   - Unfavorable labor rate and efficiency variances
   - Labor spent on the wrong priorities
   - Subcontract expenses
   - Shop congestion

3. IMPROVED INDIRECT LABOR PRODUCTIVITY thru reduction of:
   - Expediting activities
   - Material handling, movement and storage expenses
   - Production control and support manpower
   - Shop congestion

4. LOWER MATERIAL COST thru reduction of:
   - Expediting cost with vendors due to kit shortages
   - Outside processing costs
   - Air freight expense
   - Rework cost
   - Packing and shipping costs due to partial shipments

5. INCREASED PLANT THRUPUT AND UTILIZATION thru:
   - Defering the need for additional plant and equipment
   - Maintaining smooth production rates with less frantic activity at month end
   - Increase machine and tool availability due to preventative maintenance
   - Effective tool control

6. IMPROVED CUSTOMER SERVICE thru:
   - Fewer penalties for late customer deliveries
   - Fewer lost sales due to delivery and quality problems
   - Increase in sales due to high service reputation
   - Reduction is customer lead time
   - Fast and accurate response to customer inquires
   - Reduction is partial shipments
   - Fewer less-than-carload deliveries
   - More effective scheduling of field service installation
   - Improved cash flow due to less late deliveries

A FORMAL SHOP FLOOR CONTROL SYSTEM--ITS PREREQUISITES

Prerequisites for a successful shop floor control system include the following:

o An accurate and timely shop floor data base
   - Inventory and Bill of Materials
   - Work center definition
   - Routing and standards
   - Lead time elements
   - Open shop orders

o Supporting policies, procedures and disciplines
o A formal education and training program
o Management leadership and commitment
o Tools to assist such as:
   - Computer assisted shop scheduling and loading
   - Data collection devices
   - Count verification equipment
   - CRT inquiry terminals

A FORMAL SHOP FLOOR CONTROL SYSTEM--ITS FUNCTIONS

Few companies have successfully honed their shop into an efficient, cost effective competitive weapon. The tools have been available for years. The MRP crusade and the invasion of the Japanese have identified the necessity for increased productivity. The manufacturing gurus agree that we need a formal system to manage the shop. The focus of this section is to present eight essential functions of a formal shop floor control system (Figure 1).

FUNCTIONS OF A FORMAL
SHOP FLOOR CONTROL SYSTEM

PRIORITY PLANNING SYSTEM	
ORDER RELEASE CONTROL	OK?
SCHEDULE AND LOAD SHOP	OK?
PRIORITY CONTROL AND DISPATCHING	OK?
REPORT SHOP FLOOR STATUS	OK?
WIP AND LEAD TIME CONTROL	OK?
CAPACITY PLANNING	OK?
PERFORMANCE MEASUREMENT AND REPORTING	OK?

Figure 1

1. Priority Planning System

The most crucial function of formal shop floor control system is establishing the production schedule--what products need be manufactured, in what quantity and when. There are many methods for establishing a schedule. The author will discuss MRP and a non-MRP approach.

The major advantage MRP is its inherent capability to establish and maintain shop order priorities. MRP is a time-phased method to balance requirements and replenishments and identify the need for new orders, reschedules and cancellations (Figure 2).

MRP RELATIONSHIP
SHOP FLOOR INTERFACE

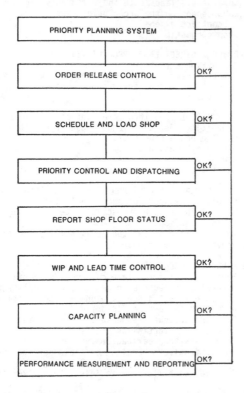

SHOP FLOOR NEEDS TO KNOW	INFORMATION IS PROVIDED BY:	
	MRP	OTHER SOURCES
WHAT	PART NUMBER	
WHEN	DUE DATE	
HOW MUCH	ORDER QUANTITY	
WHERE		WORK CENTER FILE
HOW		ROUTING FILE

Figure 23

When MRP is not applicable, another method of priority planning must be selected. In the machine shop, a typical non-MRP environment, priorities can be establshed by the production control department. The most effective approach is to maintain an accurate picture scheduled load by work center. Before scheduling a new order, production control should evaluate the requirements of the order, review the load reports and determine the earliest available schedule date.

Poor priority planning can result in missed delivery dates, high WIP inventories and low productivity. Therefore, it is important that a strong commitment be made to effective priority planning.

2. Order Release Control

The role of the order release function is to get work started in the right priority and time to assure that it will be completed on schedule. It reviews orders suggested by the priority planning system and determines if they should be released to production. The following criteria can be used to evaluate whether an order should be released:

o   Is the order's start date within the order release horizon?
o   Is the lead time sufficient to complete the order ontime?
o   Are all the materials available?
o   Is the tooling available?
o   Is there sufficient capacity?

The establishment of order release criteria is based on several important principles of shop floor control.[2]

1.   Keep backlogs off the shop floor.
     - Are difficult to control
     - Make engineering changes more expensive to implement
     - Generates more expediting and handling
     - Creates more physical problems
2.   Schedule only items that the factory can make.
     - Don't release orders with known problems such as materials or tools not available
     - Known capacity limitations or bottlenecks
3.   Release the order at the latest possible moment.
     - The shorter the scheduling period, the lower the WIP inventory
     - Since fewer orders will be in the shop, there is less handling, congestion and conflict

A shop packet is prepared for each order released. Its function is to authorize the requistion of material, provide instructions on how the item is to be manufactured and to facilitate shop reporting. Typically, the shop packet includes:

o   A pick list which identifies the parts that should be released from the stockroom.
o   A routing or process sheet that describes the sequence of operations and where they are to be performed.
o   Shop floor reporting documents such as labor, material and move tickets that facilitate accurate and timely reporting.

There is a trend toward eliminating as much physical paperwork as possible through the use of data collection devices. They can generally edit and speed-up transaction processing which will increase accuracy and the timeliness of information.

3. Schedule and Load the Shop

There are numerous scheduling and loading techniques such as backward scheduling, foreward scheduling, short-interval scheduling, OPT, infinite loading and finite loading. The selection of the appropriate technique or techniques is based on the nature of the manufacturing operation, the complexity of the product and the volume of orders.

Most of the methods utilize the concept of operational scheduling. The shop order due dates supplied by the priority planning system are offset through the use of the routing or an appropriate algorithm to establish start and due dates for each operation step. Operation scheduling is illustrated in Figures 3 and 4. Start and due dates are established for each operation on the shop order by using its routing and backward scheduling logic. A manufacturing shop calendar is used in scheduling but converted to Julian dates for reporting purposes. As the order progresses through the shop, it is easy to determine if it is on schedule.

EXPLODE

ROUTING				ORDER MASTER	
OPN	W/C	S/U	RUN	Order No.	M1234
10	F010	2.0	1.5	Part No.	A
20	A020	1.0	2.4	Quantity	10
30	A020	--	0.5	Due Date	9/28/83
40	A030	0.5	1.0		

OPERATION DETAIL

Order M1234 P/N A Qty 10 Due 9/28/83

OPN	W/C	SCHED HOURS	DATE START	DUE
10	F010	17.0		
20	A020	25.0		
30	A020	5.0		
40	A030	10.5		
		57.5		

Figure 3

BACKWARD SCHEDULING

ORDER M1234 P/N A QTY 10 DUE 9/28/83

OPN	W/C	S/U	RUN	QUE	MOVE	IQ/M	ESH
10	F010	2.0	15	2	1	--	6.4
20	A020	1.0	24	2	1	--	6.4
30	A020		5	2	1	--	6.4
40	A030	0.5	10	2	1	--	6.4

```
        10        20        30        40
     |Q|R|M|Q|R|M|Q|R|M|Q|R|M|
     97 99 102 103 105 109 110 112 113 114 116 118 119
```

OPERATION DETAIL

Order M1234 P/N A Qty 10 Due 9/28/83

OPN	W/C	SCHED HOURS	DATE START	DUE
10	F010	17.0	8/30/83	9/6/83
20	A020	25.0	9/12/83	9/15/83
30	A020	5.0	9/17/83	9/17/83
40	A030	10.5	9/25/83	9/26/83
		57.5		

Figure 4

A work center load report is prepared by sorting the data in work center sequence. The report provides production control with short term load versus capacity analysis. Overload and underload conditions can be easily detected and

alternative strategies can be evaluated that will resolve the problems before they occur. To relieve overloads, the foreman may authorize overtime, offload work to other work centers using alternate routing or when conditions are extreme, subcontract with an outside vendor.

WORK CENTER LOAD REPORT

WORK CENTER F010

PER	START	DAYS	CAP	HOURS REL	SCHED	%
0	8/27	5	32.0	17.0	52.0	163
1	9/4	4	25.6	--	41.0	160
2	9/10	6	38.4	--	27.0	71
3	9/17	3	19.2	--	22.0	116
4						
⋮						
8						

PER	0%..............100%..............200%
1	RRRRRRSSSSSSSSSSSS
2	SSSSSSSSSSSSSSSS
3	SSSSSSS
4	SSSSSSSSSSS
⋮	
8	

Figure 5

5. Priority Control and Dispatching

The informal shop floor is the mecca of the expeditor. Priorities are controlled by a variety of techniques including:

o Who screams the loudest
o Who carries the biggest stick
o Hot, Hotter, Hottest tags
o Highest $ jobs
o Gravy jobs
o Original order due dates
o Anything that can be shipped (end of month)
o Presidential order

Today's formal shop floor control system typically utilizes operational scheduling and emphasizes on-schedule performance. Its primary tool is the dispatch list which provides the foreman with a prioritized list of jobs running, waiting and scheduled for his work center (Figure 6). It's vital that the dispatch list presents an accurate picture of the work center load. If it's out of date, credibility is quickly lost. The following suggestions should be reviewed prior to implementing a dispatching list:

o It should be prepared daily to reflect current priorities and conditions.
o Its accuracy should be audited on a regular basis.
o The prioritizing rule should be simple for the foreman to understand and work with. For example, operation start date is generally rcommended over critical or slack time ratios.
o Primary emphasis should be placed on on-time schedule performance versus efficiency.
o Secondarily, the foreman should have the flexibility to alter the sequence of the orders to take advantage of common set-up and machine and skill capabilities as long as on-schedule performance is maintained.
o It should identify orders currently at the work center as well as provide visibility of orders expected to arrive within a future time frame.

FOREMAN'S DAILY REPORT

WORK CENTER NO. 4230
DESCRIPTION 2A TURRET

DATE 2/22
WEEKLY CAPACITY 112

W/O NO.	PART NO.	DESCRIPTION	QTY.	OP. NO.	OP. DUE DATE	W/O DUE DATE	SET-UP HRS	RUN HRS	PRIOR W/C	C	COMMENTS
JOBS CURRENTLY AT THIS WORK CENTER											
145	4422	SLEEVE-RET	26	50	2/20	3/15	2.2	15.6		Q	
138	4897	CONNECTOR	16	90	2/20	6/20	1.5	8.6		R	
142	3517	NIPPLE	30	50	2/22	4/15	3.7	18.5		Q	
148	3672	SV SHOE	15	70	2/27	5/01	3.4	19.7		S	
						TOTALS:	10.8	62.4			
JOBS COMING TO THIS WORK CENTER											
140	8052	RECEPTABLE	10	20	2/22	3/15	3.0	20.0	5210	R	
136	4287	COLLAR	50	70	2/29	6/13	2.6	62.2	0700	S	
130	1914	VALVE BODY	50	20	3/02	6/20	1.5	10.6	9210	H	
						TOTALS:	7.1	92.8			

Figure 6[4]

The dispatch list can be an effective management tool for the foreman. High priority orders can be identified without the need for a host of expediters. Exception conditions can be easily detected in enough to resolve most of them. For example, the foreman can identify past due orders and be ready to run them as soon as they arrive at his work center. He will have time to properly manage his resources. The foreman can properly assign order to particular workers or machines to take advantage of employee experience and machine capabilities as well as track efficiency and utilization.

5. Report Shop Floor Status

The ingredient that keeps the formal shop floor control system together is accurate and timely reporting the floor. Production activity reporting is vital to maintaining valid schedules, detecting problems and suggesting corrective action. In addition, it provides marketing with current order status and cost data meaningful to accounting.

The level of detail required from the shop floor varies by company. The type of data reported typically includes:
o Status of material
   - Issues, receipts, quantity complete, scrap, move transactions and order closure
o Status of labor
   - Time reported by operation, set-up time, run time, rework, indirect labor reporting

Production activity reporting can be obtained by manually recording of data or assisted by data collection devices such as badge readers, CRT's, bar code readers and scanners. Regardless of the method, proper disciplines, training and auditing are required to assure that the data collected from the shop follor is both accurate and timely.

6. WIP and Lead Time Control

The control of WIP has important implications on the level of inventory investment, customer lead time and factory overhead. In many companies, WIP represents 50-70 percent of the inventory investment. The level of WIP is determined by the amount of work released to the shop and the output rate from it. If you want to reduce WIP, you can reduce the number of orders released to the floor, decrease planned lead times used by MRP or increase capacity of overloaded work centers.

Typically, the majority of WIP is represented by work waiting in queues which comprise 80-90 percent of manufacturing lead time. If work center queues can be lowered, WIP inventories and lead time can be correspondingly reduced.

Several techniques for reducing WIP queues are listed below:
o By following the principles of Master Production Scheduling, overloading the shop can be controlled. One of the key principles is that the schedule must be consistent with capacity.
o When planned lead times used by MRP are reduced, fewer

orders are recommended for release with less input to the floor and capacity remaining the same, WIP queues will be worked down.
o Strict order release control can place holds on orders when capacity is not sufficient.
o Input/Output Control visibility into rates of input versus the rates of output by work center (Figure 7). If a work center is consistently underproducing, the problem must be identified and corrective action taken.
o With visibility provided by the Dispatch List, the foreman no longer needs the security of large physical queues at the work center.

INPUT/OUTPUT CONTROL

WORK CENTER NUMBER: 4230
DEPARTMENT NUMBER: 20
WORK CENTER DESC: 2A TURRET

DATE: 2/22
ACTION MESSAGE: INPUT UNDER/OVER

INPUT

WEEK	-4	-3	-2	-1	THIS WEEK	2/27	3/6	3/13	3/20	3/27	4/3	4/10
PLAN IN	115	115	115	115	115	115	115	115	115	115	115	115
ACTUAL IN	100	125	80	132								
CUM.DEV.	-15	-5	-40	-23								

TOLERANCE ± 30 HOURS

OUTPUT

WEEK	-4	-3	-2	-1	THIS WEEK	2/27	3/6	3/13	3/20	3/27	4/3	4/10
PLAN OUT	115	115	115	115	115	115	115	115	115	115	115	115
ACTUAL OUT	120	95	90	90								
CUM.DEV.	+5	-15	-40	-65								
CUM. ACT. OUT	120	215	305	395								
ACT. HRS.	160	150	165	155	ACTUAL LOAD FACTOR 395 ÷ 630 = 63%							
CUM. ACT. HRS.	160	310	475	630								

TOLERANCE ± 30 HOURS | PLANNED Q 50 HOURS | ACTUAL Q 105 HOURS

Figure 7[4]

7. Capacity Planning

Growing WIP and excessive lead times are symptoms of poor capacity planning. There are three levels of capacity planning--long term, intermediate term and short term (Figure 8). A brief description of each is found below:

o Long Term — The Production Plan and Master Production Schedule are evaluated by Rough-cut Capacity Planning to determine long-term capacity needs typically 1-2 years in the future. Its role is to identify the need for additional plant, equipment and manpower.

o Intermediate Term — MRP is evaluated by Capacity Requirements Planning to determine capacity needs in in the range of 3-12 months in the future. Its role is to identify the need for make versus buy decisions, sub contracting, redeployment of work force and alternative routing.

o Short Term — Short term capacity analysis is accomplished through released order load analysis and Input/Output Control. Its role is to identify overload and underload conditions and resolve them with overtime, outside processing of operations, alternate routing and changing the schedule.

METHODS OF CAPACITY PLANNING

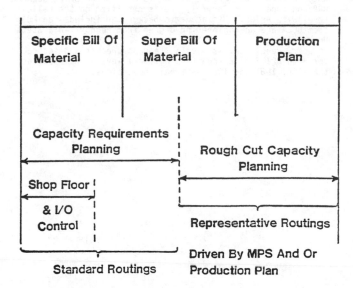

Figure 8

8. Performance Measurement and Reporting

Important to the success of a formal shop floor control system, is the establishment of an effective performance measurement and reporting. When shop personnel are measured on specific factors, they will do their best to achieve them. The measurements should have the following characteristics:

o Understandable
o Measurable
o Fair
o Achievable
o Reported on a regular basis
o Consistent with compensation plans

Examples of measurements include:

o Rate of production by work center
 - Planned versus actual in dollars and hours
 - Utilization

o WIP inventories
 - WIP value by work center
 - Queue levels by work center
 - Dollar value of inactive jobs

o On-time schedule performance
 - Operations completed on-time
 - Operations completed late and average days late
 - Jobs released with less than standard lead time

o Direct labor performance
 - Labor efficiency by work center and employee
 - Labor rate variance
 - Labor efficiency variance
 - Overtime premium expense by work center

o Overhead by work center or department
 - Rework labor
 - Indirect labor by activity

o Material cost by work center
 - Scrap value
 - Material usage variance

SHOP MOTIVATION PLANNING

Of any area in a manufacturing operation, the shop floor has been the most difficult to implement a formal system. In an APICS survey conducted in 1978, less than 30 percent of the respondents indicated that they had a formal shop floor control system. There are many reasons for this dismal statistic.

o Past failures with so called formal systems
o Pressure always on the shop to make up for poor planning
o Shop personnel often have the lowest education level and pay structure
o Shop personnel have traditionally received little job related training
o They seldom receive praise and recognition for performing well

The author surveyed a representative sample of companies that have a successful shop floor system in operation. They were asked the question, What did they do to increase the chance for success. The following list summarizes their answers:

1. Improve management skills and practices on the shop floor.
 - Establish reasonable goals
 - Resolved conflicting measurements
 - Measure and report performance on a regular basis
 - Conducted regular reviews and appraisals
 - Involved personel in decision-making
 - Established job enrichment programs

2. Organize a Quality Circle Program to enlist involvement.

3. Develop extensive, on-going training program.
4. Cultivated inside salepeople from the shop to serve as spokesmen.

5. Demonstrated management commitment to the formal through action as well as deed.

CONCLUSION

The challenge of implementing a formal shop floor control system is immense. It requires good planning, a large investment, attention to detail, and an understanding of the human aspects. The payoff can be great. Not only can productivity and profit be increased but the quality of life on the shop floor can be vastly improved. At last, shop personnel are not longer the whipping boys.

REFERENCES

1. Plossl, G., Manufacturing Control, Reston Publishing Company, Reston, Virginia, 1973.
2. Plossl, G. and Wight, O., Production and Inventory Control, Prentice-Hall, Inc., Englewood Cliffs, New Jersey, 1967, p. 251.
3. APICS Training Aid, Shop Floor Controls, APICS, Inc. Falls Church, Virginia.
4. Stevens, A. and Brooks, R., MRPII: Manufacturing Resource Planning--"The Five Day Class", Oliver Wight Education Associates, Inc., Newbury, New Hampshire.
5. Wassweiler, W., "Fundamentals of Shop Floor Control," APICS Conference Proceedings, 1980, p. 352.
6. Weeks, J., "WIP Inventory Management, Productivity and Costs," Production and Inventory Managementt, 1st Qtr., 1978, p. 40.
7. Bruhn, G., "Shop Floor Control? You Can't Control, If You Don't Know," APICS Conference Proceedings, 1979, p. 175.
8. Young, J., "Practical Dispatching," APICS Conference Proceedings, 1981, p. 175.
9. Beal, G. and Evan, R., "Performance Management: Improving the Bottom Line Activity of the P&IC Department," APICS Conference Proceedings, 1982, p. 221.
10. Van De Mark, R., "Adjust Your Capacity, Do Not Reschedule," APICS Conference Proceedings, 1981, p. 148.
11. Donkersloot, R., "Productivity Through Manufacturing Control," Production and Inventory Management, 1st Qtr., 1983, p. 103.

ABOUT THE AUTHOR

Mr. Pendleton is President of Productivity Group, a firm that specializes in products and services aimed at assisting industry in achieving its productivity goals. The firm represents for Data 3 Systems, Inc., covering Southern California, Arizona and New Mexico. Data 3 Systems offers a 3rd generation MRP II system that operates on the IBM 34/36/38. In addition, Productivity Group represents the educational products of the Forum Ltd. and the MRP II Implementation Manuals of R.F. Alban & Associates.

Mr. Pendleton's background includes 15 years experience in the sales and implementation of manufacturing systems with Arista Manufacturing System, Xerox Computer Services and IBM. He is past president of the San Fernando Valley Chapter of APICS. Mr. Pendleton is an instructor at UCLA on MRP and Shop Floor Control. He is certified on the Fellow Level with APICS. His academic background includes an MBA from UCLA and an Engineering Degree from Pennsylvania State University.

Mr. Pendleton has been a frequent speaker and instructor with APICS on a local and national level. He spoke at the 1980, 1981 and 1982 National Conventions.

Reprinted from the 1986 APICS Conference Proceedings.

CLASSIFICATION CODING FOR GROUP TECHNOLOGY
AND STANDARDIZATION
John N. Petroff, CPIM
Comserv Corporation

Classification Coding is not an end in itself, but a necessary tool in the analysis and development of Group Technology and Standardization most notably. Once available, however, many other benefits will emerge. A good system is non-trivial and must be developed and implemented with care and skill.

For purposes of this presentation, I would like to define Classification Coding as follows: "A method of putting components into groups according to their physical characteristics such that similarities can be identified and analyzed." A component in this sense includes everything from raw material to finished product, purchased or manufactured in-house.

To better understand the necessary characteristics of Classification Coding, we should first review Group Technology and Standardization.

Group Technology is the practice of grouping dissimilar machines together in the factory to make similar parts. This is directly opposite from the usual, functional, factory layout, where machines are grouped together according to their similarity, then called on to make dissimilar parts. Figure 1 shows the conventional process-type layout. This illustration also shows the typical spaghetti-bowl routing which occurs in such a layout. Materials management professionals also will appreciate that there is a queue in front of each work center.

Figure 2 shows a Group Technology version of the same factory. Here, the machines have been rearranged according to the three main family groups of components being manufactured. Once started, each piece flows from machine to machine without pause. This reduces throughput time typically by four-fifths. And since queue time occurs only at the start of the Group Technology cell, it is also reduced by four-fifths. There are a number of other attractive benefits of Group technology, but this subject lies outside the scope of this presentation.

Considering that Group Technology requires rearranging the factory, preparatory analysis must be well-done. One requirement is to analyze

PROCESS—TYPE LAYOUT

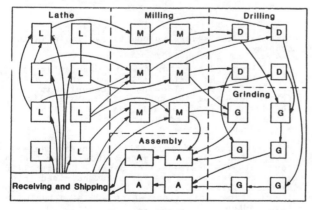

Figure 1

GROUP TECHNOLOGY LAYOUT

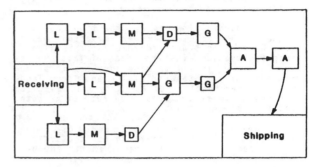

Figure 2

all components according to manufacturing similarities. In small factories, or where production is simple, this analysis could perhaps be done intuitively or by simple manual methods. But in most cases some sort of computerized analysis is the only feasible way to do a complete study. In these cases, then, some sort of comprehensive classification coding device is needed which will list parts according to manufacturing similarity.

Standardization can be an engineering specialty on its own, but simply put it means don't reinvent the wheel.

A standardized approach to component design proceeds in the following sequence:
1. Use an existing component as is.
2. Slightly modify an existing component.
   a. The modified version is interchangeable, and the component's revision level is raised.
   b. The modified version is not interchangeable, and a new part number is started.
3. Take design tips from existing components.
4. Start from scratch.

The advantages of standardization are very attractive and include such things as
* Lower design cost
* Faster design process
* Less inventory
    Fewer stock locations
    Lower investment
* Lower unit costs
* Planning efficiency
    Fewer items
    Fewer stockouts
* Outside authorities
    Customer's design
    Government contracts
    Regulatory authorities
* Simplified tool design
* Facilitates equipment purchase

Design costs are lower because new designs are avoided. Starting a new part costs anywhere from hundreds to thousands of dollars each. Using an existing part avoids this cost altogether. Using a revised version of an existing one sharply reduces the design cost.

Standardization results in many fewer components used in manufacturing, thereby avoiding inventory on each. With higher usage of fewer components inventory usage becomes more stable and manageable, leading to lower investment. Higher volume also leads to lower unit cost.

With fewer items to manufacture or procure,

planning is less cumbersome, and usage less lumpy. This results in fewer stockouts

In a government procurement environment, it often is very difficult to get permission to use a new component. Getting approval for one already being used is far easier.

Standardization has an impact on tool design. Higher volume of fewer variations means that better tools are affordable. This also supports the just-in-time ideas of fast change-over. Equipment and machine purchase is affected similarly. Standardiztaion and Group Technology taken together create many new selection and design considerations with respect to both tooling and equipment.

Bearing in mind the basic needs of Group Technology and Standardization for classification codes, the following requirements emerge for a good classification coding system.

1. Universal.
A classification coding system should be able to catalog the universe. Change is a fact of life, and a number of writers and lecturers point out that the pace of change is accelerating. This means that a classification coding system must be able to expand to encompass unexpected, new demands.

2. Physical Characteristics.
The code should classify each item according to its physical characteristics which are permanent over time and permanent regardless of application. Classification can not be according to how used or where used. For example, "Standoff" is a description of use and no good for analysis. Describing such an item as a piece part, made of steel, threaded at both ends, approximately 2 inches long and 1/4 inch in diameter, is a useful classification.

3. Discrete.
It is important that the system bring similar items together, and exclude interlopers. Moreover, it is very useful that the system allow selection and listing at cascading levels of detail, from fairly general at one end of the spectrum to quite specific at the other. In addition it is necessary that each item have only one code.

4. Computable.
In this day and age, it can be assumed that a computer is available for use. This is especially true of companies using MRP software, which universally have an item master file already available. The classification coding system should be crafted so sorting, selecting, and listing is flexible, easy, and on demand. Listing should be on a terminal's screen if possible, and in every case in printed form.

5. Separate Field on the Item Master
Many companies make the mistake of trying to imbed some sort of classification into either the part number or the description. Neither can or ever works. It is necessary to have a separate field on the item master (or elsewhere) to house the classification code.

Recognizing that this is contrary to common orthodoxy, let's explore this point further. There is a general law that applies here, Petroff's 27th Law of System Design: You can't have one data element serve two functions. Corollary #1: If you do, the multiple demands will soon diverge and eventually become mutually exclusive resulting in at least one function becoming incapacitated. Corolary #2: You can't do a sort on a language field and be satisfied with the result.

Corolary #2 is almost always violated in the description field of engineering drawings.

Its the old "bolt, hex" syndrome. This practice never works for even the humble hex bolt, much less for more complicated manufactured items. No amount of red tape and discipline in the engineering department is going to accommodate parts of similar physical characteristics with widely divergent uses. One engineer will call a component a flange. A similar part is called a support elsewhere. Yet another is called a bracket. All are good names, considering their applications, yet useless as classifications. Even after spending a lot of energy and expense at policing the description field, there is no company which can do an alphabetic sort on the description field and come up with a useable list. This even includes those companies who have made the description field into a series of data fields by making it several lines and hundreds of bytes long. There is no way to avoid Petroff's 27th law.

The above requirements describe an ambitious classification system, one that would be very difficult to construct by a company with its own resources. To do so would require a major development project, and many months. Luckily there are a number of serviceable proprietary products on the market that spare the user from reinventing that wheel. This is similar to MRP software, where almost everyone is turning to commercial sources.

For purposes of illustration I will draw most heavily from the Brisch-Birn system, which

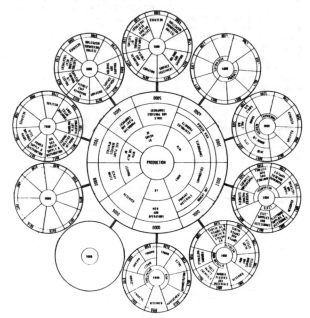

Figure 3

is one of the several products available in this country.

Figures 3 & 4 show how the manufacturing universe can be divided into a hierarchy, and is the first step in allowing the computer to retrieve data from the general to the specific. The world of production is divided into the categories of "By, From, Into, By Means Of, and With the Help Of"

Taking one of production's general classes, 1000, Primary Metals, Figure 5 shows them broken down into the next level of detail, Non-metallic and Metallic, which are further subdivided into nine classes, 1100 through 1900. Not shown are the further subdivisions which would go two more levels deep.

Figure 6 shows Commodities, class 2000 broken down into its nine divisions, 2100 - 2900. And Figure 7 shows the same for class 3000, Piece Parts. There would be a similar breakdown for each of the other categories.

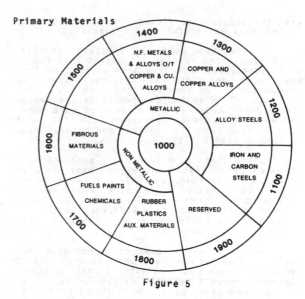

Primary Materials

Figure 5

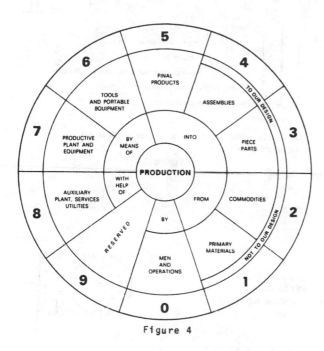

Figure 4

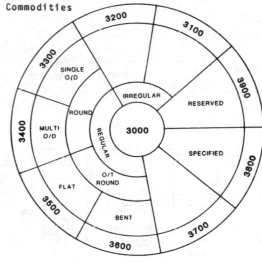

Commodities

Figure 6

To illustrate how a common piece part would be classified, we can refer to Figure 8 which shows a typical machined component. Figure 9 shows how we would step through a hierarchy of detail. First we see that our component is round with multiple diameters. Within that group we further refine our definition by designating that our part has a straight centerline and blind holes. Within that class we can quickly determine that its maximum dimension is at one end, and its diameter is between three and four inches.

This example illustrates that it is easy to give a component its correct code. But this also should show that the basic system must be fully in place ahead of time, and correctly developed. A poorly designed system soon would break down in ambiguity and confusion.

Also, although it is easy to classify one component, converting an existing population of thousands of components, even spending just a few seconds on each one, aggregates into a huge project. The file conversion problem, together

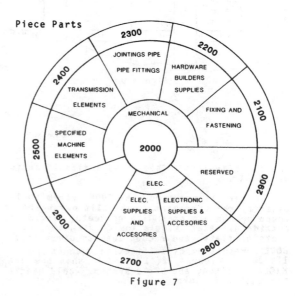

Piece Parts

Figure 7

with the acquisition and development cost of the system must be carefully cost-justified.

To illustrate cost justification, in 1979, one medium-sized company discovered that they could save $1500 each time they avoided making a new design, and $1400 when they could modify an existing one. In one year they made 150 searches, 50 of which resulted in design avoidance. Their measurable cost savings were augmented by noticeable improvements in other areas such as procurement, tooling, and general manufacturing flexibility.

Notice that the hierarchical approach would allow us to do different analyses based on that scheme. For example, we could ask the computer to give us a list of all straight round parts with multiple diameters. They would all have the code 341xx and 342xx. Reference to the index of codes would reveal any number of possible selection arguments.

There are several commercial products available, and we can review some of them briefly by seeing how each would classify a plain washer. Figure 10 shows a Brisch-Birn derivative calling our washer a piece part, round with a straight centerline, metallic, short, with a single outside diameter, single centerhole, and specifying

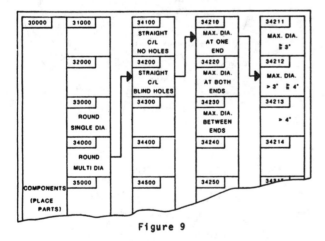

Figure 8

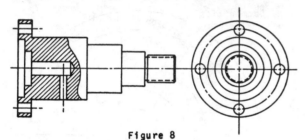

Figure 9

the two diameters. This gives a classification of 311312.

Figure 11 shows how the CODE system could classify the same part. It calls our washer a round concentric part with no teeth, single outside diameter, single inside diameter, no slots or flats, and recognizes its dimensions. CODE's resulting classification code is 11200061. Figures 12, 13, and 14 show how the MICLASS, TEKLA, and OPITZ systems would handle the washer in turn.

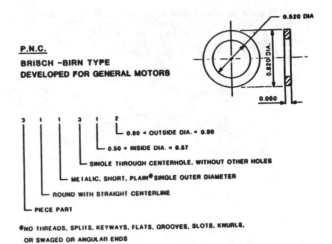

Figure 10

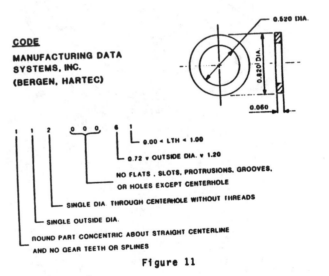

Figure 11

MICLASS
(T.N.O.)

ROUND PART WITH SINGLE OUTSIDE AND DIAMETERS WITHOUT FACES, THREADS, SLOTS, GROOVES, SPLINES, OR ADDITIONAL HOLES. THE OUTSIDE DIAMETER AND LENGTH ARE WITHIN CERTAIN SIZE RANGES.

Figure 12

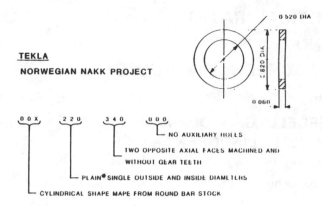

TEKLA

NORWEGIAN NAKK PROJECT

0 0 X   2 2 0   3 4 0   0 0 0

— NO AUXILIARY HOLES

— TWO OPPOSITE AXIAL FACES MACHINED AND
WITHOUT GEAR TEETH

— PLAIN*SINGLE OUTSIDE AND INSIDE DIAMETERS

— CYLINDRICAL SHAPE MAPE FROM ROUND BAR STOCK

*NO THREADS, GROOVES, OR SLOTS

Figure 13

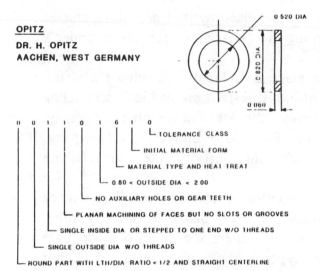

OPITZ

DR. H. OPITZ
AACHEN, WEST GERMANY

0 0 1 1 0 1 6 1 0

— TOLERANCE CLASS

— INITIAL MATERIAL FORM

— MATERIAL TYPE AND HEAT TREAT

— 0.80 < OUTSIDE DIA < 2.00

— NO AUXILIARY HOLES OR GEAR TEETH

— PLANAR MACHINING OF FACES BUT NO SLOTS OR GROOVES

— SINGLE INSIDE DIA OR STEPPED TO ONE END W/O THREADS

— SINGLE OUTSIDE DIA W/O THREADS

— ROUND PART WITH LTH/DIA RATIO < 1/2 AND STRAIGHT CENTERLINE

Figure 14

In summary, Classification Coding is needed to support thorough development of Group Technology and Standardization. There are a number of difficult design requirements for a classification system, such as universal and complete applicability, a separate field in the item master, and fast and accurate data retrieval. The needed design features can mainly be accommodated with commercial products and the use of a computer. Although not cheap or easy, a good classification coding implementation could easily pay itself back in less than two years.

REFERENCES

SYSTEMS

Brisch System

Rrisch-Birn & Partners, Ltd
1656 Southeast Tenth Terrace
Fourt Lauderdale, FL 33316

Miclass System

TNO US Office
176 Second Avenue
Waltham, MA 02154

Code System

Hartec Corp
Manufacturing Data Systems, Inc
3350 E. Atlantic Blvd
Pompano Beach, FL 33061

BOOKS & PEROIDICALS

Hyde, William F. Classification Coding, and Data Base Standardization. New York; Marcel Dekker, Inc., 1981

------. Group Technology an Overviw and Bibliography, MDC 76-601. Cincinnatti; Machinability Data Center

Opitz, H. A Classification to Describe Workpieces. Oxford, England; Pergamon Press

Groover, Mikell O. Automation Production Systems and Computer Aided Manufacturing. Englewood Cliffs, NJ: Prentice Hall, 1980

Spencer, Michael S. "Scheduling Components for Group Technology Lines (A New Application for MRP)", Production & Inventory Management, 4th Quarter, 1980

John Petroff, CPIM, is an Executive Consultant at Comserv Corporation. a leading vendor of commercial software for manufacturers. Petroff is a Past President of The Twin Cities Chapter and was a founder of the Arabian Gulf Chapter. He has over 25 years of experience in consulting, materials management, and data processing management. In addition to the CPIM, Petroff has BS and MBA degrees, holds the Certificate in Data Processing, and is a Certified Systems Professional.

Reprinted from *Production and Inventory Management*, Vol. 12, No. 4 (1971).

UPDATING CRITICAL RATIO
AND
SLACK-TIME PRIORITY SCHEDULING RULES

by

A. O. PUTNAM, R. EVERDELL, G. H. DORMAN,
R. R. CRONAN, and L. H. LINDGREN

Rath & Strong, Inc.

Lexington, Massachusetts

I. INTRODUCTION

Over the past few years, many papers have been written describing studies and reporting theoretical results regarding the behavior of job shops under a variety of priority dispatching rules.

Subsequent applications have taken place in isolated companies (in different geographic locations and in different industries). These included scheduling systems at the Hughes Aircraft Company, the Western Electric Company, Texas Instruments Corporation, and the Fairfield Manufacturing Company. Each of these systems makes use of a scheduling priority rule known as the Slack-Time priority rule.[1]

Concurrently with the developments mentioned above, A. O. Putnam, of Rath & Strong, was developing scheduling systems based on priority rules, relating remaining standard lead time to forecasted stockout or date due. The first application of this type of rule was made in Cabot Machinery Division in 1963, and subsequently described in the *American Machinist*, 1964,[2] and *Unified Operations Management*, McGraw-Hill Book Company, 1963.[3] During the same year, applications were made at the Worcester Division of the Geo. J. Meyer Manufacturing Company (now a Division of A-T-O, Inc.). Subsequently, Robert R. Cronan, of Rath & Strong, described these rules more completely in a paper issued by the American Production and Inventory Control Society, Inc. (APICS) as Training Kit #2.[4] This set of rules is actually a family of rules, since variants of the basic ratio have been implemented for use with fixed due dates, dynamic due dates, and manufacture for stock replenishment. While Critical Ratio rules have not been studied in any of the major simulation studies reported to date, the elements employed are similar to (order and shop) parameters used in the Slack-Time

---

[1]Colley, John L. *Systems and Procedures Journal*, July, 1968.

[2]Putnam, A. O. *American Machinist*, February 17, 1964.

[3]Putnam, A. O., Barlow, E. R., Stilian, G. *Unified Operations Management*.

[4]Cronan, R. R. American Production & Inventory Control Society, Inc. National Training Kit #2 on Critical Ratio Scheduling. (and others)

rules and should intuitively lead to similar results. In fact, the rule designated as a Slack-Time priority in the Fairfield Manufacturing Company system is the inverse of one version of the Critical Ratio rule just mentioned.

The purpose of this paper is to report the results of a number of practical installations of this general family of rules that, to our knowledge, have dominated the implementation of practical scheduling systems. The paper discusses some of the details and problems (not heretofore published) involved in the use of the rules, reports progress to date in a number of companies and draws some practical conclusions regarding the likely success of such systems in the future.

II. THE FAMILY OF DYNAMIC DUE DATE/LEAD TIME PRESSURE INDEXES

The practical application of priority rules, which have the objective of the best performance to date due, has been dominated by Minimum Slack Time per Operation,[5] and Critical Ratio.[2,3,4]

The purpose of this paper is to compare their relative effectiveness and to add some recent modifications.

A.   *Slack-Time Rules*

Minimum Slack Time was developed to assign relative priorities to jobs in queue at various operations. It later became a part of Program Evaluation Review Technique (PERT) scheduling techniques, and the Critical Path Method (CPM), both of which emphasized the network path with the least amount of slack. If valid end dates were established for jobs in independent networks, the relative slack time for each could be computed even though the paths could not be linked practically in an overall PERT network. The other factor needed, in addition to end dates, was knowledge of the actual processing or "make" time (i.e., the time the job is actually on the machine). Now, if a progress report would show the status of each job including the remaining (not completed) operations, a comparison of the work left (process time remaining) to the total time left could be made. Slack time is what is left after removing the process time remaining from the total time left until due date, or

Slack Time = (Date Due-Date Now) − (Processing Time Remaining).

The first version of the rule ranked jobs in priority solely by the *Slack Time Remaining* factor. However, if two jobs have the same slack time, the job with the most operations remaining is the more critical job. Jobs just

---

[5]See for instance, the review in *Journal of Industrial Engineering*, July, 1968.

released might be the ones in the most serious trouble, even though they have more slack time than those near completion. Thus, the rule may be modified to compute the Slack Time per Remaining Operation:

$$\frac{(\text{Date Due} - \text{Date Now}) - (\text{Processing Time Remaining})}{\text{No. of Operations Remaining}}$$

Job No.	Slack Time	Operations Left	Slack Time per Operation
1	10 Hrs.	1	10 Hrs.
2	50 Hrs.	20	2½ Hrs.

Job #2 would be given priority over Job #1 based on the lowest slack time per operation.

This rule was tested (along with a total of twenty-six other priority rules) in 1963,[6] and was found to provide the lowest variance among those tested when measuring the deviations of actual order completion dates from due dates. This criterion has come to be the most commonly used measure of schedule performance and has led to considerable interest in the Minimum Slack Time per Operation priority rule.

B. *Critical Ratio Rule*

In parallel with the developments discussed above, and independently, another priority rule called the Critical Ratio was developed. This rule was not among those tested in the computer simulations mentioned above. While the behavior of shop performance under the Critical Ratio criterion has not been simulated, this sequencing rule has most of the properties of the Slack Time per Operation rule. Critical Ratio was a normal outgrowth of the concepts of operational due-dating and work center backlog (queue) control that have been used widely in job shop manufacturing. The Critical Ratio differs from the Slack Time rule in two important ways.

1. The date due is constantly revised by continued up-to-date review of the current inventory position (or date of the earliest requirements that will be satisfied by the order being scheduled). The Slack Time per Operation rule was shown to be the best of those studied for fixed due dates. It would have to be modified to handle the scheduling of inventory replenishments.

2. Instead of using total slack time remaining (which can also be defined as total time *remaining* for queues of "move and wait"), Critical Ratio

---

[6]Jackson, J. R., Conway, R. W. "An Experimental Investigation of Priority Assignments in a Job Shop." Rand Corp., Memorandum RM-3789-PR, February, 1964.

looks at the sum of the *predetermined* standard move and wait allowances for *each* remaining operation. In other words, it recognizes and makes use of individual move and wait allowances to provide different queue sizes at different production operations.

In addition to these significant differences, there is a mathematical difference in computation of the priority sequencing number. Critical Ratio is computed as follows:

$$\left(\frac{\text{Current Date Due} - \text{Date Now}}{\text{Lead Time Remaining}} \right)$$

Where: Lead Time Remaining = Processing Time Remaining *plus* Expected Queue Time Remaining.

This is the current basic formula that evolved from Arnold Putnam's original work first published in 1960. The American Production & Inventory Control Society, Inc. (APICS) National Training Kit #2 has a more complete treatment of the revised basic formulas as presently recommended for use.

C.   *Comparison of Slack Time and Critical Ratio*

The Critical Ratio rule compares the time remaining until the latest revised date due to time remaining for processing and planned slack, while Slack-Time-oriented rules compare actual slack remaining to time remaining based on fixed due dates. The expression (Date Due − Date Now) is identical for each rule. Although the Minimum Slack per Operation rule was designed for fixed due dates, the rule can be adapted to use continually updated due dates. The Critical Ratio concept of examining the inventory status to make necessary revisions to dates due will improve the performance of the Minimum Slack Time per Operation rule substantially. Critical Ratio calculations normally refer to a requirements planning subsystem during each priority computation to take into account any due-date revision caused by either a change in requirement dates or a change in available inventory. For stock replenishment orders, the direct computation from inventory records of the days of stock remaining provides a dynamically updated equivalent to the expression (Date Due − Date Now). APICS National Training Kit #2 contains the various formulas used. The difference in the two rules lies with the method of handling the time remaining to complete the order and the two major elements in that time remaining: processing time and slack time. It is not significant to the relative priority ranking that one formulation subtracts Processing Time Remaining from the days left to delivery in the numerator, whereas the other adds Processing Time Remaining to Queue Time Remaining in the denominator and creates a ratio. It is significant, however, that Critical

Ratio recognizes predetermined queue allowances per operation, which may differ from operation to operation in the interest of operating efficiency. Taking the difference in planned lead time into consideration should improve the scheduling process. This incorporates the idea that the scheduling process must not only strive for the lowest variance to date due but must also recognize an optimum balance between the return on inventory invested in work-in-process (queue allowances) and a satisfactory utilization of any work center. The mathematical queuing theory of waiting lines suggests that in a job lot environment, total machine utilization can be improved (with the same total work-in-process level) by using optimum queue allowances per machine group rather than evenly distributing the queues throughout. (Note: This results from differences in average processing time from queue to queue, among other things).

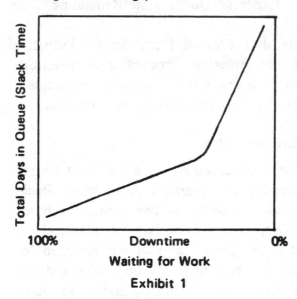

Exhibit 1

The foregoing statement is based on the fact that the downtime attributable to waiting for work is a function of the level of work in queues. (Exhibit 1)

Investment in work-in-process gives a rapid improvement in machine utilization up to a point of diminishing returns. At this critical point, additional work-in-process (and therefore lead time) must increase at a far greater rate than improvement in utilization. The relationship suggests that a trade-off between utilization and work-in-process must be made. This is a complex relationship that only a shop simulator could establish, and it will vary from one facility to another. However, it is suggested that using move and wait allowances specific to each production work center will distribute a greater portion of the slack time to those machine groups requiring higher queues and produce better utilization with the same total work-in-process. It is between work centers that have the greatest independent random variations in uptime to downtime (down for reasons other than waiting for work) that the largest wait allowances are required. It is also important to be able to recognize significant differences in move elements for each operation. A final finishing operation such as anodizing might have to be done by an outside source. The longer move time required must be preserved by the priority system, which does not occur with Slack Time rules.

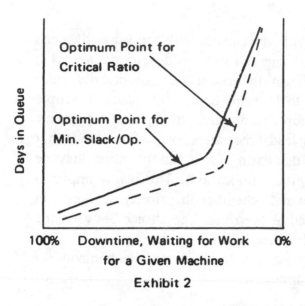

Optimum Point for
Critical Ratio

Optimum Point for
Min. Slack/Op.

Days in Queue

100%   Downtime, Waiting for Work   0%
for a Given Machine

Exhibit 2

The Critical Ratio rule, since it operates with predetermined queue allowances of different lengths within the shop, will preserve the prescribed balance in planned queues from machine center to machine center. Sustaining the planned balance in queues is necessary for optimizing investment in work-in-process inventories. The difference is shown graphically in Exhibit 2. In one application of the Minimum Slack per Operation rule, it was recognized[7] that total work-in-process must be controlled by order release procedures to maintain the necessary total slack time, i.e., to operate close to the optimum point. Under Critical Ratio, the same control of work-in-process is achieved by releasing orders only at Start Date (which is Date Due − Total Lead Time, where TLT = Total Processing Time + Total Wait and Move Allowances or its equivalent, Total Standard or Allowed Slack Time). In each case, the amount of total work required to operate at the selected level of machine utilization is preserved by the order release procedure (always assuming a balanced production facility). Once orders are released under such procedures, the rules will operate differently only when queue allowances vary between production centers.

1. Similarities

It can be stated that the Critical Ratio and Slack Time rules are basically similar. Both rules apply most of the same elements and will produce the same priority sequence within each work center wherever queues are evenly distributed throughout the production facility. As companies develop lead times that are specific to the routing of each part and approach optimum queues for each work center, Critical Ratio offers significant advantages. The use of continually revised due dates instead of fixed due dates is important but can be applied to both rules.

Both rules require: an effective master scheduling aggregate loading system to control the total load, a shop whose man-hour capacity in each work center is balanced to the total load, and an order release procedure that recognizes either the total standard lead time or the optimum level of work-in-process in order to produce optimum results.

---

[7]Colley, John L., Jr. "Computer-Based Job Shop Scheduling Systems," *Systems and Procedures Journal*, July/August 1968.

2. *Differences*

Generally the selection of the rule depends initially on how advanced a company may be in applying queuing and shop loading principles. It is possible in some companies to begin the application of priority rules sooner, if they do not know their lead times, by using a simple Minimum Slack Time per Operation. Eventually, the Critical Ratio rule will be a useful refinement when lead times are known. Companies that may have employed operational due-dating for a suitable time may be able to apply Critical Ratio in initial applications. The major improvement comes from using daily revised schedules in priority sequence in place of fixed due dates plus expedite overrides. The choice between the two rules is a refinement to the dynamic scheduling concept.

The following examples are presented to illustrate the behavior of orders under the two rules being discussed.

CASE 1

The results of the two rules are similar when an order progresses according to planned lead time.

Operation Number	1	2	3	4	5	Job Flow
Processing Time	.5	.5	.5	.5	.5	2.5 days
Total Flow Time	2.5	2.5	2.5	2.5	2.5	12.5 days
Planned Time in Queue	2.0	2.0	2.0	2.0	2.0	10.0 days

Slack Time per Operation		Critical Ratio	
Operation No.	Days of Slack per Operation	Operation No.	Critical Ratio
1	$\frac{10}{5} = 2$	1	$\frac{12.5}{12.5} = 1.00$
2	$\frac{8}{4} = 2$	2	$\frac{10.0}{10.0} = 1.00$
3	$\frac{6}{3} = 2$	3	$\frac{7.5}{7.5} = 1.00$
4	$\frac{4}{2} = 2$	4	$\frac{5.5}{5.5} = 1.00$
5	$\frac{2}{1} = 2$	5	$\frac{2.5}{2.5} = 1.00$

CASE 2

Differences occur when operation and queue times vary, with Critical Ratio providing a more accurate estimate than the Minimum Slack Time rule.

(Major Operations Near Start of Process)

Operation No.	1	2	3	4	5	Job Flow
Processing Time	.5	1	.25	.25	.5	2.5 days
Total Time	1.75	6	1.5	1.5	1.75	12.5 days
Slack Time	1.25	5	1.25	1.25	1.25	10.0 days

Days of Slack per Operation			Critical Ratio	
Operation No.	Days of Slack per Operation		Operation No.	Critical Ratio
1	$\dfrac{10}{5} = 2.0$		1	$\dfrac{12.5}{12.5} = 1.00$
2	$\dfrac{8.75}{4} = 2.2$		2	$\dfrac{10.75}{10.75} = 1.00$
3	$\dfrac{3.75}{3} = 1.25$		3	$\dfrac{4.75}{4.75} = 1.00$
4	$\dfrac{2.50}{2} = 1.25$		4	$\dfrac{3.25}{3.25} = 1.00$
5	$\dfrac{1.25}{1} = 1.25$		5	$\dfrac{1.75}{1.75} = 1.00$

While the true situation indicates that the job is on schedule, the Slack Time per Operation rises by 10% before Operation 2 with the large move and wait requirement and then falls by almost 50% giving undesirable indications in both directions.

On the other hand, if the major operation is at the end of the process, the Slack Time rule gives a false sense of extra slack in the early operations whereas the job is actually on schedule with no excess time above the desired move and wait allowance. Minimum Slack Time per Operation rules also do not provide a good indication of real need in the early operations when the total slack is likely to be large.

III. NEW DEVELOPMENTS IN CRITICAL RATIO

A. *Black & Decker's Compression of Total Queue and Time*

Variation of Critical Ratio has been developed by the Black & Decker Manufacturing Co.,[8] where the compression of slack (queue) is watched until the slack is gone, and then Critical Ratio is used. The following is quoted from a previously unpublished article (Exhibit 3).

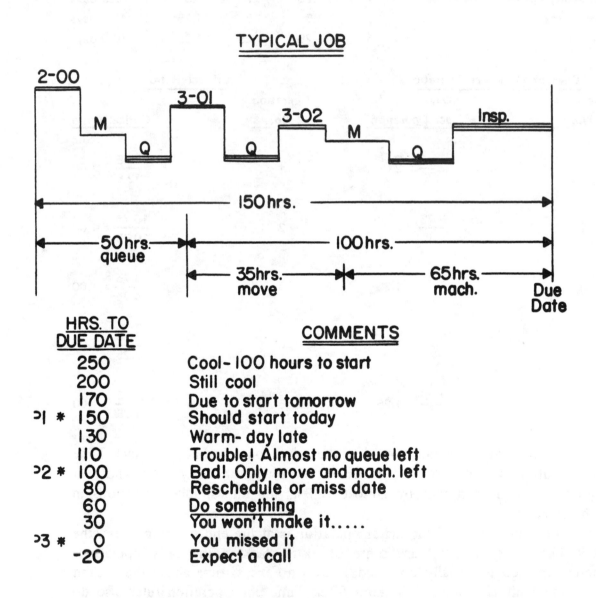

TYPICAL JOB

HRS. TO DUE DATE	COMMENTS
250	Cool- 100 hours to start
200	Still cool
170	Due to start tomorrow
>1 * 150	Should start today
130	Warm- day late
110	Trouble! Almost no queue left
>2 * 100	Bad! Only move and mach. left
80	Reschedule or miss date
60	Do something
30	You won't make it.....
>3 * 0	You missed it
-20	Expect a call

*See comparison QR/CR. and method 41

Exhibit 3. Typical Job

---

[8]Developed by Robert Haddox, Manager of Management Information Systems and his associates.

Critical Ratio (Exhibit 4)

"Critical Ratio" is calculated by dividing the time left to the date due by the work remaining to the date due. As the graph shows, the value of the ratio decreases as the job becomes late. The ratio also gives us two distinct values: when the job is on time, and when there is no time left. It will not, however, warn us when the queue has been depleted.

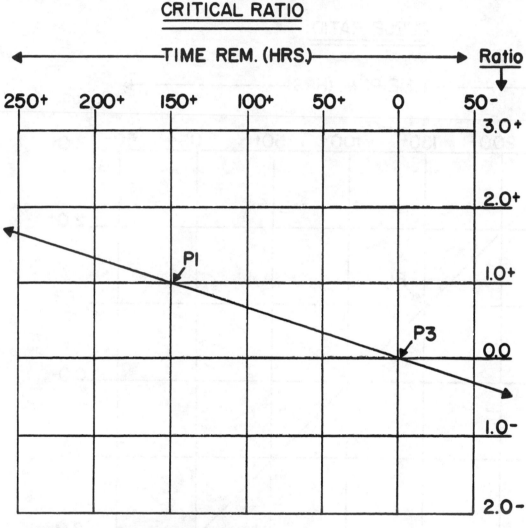

CRITICAL RATIO

$$\text{Ratio} = \frac{\text{Time Remaining}}{\text{Work Remaining*}}$$

P1 <u>always</u> represents "on schedule"

P3 <u>always</u> represents "no time left"

*Defined as sum of scheduled move, scheduled queue and oper. times.

Exhibit 4. Critical Ratio

Queue Ratio (Exhibit 5)

"Queue Ratio" is calculated by dividing the hours of slack left in the job by the queue originally scheduled between the start of the operation being considered and the scheduled date due. The ratio decreases as the job becomes late. It (like "Critical Ratio") gives a pair of distinct points: when the job is on time, and when the queue has been depleted and only move and machine times remain. "Queue Ratio" will *not* tell us when there is no time at all left.

QUEUE RATIO

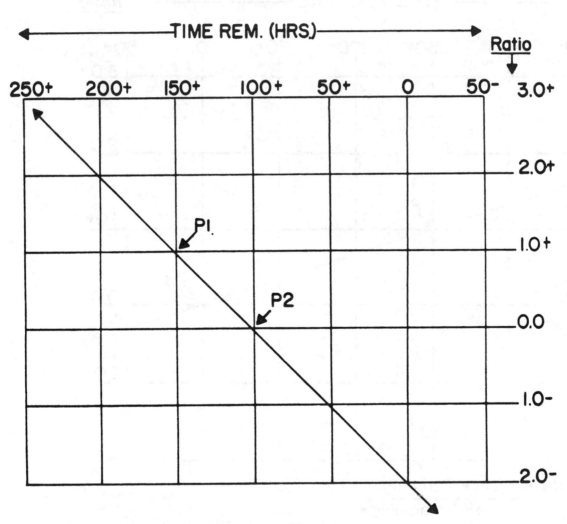

$$\text{Ratio} = \frac{\text{Time Rem-Op Rem-Transit}}{\text{Std. Sched. Queue}}$$

PI <u>always</u> represents "on schedule"
P2 <u>always</u> represents "queue gone"

Exhibit 5. Queue Ratio

Comparison (Exhibit 6)

Both "Critical Ratio" and "Queue Ratio" are drawn on the same grid. The three major peg-points are labeled P1, P2, and P3. Unfortunately, neither method will produce all three points.

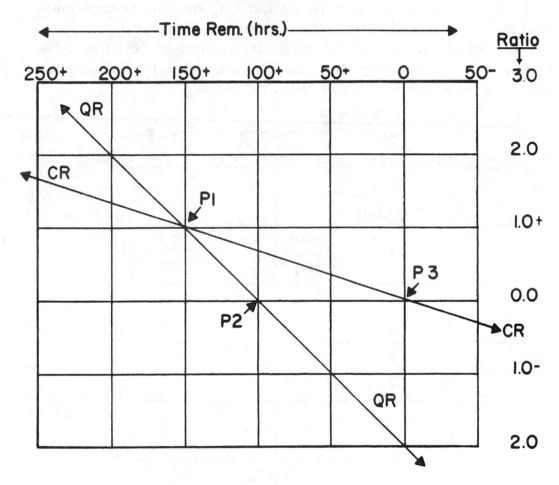

COMPARISON
QR and CR

P1 <u>always</u> represents "on schedule"
P2 <u>always</u> represents "queue gone"
P3 <u>always</u> represents "no time left"

Exhibit 6. Comparison QR and CR

Method-41 (Exhibit 7)

"Method-41" is a composite of "Critical Ratio" and "Queue Ratio." It incorporates the good points of each.

The graph is composed of two portions, each generated by a different formula. The transition from one to the other takes place at P2, the time at which queue is depleted.

To the left of P2 (there is still some que left) the ratio is found by dividing the "Critical Ratio" into the "Queue Ratio." This produces a curved line passing through P1 to P2. The curve also increases its rate of decrease as the job becomes later. This is important because the delay of a day becomes more important as the job becomes late than when it is early.

To the right of P2 (when there is no queue left and the job is in trouble) the curve drops steeply from P2 through P3 (the point when no time is left). The formula is such that the curve will always have a value of −5.0 when time runs out. This and the fact that the curve becomes quite steep serve to warn us that we are rapidly heading for trouble.

This method provides all the information desired in objectives of a method (read earlier) except two; namely, 2c1a and 2c1b, regarding the relationship between the remaining queue and one day.

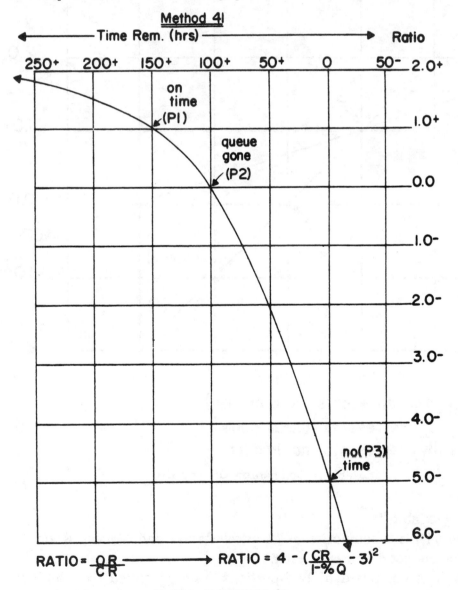

Exhibit 7. Method 41

B. *Slack Compression Ratio at Hughes Aircraft*

In 1968, Hughes Aircraft changed from their minimum Slack per Remaining Operation to a Slack Compression Ratio Plan. The objective was to overcome the assumption that all available slack time should be distributed equally among operations, to compute the priority sequence number for Work Centers beyond the current job location, and to provide shop load by center and week for all open jobs. As a result, they have developed an Operational Back Dating with compression rule that they feel is an improvement over the original Minimum Slack Time per Operation approach.

Basically, a start date for each Work Center is computed daily by subtracting in reverse routing sequence the processing time and move and wait allowance (queue time) for each operation from the end date due. By this means, operational start dates are generated and maintained. Each Work Center Schedule shows jobs sequenced by start date for each center including jobs one and two operations away. Of course, job location as of last reported job status is shown.

The refinement on the classical back-dating approach recognized the psychological problem of having a job due to start prior to its arrival date. If the start date for any Work Center beyond the last completed operation is earlier than the current date, the start date for all Work Centers will be recomputed by reducing the standard queue allowance using a compression factor computed by the formula:

$$\text{Compression Ratio} = \frac{(\text{Date Due} - \text{Now}) - (\text{Processing Time Remaining})}{(\text{Standard Move and Wait Time Remaining})}$$

$$= \frac{\text{Actual Queue Remaining}}{\text{Standard Queue Remaining}}$$

Thus, if the actual queue left is only 50% of the standard allowance, the slack adjustment factor would be .5. All operational start dates would be refigured, allowing .5 times the standard queue allowed for each operation. The Work Center Schedule always shows the jobs in start date sequence, and within each date, sorted by ascending per cent slack remaining, if the job has been compressed. There is also a minimum allowable-slack-remaining percentage that is set by management decision. Any job with less than the minimum allowed slack will be indicated on the Work Center Schedule and be highlighted for special handling. Virtually no priority overrides are allowed, and no "hot lists" are maintained.

Evaluating this system indicates that it has many attractive features, ranking jobs close to Critical Ratio, but not exactly the same. It has a major "human" benefit in that it works with more "meaningful" numbers. There are only two readily apparent limitations with the Work Center start dates:

1) There is no tie-breaking capability, and

2) The number of operations remaining is not recognized in the priority calculations.

As an example, consider three jobs all due to start tomorrow so that they would be ranked the same under this scheme, and consider three Critical Ratios for the three jobs:

$$1) \quad \frac{4 \text{ Days to Date Due}}{3 \text{ Days of L.T.R.}} = 1.33 \text{ C.R.}$$

$$2) \quad \frac{10 \text{ Days to Date Due}}{9 \text{ Days of L.T.R.}} = 1.10 \text{ C.R.}$$

$$3) \quad \frac{50 \text{ Days to Date Due}}{49 \text{ Days of L.T.R.}} = 1.02 \text{ C.R.}$$

Although each job is due to start in the center the next day, many would consider the one with the most operations remaining (i.e., the job with the longest lead time remaining) to be more critical than one with fewer operations remaining. In that case, Critical Ratio would provide the better rank order. The reports at Hughes, however, do show the remaining hours per job as a guide to the schedulers who can process the ones with the greatest hours remaining first.

C. *Modifications by Stromberg-Carlson*

In 1966, the Production Control group at Stromberg-Carlson[9] initiated the design of a Machine Schedule System involving modified Critical Ratio priority sequencing. Several interesting variations were made.

1. *Continual Overlap*

Not being a typical job-lot environment, in that the production lots may run for several days on a machine, the system controls on operation start date not end date, and schedules operation overlap. After the start date in Operation 1, the job is available to start the next operation on start date for Operation 1 plus the move and wait allowance for Operation 2. In this fashion, processing times will overlap (Exhibit 8).

---

[9] Stromberg-Carlson, 100 Carlson Road, Rochester, New York. A subsidiary of General Dynamics Corp.

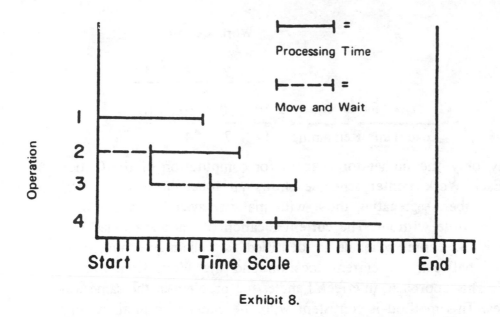

Exhibit 8.

The only caution using this approach, which assures maximum overlap, is that no succeeding operation be fast enough to run out of parts available from the prior center. Overlapping vastly reduces lead times and work in process, without loss in utilization. With maximum overlap, total lead time equals the sum of queues plus longest single machine processing time (of all operations in the routing).

2. *Predicting Arrival*

A clever concept is used to overcome the problem of recognizing when a job is not likely to meet schedule even with proper sequencing (the problem tackled by Black & Decker). Whenever the Critical Ratio is less than 1.0, an estimated completion date is computed by using the Critical Ratio (down to a minimum of 0.1) as a decimal to multiply the remaining move and wait time (for established compression of slack) and add that to the longest remaining maching processing time, also multiplied by the Ratio (down to a minimum of 0.5). The sum of these two computations added to the current date and any allowance for problem resolution gives the expected arrival date. When this date is later than the end date due, the job requires special handling.

3. *Look Ahead Capability*

In all priority sequencing systems, properly handling "jobs coming" has been a problem. The S-C MSS system has developed a simple solution. The Critical Ratio for each job in each work center is computed as though it were in that center:

		1	2	3	4
Date Due − Now	=	10	10	10	10
Lead Time Remaining		12	7	4	1

Each day only the numerator changes for computation of the Critical Ratio. Each Work Center schedule shows all jobs above a "cut-off" priority number, segregating those with material available in the Work Center and those without. The current location of "not available" jobs on each Work Center schedule is identified as well as the number of operations between its current location and the Work Center being reviewed. This approach, in effect, handles the problem in the same way as Hughes. This method is consistent with the experience in all systems that the ability to predict job arrivals beyond a single move has proved to be limited severely by the large number of unpredictable causes affecting job progress. At Stromberg, if a job arrives and is not on the schedule, it is assumed to be ahead of time and would not be assigned to a machine. Any job that arrives which is on the schedule will always be slotted in in the proper relative position. If, for some reason, a job does get started ahead of schedule, it will be carried only on the schedule of the Work Center containing the material.

D. *Methods of Adjusting Ratios for Overdue Jobs*

All of the rules with ratios have had difficulty in measuring lateness when the order becomes "past due". Dividing the overdue days by the number of operations remaining or by standard lead time remaining merely results in a negative ratio in which the value closer to zero is in greater trouble than the job with the higher negative value.

Some companies (e.g., Jones & Lamson)[10] have modified the standard Critical Ratio formula to subtract the lead time remaining rather than dividing by it. This results in a "ratio" or priority number equal to 0.0 rather than 1.0 when exactly on schedule. It also will be negative as soon as it gets behind schedule, whether or not it is past due for completion. This loses the past-due recognition point. On the other hand, it maintains the priority continuum even as the number goes negative. The lower the number (also the more negative), the more critical the job. Another reading that can be made directly from the priority number in this case is the actual amount of time ahead of or behind schedule.

---

[10]Jones & Lamson Machine, Division of Waterbury Farrel, of Textron, Inc.

The priority sequence (Table 1) could have been improved further by subtracting the slack and move time from the lead time and reranking the jobs based on process time plus time overdue.

J & L CRITICAL RATIO = DATE DUE-DATE NOW − LEAD TIME REMAINING IF DATE NOW = 10					
Job No.	Date Due	Actual Time Remaining	Lead Time Remaining	Critical Ratio Std	Critical Ratio J & L
1	20	10	5	2.0	5
2	20	10	10	1.0	0
3	20	10	25	.4	−15
4	10	0	5	0.0	− 5
5	10	0	10	0.0	−10
6	10	0	25	0.0	−25
7	5	−5	5	−1.0	−10
8	5	−5	10	−0.5	−15
9	5	−5	25	−0.2	−30

Table 1. Example

Ranking with this revised computation (Table 2) changes the position of 3 out of the 9 jobs. Job 3 changed dramatically as the process time alone was not great enough to make it overdue. *The conclusion can be drawn that when process time is a small but varying per cent of lead time and the slack and move time can be compressed by priority sequencing, ranking is improved using days overdue plus process time remaining rather than total lead time remaining.* One of the "best" ranking schemes at the present time appears to be:

Job No.	Due Date	Actual Time Remaining	Lead Time Remaining	Process Time Remaining	J&L	Rank	Revised Computation	Rank
1	20	10	5	1	+5	9	9	9
2	20	10	10	2	0	8	8	8
3	20	10	25	5	−15	4	5	7
4	10	0	5	2	−5	7	−2	6
5	10	0	10	5	−10	5	−5	5
6	10	0	25	12	−25	2	−12	2
7	5	−5	5	3	−10	6	−8	4
8	5	−5	10	7	−15	3	−12	3
9	5	−5	25	16	−30	1	−21	1

Table 2. Example

Use Critical Ratio with full lead times until the job is below 1.00.

Use a compression ratio from 1.00 down to full compression.

Use the process time remaining plus days overdue when the priority computation becomes zero or negative or, more correctly, whenever the move and wait time has been used up.

Though considerable effort has been expended to develop a continuous Critical Ratio rule where the greater minus values indicate the correct ranking of the jobs, no such calculation has yet been devised.

E. *Critical Ratio for Split Lots*

Critical Ratio has been modified to cover split lots by calculating the ratio on those sent ahead and performing a separate calculation on the following portion.

The problem becomes more difficult where the lot is stretched over two or more operations so that portions are being overlapped. In some cases it is sufficient to compute the ratio on the arrival of the front end of the lot, which will satisfy some of the requirements. Perhaps, the most foolproof method is to design the program to compute a ratio for each quantity remaining at each station. Of course, the Stromberg-Carlson approach avoids this problem by keying on start dates, but this implies a continual overlapping (or splitting).

IV. OPERATING RESULTS WITH CRITICAL RATIO

There are sufficient Critical Ratio applications to generalize upon management reactions as well as operating results.

1. Line supervisors are most enthusiastic about its simplicity and timeliness. They are tired of old dates, conflicting orders, color priority schemes, and the like.
2. Production control men generally are excited about the ease with which it updates and ranks priorities in the plant without a lot of chasing. A few miss the power of directly establishing priorities, and a few abuse their override privilege.
3. Management universally likes the listing of the work available by priority groupings and the separation of critical, on-time, and slack workload

figures upon which they can base more accurate decisions on overtime and manpower. There is some procrastination when it comes to shrinking queues through temporary increases in output above the input until the desired level is achieved.

Exhibit 9 shows the dramatic results that can be produced when input-output is controlled and priorities are followed down to final due date.[11]

This performance was achieved at Moog, Inc., in East Aurora, New York. The narrowing of the distribution of job completions around the due date from 90 days (+30 to −60) to 35 days (+20 to −15) is adequate testimony to the control power of a properly used Critical Ratio system. This is a 2½ to 1 improvement. The target for 1970 is a 15 day variation. This is an additional 2 to 1 improvement.

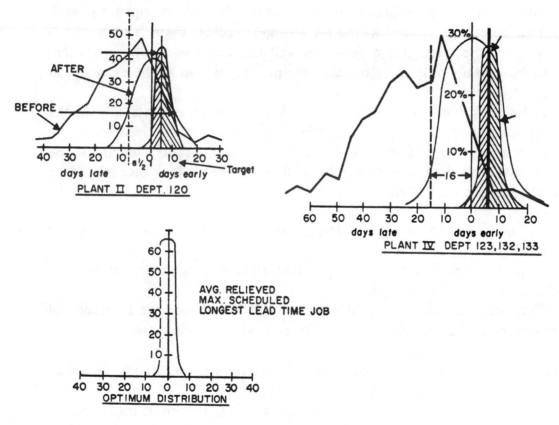

Exhibit 9

V. SUMMARY

Because of the extensive literature on the "Shortest Processing Time First" sequencing rule (often called the SPIT system), which was studied by many

---

[11]L.H. Lindgren, Principal, Rath & Strong, designed further modifications at Moog to increase the ratio for jobs with many operations (conflicts) before due date. Mr. Lindgren was instrumental in the performance graphs shown in Exhibit 10.

early students of various priority approaches, it has received considerable attention in industry. It can be shown that it will reduce the *number* of jobs that are late, but when used in industry (particularly in shops feeding assembly) tends to affect adversely the key long lead "A" items that have a major effect on customer service, level of work-in-process inventory, and can delay many assemblies all waiting for a few key parts. The slack time family of rules, of which Critical Ratio is one, are those which rather than minimizing *number* of jobs late, minimize the variance of arrivals around end date due.[12]

Both Critical Ratio and Minimum Slack rules can recognize the importance of the date due, and both recognize time left for manufacturing. The significant difference is that Critical Ratio recognizes the variation in slack time per operation while Minimum Slack treats all slack as equal for each remaining operation. If the operations are about equal, there is little difference between the rules. If the move and wait times vary widely by operation, then Critical Ratio gives the more accurate picture, as seen in the examples in this report.

For the future, a "composite" approach holds promise. Note that in the modifications used and reported herein, there is increasing recognition of several categories of priority within the slack time concepts, which can be handled by more than one computation to sequence all jobs properly. As a suggested approach consider:

Top Priority – Assembly line down, customer order past due, or item is stocked out.

Sequencing rule is either the job that is furthest past due or the one related to a favored customer.

The customer-oriented priority sequence is least conducive to numerical sequencing as each job or group of jobs is almost a special case.

Second Priority – Not yet "passed due," but no slack remaining. Sequencing rule depends on time left and operations left.

These items also require some special handling, as there is no allowance for normal moving. They may have to be hand carried and/or overlapped.

Third Priority – Those items with enough slack remaining at least to cover moving so that following the priority sequence will probably bring the job in on time. This area is where the original rules without modification work best.

---

[12]Reference footnote [1]. These studies show that the "Shortest Processing Time First" rule may have some value in breaking ties between jobs with the same priority sequence. However, the High-Low sequence rules referred to in reference footnote [4] may have more desirable tie-breaking qualities.

A necessary word of caution: It has been shown that no priority sequencing scheme will operate if more than 10% to 20% of the jobs are in the first and second category.

It has been stated by experienced practitioners, and bears repeating, that there are five critical prerequisites for the effective use of priority scheduling techniques:

1. An overall "aggregate production plan" (Master Schedule) that recognizes capacity, prior load, and lead time restraints and generates realistic finished product due dates.

2. A "requirements planning" subsystem, whenever assemblies are involved, to properly compute and maintain the end item due dates on component shop orders. An "inventory control" subsystem where stock replenishment is involved.

3. Maintenance of accurate lead times (without hidden safety allowances) through use of engineered process times and standard move and wait allowances.

4. Control of work-in-process to the levels allowed by lead time computations through work center capacity balancing and queue control (Input/Output and Queue Control), in conjunction with controlled release of orders to the shop.

5. Accurate progress reporting.

It should also be noted from comments made by those who have long experience using priority rules that allowing manual priority overrides can be a dangerous practice. Expeditors and planners often find they can very effectively "push" favorite items or projects by this approach. Any significant or uncontrolled use of overrides can destroy the whole concept. Overrides often creep in when excessive delinquency sets in (observed when the distribution of arrivals is no longer centered around "on time"). The proper way to correct this condition is to break bottlenecks and reduce queues to normal by short-term increases in capacity and to reschedule the remaining work through the Master Schedule.

With proper concern for the prerequisites and careful maintenance of the priority computation, use of sequencing rules has achieved consistent performance to date due of 95%, with a minimum level of work in process. In the last analysis, the final service level (90%, 95%, or 99%) depends on (1) the number and degree of unpredictable problems such as machine breakdown, raw material shortages, abnormal yield losses, or absenteeism, and (2) the degree to which items in the Master Schedule are scheduled or rescheduled to a date earlier than the current date plus the normal lead time.

About the Authors—

ARNOLD O. PUTNAM *is President of Rath and Strong, Inc. He received his B.S. degree in industrial engineering from Lehigh University and his M.S. degree in business and engineering administration from Massachusetts Institute of Technology. In addition, he is a founding member of the Institute of Management Consultants and is a Certified Management Consultant. Mr. Putnam is the author of articles in THE HANDBOOK OF QUALITY CONTROL and the APICS HANDBOOK. He is a frequent lecturer and course leader at the American Management Association and many other professional societies and has served as a Director of the APICS Boston Chapter and on the Advisory Board of the Production Planning and Control Division of AIIE.*

ROMEYN EVERDELL *is Vice President and Director of Information & Control Systems with Rath & Strong, Inc. He received his A.B. with honors in chemistry from Williams College. Mr. Everdell is a member of APICS. He is a frequent lecturer for AMA, APICS, ASQC, AIIE, SAM and training programs for the University of Connecticut.*

GERALD H. DORMAN *is Vice President and Associate Director of Information and Control Systems with Rath and Strong, Inc. He received his A.B. and M.B.A. degrees from Harvard University, with emphasis on mathematics, production, and general administration. Mr. Dorman has written The Purchasing Function and a Case in Inventory Control published in the American Management Association's Management Report Number 68. He is a member of APICS and has served as a guest speaker for AMA and other professional societies.*

ROBERT R. CRONAN *is a Principal with Rath & Strong, Inc. He holds A.B. and M.B.A. degrees from Harvard University. Mr. Cronan wrote the Second National Training Aid for APICS on critical ratio scheduling and has lectured at various professional societies.*

LEROY H. LINDGREN *is a Principal and a consultant in total systems with Rath and Strong, Inc. He received his B.S. in Industrial Engineering from the Illinois Institute of Technology and attended Lewis Institute of Technology and Yale University for graduate study. He has lectured on both production and inventory control and quality control for various professional organizations.*

As a member of the IMC, Mr. Lindgren is a Certified Management Consultant, and a registered Quality Engineer with ASQC. He is Chairman of a committee of SME that is preparing a MIS book as part of a series of books sponsored by the Society.

Reprinted from the APICS 1982 Conference Proceedings.

ACHIEVING ACCURACY IN SHOP-FLOOR PRODUCTION REPORTING

Joel M. Schipper, CPIM*
Peat, Marwick, Mitchell & Co.

INTRODUCTION

Achieving accuracy in shop floor production reporting transactions -- Order Release/Close-out, Stock Issue/Receipt, Operation Start/End, Scrap/Rework Reporting, and Move Reporting -- is a subject of tremendous interest. The next pages will look at: why accuracy is difficult to achieve; how can we control these transactions; tips about data collection; and how to improve your present shop floor data collection system.

ACCURACY: WHY?

What if production reporting is not 100% accurate all the time? Besides over or underproducing, you destroy the trust needed to support an effective manufacturing control system (MCS). A formal, computer-based MCS is impossible if shop floor data is high, low, early, late, not at all, or is given for the wrong products or jobs because:

(1) Computer prepared reports that contain inaccurate information usually earn a quick trip to the "circular file".

(2) Computer reports with untrustworthy content or timing throw every planner and foreman back to the old "back-of-the-envelope" systems faster than dandelions in Spring.

(3) Accurate production data allows planning data (eg, the real routings, real work center capacities, real operation standards, real queue time estimates, and real job status information) to be audited, verified, and finally utilized for planning and releasing makable amounts of work into the factory.

(4) Finally, payrolls based on production reports can stop the "late," "low," and "not-at-all" reporting mistakes, but often cannot eliminate the "early,", "high," and "wrong product" mistakes.

OBSTACLES TO ACCURACY

First, you may be using the wrong collection methodology. Not only does the methodology have to be easy, obvious, "user friendly," and convenient, but it is possible to have an inappropriate combination of production environments and production reporting techniques. Fabrication or assembly, long or short lead time, one piece or big lots, high or low volume environments all have their own unique data collection requirements.

Take a wire drawing, plating, and stranding factory where semi-finished wire is kept in open floor racks. Production reporting assumes a standard consumed (input) wire for each produced (from the next operation) wire. But more than one input wire can be used under certain circumstances. A once-a-day production reporting technique based upon scraps of paper from the previous three shifts is inappropriate because the day-shift foreman making the "real" entries cannot be sure whether standard or substitute input wire was used (unless someone took the trouble to specifically note otherwise).

Have you ever thought that automated data collection leads to more accuracy all by itself. What if automated collection machines are installed where assembly work is part of an incentive pay system, and that workers are expected to enter their own production data. But inspection tags are stilled being turned in by Q.C. Which count is the "production"? If Q.C. is the determining factor, then perhaps the worker oriented collection machines are the wrong collection methodology.

But even with a correct methodology, the collection tools may be inadequate or inapprpriate. For example, if we are trying to record production on an operation by operation basis, have we installed automated recording equipment? Clerks cannot usually keep up with manual posting of operational status, particularly in high volume, fast moving, and/or short lead time assembly environments. Or, if we are trying to record stock issues of small parts, have we installed accurate and easy to use scales? Handcounting is usually slow and error-prone. Finally, if we are trying to use checkpoint or delay type reporting techniques, have we adjusted our inspection techniques? If we inspect after each operation, then rejects will not be noted, and production requirements adjusted, until the next checkpoint.

The second obstacle is spending too much time and effort for the value of the collected data. A blizzard of material identification tags or an avalanche of production forms will quickly put an end to accuracy. For example, take a dispatch list for a work center so large that -- even if all the job data were accurate -- the list is still useless because the physical jobs would be spread over too large an area, and hence be difficult to locate, move, setup, and run. It wouldn't take long before the need for an accurate list would be questioned, and accurate reporting would decline.

A third obstacle can be the length of time required to summarize and distribute worthwhile information. Timely and purposeful reporting of collected data is a key support for a formal data collection program. If supposedly useful data is not made available until after the time when decisions must be made -- and so those decisions are made in the dark by the seat of someone's pants -- then requests for accurate data collection will fall on deaf ears.

For example, batch processing through remote job entry (RJE) units to corporate host computers may take three to five days to enter, edit, correct, and finally report shop floor data. While data collection devices with on-line editing of transactions reasonableness can overcome the timeliness barrier, only education and a constant show of management concern can tell workers why they should care to properly complete and correct the transactions.

Education is the fourth obstacle because we always assume our people can read and count. But not all factory workers are fully literate or sure of their arithmetic. And many who are literate, have their literacy in other languages (eg., Spanish), not in English. Few data collection programs or inhouse training programs are geared towards non-English speaking workers. Is their limited English is strong enough to understand technical, systems documentation? And even if the answer is "yes," was it completed before implementation, and were the workers tested on their ability to handle CRT's or other automated devices?

Motivation (fifth obstacle) starts with few people getting excited about systems that complicate their jobs, and do it without first getting their opinions or ideas about what they think needs to be done to collect accurate production reports. And, do your people sense that management expects accurate shop floor production reporting? After all, why change now if poor data has been tolerated since Day One! How can you communciate the new urgency, the new importance of accuracy? And is it clear as to who is responsible to make the new transactions, and when; and who is accountable for seeing that the responsible person actually gets the job done. And, few people can "keep up the good work" without knowing "how good" it was. Motivation thrives on feedback about the number and percentage of accurate transactions, and on the accomplishments (or embarrassments) that result from those efforts (eg, special orders being done or not done on time).

The sixth obstacle is self-inflicted through improper P&IC practices, such as releasing shop orders before the starting work centers are ready to accept those orders. A quick way to make a joke out of a dispatch report is to make it several pages long with dozens of orders that everyone knows can't be worked on for at least two weeks. Yet this can be perfectly plausible when planners are measured on their speed in getting jobs specified and "into the system". Although getting planned orders into the system early is a good idea, it is not a good idea to release them (a mistake which could be easily to make).

Another example is kiting ahead of time, not so much to identify shortages, but simply to take advantage of summer help or limited duty workers who need "something to do". Advance kits get "robbed", and so do your inventory record accuracy levels.

The last obstacle is the lack of solid audit programs to first determine if collected data is accurate; second, determine the causes of inaccurate data; and third, to take effective, management supported action to permanently fix those problems.

"Cycle count" production data. Did those jobs and pieces really move, go to scrap or stock, or come back from rework? Did it really take an extra hour to set the machine or to run 100 pieces? And if not, then why was it reported that way?

CRITERIA FOR TRANSACTION ACCURACY

Each of the shop floor production reporting transactions has its own criteria for accuracy, including: the controls that guard against not making a transaction; the key data required for an accurate transaction; the principle edits for that data; and the checkpoints that can indicate complete (or reasonable) transactions.

ORDER RELEASE:

Control
Released planned orders when due dates equal the cumulative product lead time
Key data
Due Date;
Order Quantity
Edits
Due date within cumulative product lead time;
Order number not previously released
Completeness
Check sequenced listings of manufacturing orders for release of all planned orders.

STOCK ISSUES:

Control
Use batches of picking lists or issuing material requisitions;
Review each unplanned issue
Key Data
Manufacturing order number;
Planned or Unplanned order code;
Quantity Issued
Edits
Only released orders can be picked;
Unplanned issues must follow initial order issues;
Completeness
Maintain control list of pick list or M.R. batches

OPERATION BEGIN:

Control
Verify that operation begin transactions are submitted before production quantity reports from that operation
Key Data
Manufacturing order number
Edits
Previous operation number
Completeness
Review dated listings of operations due to begin after previous operation ends

OPERATION END:

Control
Verify that operation ends precede subsequent inspection and/or move reports
Key Data
Manufacturing order number;
Quantity completed

Edits
Total Quantity completed vs. order quantity
Completeness
Review dated listings of all open operations

SCRAP AND REWORK:

Control
Require rework transactions for every move out of a rework work center
Key Data
Manufacturing order number;
Quantity reworked or scrapped
Edits
Total quantity reported complete on the order plus the total quantity scrapped and reworked to-date less than or equal to the order quantity (unless planned yields are exceeded).
Completeness
Review every operation close where the quantity complete was less than the order quantity requires a scrap or rework transaction

MOVE REPORTS:

Control
Require move reports after every operation end transaction
Key Data
Manufacturing order number;
Quantity moved
Edits
Quantity reported complete vs. the quantity moved
Completeness
Check for a move report within an expected time after an operation end transaction

STOCK RECEIPTS:

Control
Require stock receipts after a final operation close and accompanying move report transactions;
Review each unplanned receipt
Key Data
Manufacturing order number;
Quantity Received;
Planned or unplanned receipt code
Edits
Quantity received equals the quantity moved and equals the quantity reported complete from the final operation;
Unplanned receipts should only be for components issued to open manufacturing orders
Completeness
Review dated lists of final operation ends

ORDER CLOSEOUT:

Control
Review released orders that are late against planned due dates
Key data
Manufacturing order number
Edits
Order number not previously released;
Final operation end transaction not received;
Total quantity complete plus scrapped plus reworked not equal to order quantity
Completeness
Review listings of orders with final operation end transactions or stock receipts

FOUR SIMPLE IDEAS FOR ACCURACY

Regardless of whether you have automated data collection systems or old-fashioned, paper and pencil methods, these ideas "must" be utilized in order to collect accurate shop floor data. Ignoring them will certainly add many hours of aggrevation to an already difficult task.

CLARITY -- No one wants to guess at the information to be entered on a CRT or to be written down. You've gone wrong if:

o Wrong data is being entered that would have been correct in a different screen field or elsewhere on the form

o Data fields are omitted if not forced to be entered by the computer, or if skipped on a paperwork form

o Entire transactions are skipped if the confusing data field is one required by the computer.

FRIENDLINESS -- "User-friendly" means that data prompts are understandable, computer jargon is omitted from CRT screens, and that editing and error messages are simple and clear. Use a foreign language if necessary. In a paperwork system, you know that the forms are not user-friendly when:

o Entries are scrunched so small that keypunchers are making mistakes

o Entries are spread over several lines, spaces, or blocks instead of being neatly entered in the intended spots.

MINIMALNESS -- This means having workers enter the least amount of data to the machine or CRT. With paperwork forms, minimalness is having office clerks complete as much as possible (such as job number, product number, and scheduled quantity) before sending the paperwork out onto the shop floor. Leave a minimum of data to be completed by the factory. Problems occur when:

o There are a lot of complaints about too much key entry work or pencil pushing

o Entries are made far after the work was completed (eg, the next day shift), and/or they are made from machine logs or other informal "collection" records.

COMPLETENESS -- Computerized systems get around this problem by comparing scheduled work with actual reported work to highlight jobs that may not have been reported. Paperwork systems account for documents numbered at issuance or issued in batches with batch control lists, with follow-up at prompt, regular intervals. This type of problem is usually uncovered by cycle counts of finished goods or work-in-process.

MEASURING AND REWARDING ACCURACY

Suppose you do everything suggested so far. How can you tell how well you're doing?

First, accuracy must be the number of times -- within like transactions -- that the reported transactions are absolutely correct with respect to manufacturing order number, quantity count, and date. Thus, 95% reporting accuracy means that 95% of all transactions of a given type (eg, move reports) are perfectly correct. Just like in cycle counting. The quantity count may have a tolerance for production pieces not hand or machine counted (eg, weighed), but there is no tolerance for wrong order numbers or dates.

Second, the measurements must be made regularly, and with the concurrence of all manufacturing supervision and management as to the methods of sampling, auditing, determination of accuracy, and reporting of results. There is no other way to develop acceptable statistics.

Third, there supervisors and foremen must acknowledge that company and manufacturing management expect a certain degree of accuracy, and that accuracy itself is as important as actual production.

Fourth, the supervisory group must feel that they can control accuracy. For example, paperwork forms and data collection machines must be well documented; audit and feedback procedures must exist for supervision to monitor transaction completeness; responsibilities must be clearly defined so supervision can follow up on errors with the correct persons.

Fifth, tangible rewards may be appropriate (eg, monetary bonuses or changes in grade levels) for clear achievement of openly acknowledged accuracy objectives.

IMPROVING THE PRESENT SYSTEM

Consider the following intermediate "bridges" to move from your present (assumed to be a manual, paperwork production reporting) system to the installation of improved data collection systems.

(1) Begin with a formal statment from management that success is as important a priority as any other project in the manufacturing department. This is because the successful installation involves changing people's ways and motvations -- difficult items under the best of conditions. It will be tempting to push the project into second place behind other, easier projects -- where it will fail -- unless it starts and stays the Number One project in manufacturing. The project is serious when the job security of the project leader is on-the-line. And it's not fair to expect a part time project leader to do a good job. Part time means something else is the Number One concern. Only full-time efforts can hope to succeed.

(2) Redesign present paperwork forms to include new (future) data elements. If you will capture future data by machine group within work center, then include a machine group entry spot on the new forms. It doesn't matter that you won't actually fill in that field now; just having it visible every time production workers use the form will provide an opportunity to have people think about and discuss that new piece of information.

(3) Review what will be key entered by shop floor personnel, and rearrange pen and pencil reporting so that they switch now to only writing down what they will be keying in the future. If necessary, shift all the other writing to office staff. In the wire factory, the computer would have automatically supplied the input wire type specified by the bill of material or as overriden by a production planner, leaving shop floor personnel to only enter an order number and quantity produced. Paperwork was changed so that the office completed the input and output wire types and order number before the paperwork went into the factory.

(4) Integrate back-of-the-envelope methods into the bridge system. Study why people record information informally, and take specific steps to conveniently, easily, and simply capture that information. Suppose a machine had a clipboard attached with scrap paper so machine operators could record production quantities that were later collected and rewritten onto offical production reports. It may be easy to replace the scrap papers with the bridge system pre-formatted and pre-completed shop floor reporting forms so that instead of making informal entries, operators were making the real entries.

(5) Resolve implementation issues at the shop floor level. Only a "working" committee of foreman and supervision can actually approve and implement workable resolutions to sticky questions such as: how to handle third shift stockroom issues from unmanned stock rooms; where to phsically locate CRT's; and so forth.

(6) The intermediate bridging system must provide for the maximum amount of flexibility in allowing factory workers to report what actually happens. For example, forms and CRT's should provide opportunities for situations such as: operations happening out of sequence; operations not on the routing; rework transactions; and machine utilization data.

(7) Audit actual data and report the results. An ABC approach that takes into account large work orders, difficult operations, and scrap and rework transactions will help place the auditing efforts where the most accuracy problems are suspected to be greatest and where accuracy is most important. Take management actions to revise and enforce the procedures that lead to accuracy.

(8) The pilot or intermediate bridge system represents a serious dress rehearsal. The transactions are as important as any that will be made in the future, and therefore this is the right time to assign and enforce the responsibilities and accountabilities for accuracy that make the automated system "fly."

(9) As you move to the new system, remember to:

o Give exams to everyone to prove their operational knowledge of forms, procedures, and electronic data collection machines in formal, testing environments before you let them use the system.

o Train newcomers the same as you trained the folks who were there when the system started up.

o Start-up ASAP after you've demonstrated that new electronic hardware works mechanically, and after you've demonstrated your ability to generate accurate transactions in the bridge system; ie, don't let enthusiasm and knowledge fade away

o Keep on auditing, measuring, and reporting accuracy levels

o Keep on taking actions to correct the causes of errors.

o Keep factory supervision and management meeting on a regular basis: to review and approve procedural changes; to ride herd on the person(s) responsible for keeping documentation up-to-date; and to raise issues that need investigation and perhaps top management intervention.

CONCLUSION

The best thing you'll probably ever hear about an accurate shop floor data collection system is "nothing at all" -- a welcome silence of complaints.

Author Biography

Joel M. Schipper is a Senior Consultant in the New England Management Consulting Department of Peat, Marwick, Mitchell & Co, and specializes in the management of manufacturing and distribution businesses and their supporting control systems. His industry experience ranges from electronics to chemicals, wire drawing to fashion clothing manufacturing, and he held prior positions with DuPont and Playtex. Mr. Schipper is certified at the fellow level by APICS, holds the Certificate in Data Processing, and has B.S. and M.S.I.E. degrees from Syracuse University.

THE JAPANESE APPROACH TO PRODUCTIVITY

Kenneth A. Wantuck, CPIM*
The Bendix Corporation

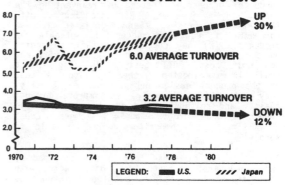

INVENTORY TURNOVER — 1970-1978

UP 30%

6.0 AVERAGE TURNOVER

3.2 AVERAGE TURNOVER

DOWN 12%

LEGEND: ▬ U.S. ⁄⁄⁄⁄ Japan

Note: Inventory turnover = cost of goods sold/inventory.

Figure 2

This special 3-hour presentation will be given by both Mr. Kenneth A. Wantuck and Mr. Leonard J. Ricard, General Motors.

The following paper was submitted by Mr. Wantuck.

The increasing penetration of the Japanese "Manufacturing Machine" in selected American markets has received widespread coverage in the media. The impact on our automotive industry has been of sufficient magnitude to make it a national issue. It is prudent for us to examine what the Japanese are doing in the area of productivity, to isolate the significant factors in their approach, and to determine which things we might emulate to our advantage.

Everyone is aware, to some degree, of the inroads the Japanese have made in U.S. markets. Product areas, such as television, video-recorders, cameras, watches, motorcycles and even shipbuilding, have become dominated by them. Of particular concern today are machine tools and automotive products, but an impact will soon be felt in the aerospace-electronics field. In all areas, we know that, not only do the Japanese compete with us at competitive prices, but the level of quality they have been demonstrating in recent years has been phenomenal.

For example, consider a study done by the Hertz Corporation in 1977. The objective was to determine which cars in their fleet had the lowest number of repairs for the first 12,000 miles of operation, the warranty period. Ford, Chevrolet and Pinto automobiles produced similar results. Each experienced three to four repairs per vehicle. On the other hand, Toyota repairs were significantly lower, only one-eighth as great. In this case, as shown in Figure 1, Japanese quality was better by almost an order of magnitude.

THE QUASAR STORY

Many people believe these accomplishments are attributable to cultural differences. They envision the Japanese dedicating their lives to their companies and working long hours for substandard wages, which would be unthinkable in America. The evidence, however, is contrary to these distorted notions. Consider the following. In 1977, a Japanese company named Matsushita purchased the Quasar television plant, in Chicago, from Motorola. The plant had been losing money consistently. In the purchase contract, Matsushita agreed that all of the hourly personnel would be retained. Two years later, as shown in Figure 3, they still had essentially the same one thousand hourly employees and had managed to reduce the indirect staff by 50%. Yet, during that period, daily production had doubled. The quality, as measured by the number of repairs done in-house, improved more than twenty fold. Outside quality indicators also improved. Where Motorola had spent an average amount of $16 million a year on warranty costs, Matsushita expenditures were $2 million. (That's for twice as many TV sets, so it's really a sixteen-to-one ratio.) These are big differences, achieved in the U.S. with American workers. The issue is how do the Japanese do this and what can we learn from them?

1977 HERTZ REPAIR STUDY:

MODEL	REPAIRS PER 100 VEHICLES
FORD	326
CHEVROLET	425
PINTO	306
TOYOTA	55

Figure 1

QUASAR PLANT PRODUCTIVITY

	UNDER MOTOROLA	UNDER MATSUSHITA (1)
DIRECT LABOR EMPLOYEES	1,000	1,000 (2)
INDIRECT EMPLOYEES	600	300
	1,600	1,300
DAILY PRODUCTION	1,000	2,000
ASSEMBLY REPAIRS	130%	6%
ANNUAL WARRANTY COST	$16 M	$2 M

NOTES
(1) 2 YEARS LATER
(2) SAME PEOPLE

Figure 3

Another interesting thing is that they've been able to accomplish this with much lower investments. Figure 2 is a graph of inventory turnovers for the Japanese and U.S. Electronics Industries. They turn their inventories approximately double the rate we turn ours. Of equal importance is that they are continually getting better while we are actually deteriorating about 10% over the time period shown on the chart.

ISOLATING THE ELEMENTS

First, it's important to understand that the Japanese, as a nation, have had one fundamental economic goal since 1945: full employment through industrialization. The strategy employed to achieve it called for obtaining market dominance in very select product areas. They very carefully chose those industries where they believed they could become dominant and concentrated on them, rather than diluting their efforts over a broad spectrum.

Their tactics were threefold: (1) They imported their technology. (The entire Japanese semiconductor industry was built around a $25,000 purchase from TI for the rights to the basic semiconductor process.) Instead of reinventing the wheel, they avoided major R&D expenditures, with the attendant risks, then negotiated license agreements to make the successful, workable new products. (2) They concentrated their ingenuity on the factory to achieve high productivity and low unit cost. The best engineering talent available was directed to the shop floor, instead of the product design department. (3) Finally, they embarked on a drive to improve product quality and reliability to the highest possible levels in order to give their customers product reliability that competitors were not able to supply.

Implementation of these tactics was governed by two fundamental concepts (most of us agree with these things in principle, but the difference is the degree to which the Japanese practice them): (1) they are firm believers that in every way, shape and form you must ELIMINATE WASTE and (2) they practice a great RESPECT FOR PEOPLE. We will explore these two areas in more depth.

When the Japanese talk about waste, the definition given by Mr. F. Cho, from Toyota, probably states it as well as anything. He calls it "...anything other than the minimum amount of equipment, materials, parts and workers (working time) which are absolutely essential to production..." That means no surplus, no safety stock. That means nothing is banked. If you can't use it now you don't make it now because it's waste. There are seven basic elements under this concept and another seven under respect for people which will be discussed further:

ELIMINATION OF WASTE	RESPECT FOR PEOPLE
o Focused Factory Networks	o Lifetime Employment
o Group Technology	o Company Unions
o Q.C. at the Source	o Attitude Toward Workers
o Just-In-Time Production	o Automation/ Robotics
o Uniform Plant Load	o Bottom-Round Management
o Kanban P.C. System	o Subcontractor Networks
o Minimized Set Up Time	o Quality Circles

FOCUSED FACTORY NETWORKS

The first element is Focused Factory Networks. Instead of building a large manufacturing facility that does everything (highly vertically integrated) the Japanese build small plants that are specialized. There are several reasons for doing this. First, it's very difficult to manage a large installation; the bigger it gets the more bureaucratic it gets. Their management style does not lend itself to this kind of environment.

When a plant is specifically designed to do a specific thing it can be constructed and operated more economically than its universal counterpart. It's comparable to buying a special machine tool to do a critical job instead of trying to adapt a universal tool. There are less than 750 plants in Japan that have as many as a thousand employees. When we talk about the Japanese approach to productivity and the impressive things they're doing, we're talking primarily about the middle group, where most of their model manufacturing plants fit.

Two illustrative examples have been cited by the Ford Motor Company. The Escort automobile needed a trans-axle which was going to require a $300 million expansion at their plant in Batavia, Ohio. They asked the Japanese for an equivalent quotation and Toyo-Kogyo offered to construct a brand new plant with the same rate of output at a competitive unit price for $100 million, a one-third ratio. A second example relates to the Ford Valencia engine plant, which produces two engines per employee per day, and requires 900,000 square feet of floor space. An almost identical engine is produced by the Toyota Motor Company in Japan, where they make nine engines per employee per day in a plant that has only 300,000 square feet of space. The issue is not only productivity per person but also a much lower capital investment in order to achieve this manufacturing capability.

GROUP TECHNOLOGY

Inside the plant they employ a technique called group technology. Incidentally, group technology is nothing new to America; it was invented here, like so many of the techniques the Japanese successfully employ, but it hasn't been practiced very much in the U.S. A simplified diagram of the technique is shown in Figure 4. The lower portion shows the way we operate our plants today. Most companies process a job and send it from department to department because that's the way our plants are organized (saw department, grinders, lathes, etc.). Each machine in those departments is usually manned by a person who specializes in that function. Getting a job through a shop can be a long and complicated process because there's a lot of waiting time and moving time involved (usually between 90% and 95% of the total processing time).

GROUP TECHNOLOGY
MANUFACTURING CELLS . . .

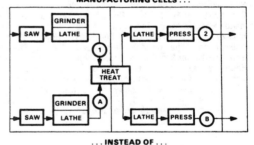

. . . INSTEAD OF . . .
. . . DEPARTMENTAL SPECIALTY

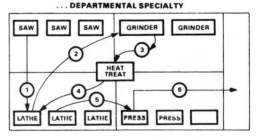

Figure 4

The Japanese, on the other hand, consider all of the operations required to make a part and try to group those machines together. The upper part of Figure 4 shows clusters of dissimilar machines that are designed to be a work center for a given part or family of parts. One operator runs all three machines shown in the upper left-hand corner, which increases the utility of the individual operator and eliminates the move and queue time between operations in a given cluster. Thus, not only does productivity go up, but work-in-process inventory comes down dramatically. In order to achieve this people have to be flexible, and in order to be flexible people must identify with their company and have a high degree of job security.

LIFETIME EMPLOYMENT

Much has been written about the Japanese concept of "Lifetime Employment." When a Japanese worker is hired for a permanent position with a major industrial firm, he has a job with that company for life (or until retirement age) provided he works diligently. If economic conditions deteriorate, the company will maintain the payroll almost to the point of going out of business. We should understand, though, that these kinds of benefits only apply to permanent workers, who constitute about one-third of the work force in Japan. What's important is that the concept is pervasive. When people can identify with the company as the place they're going to spend their working life, not just an interim place to get a pay check, then they have a tendency to be more flexible and to want to do all they can do in order to help achieve the goals of the company.

COMPANY UNIONS

When MacArthur introduced the union concept to Japan during the World War II reconstruction period, he undoubtedly had in mind trade unions, but the Japanese didn't think that way. A Japanese worker at Toyota was concerned about Toyota. He really didn't identify with the other automobile manufacturing employees in the rest of the country. He identified not with the kind of work he was doing but rather with the company for whom he was working. So Toyota formed a union which included everybody who worked for Toyota; it didn't matter what their skill was. The objective of both the union and management was to make the company as healthy as possible so there would be benefits accruing to the people in a secure and shared method. The resulting relationship was cooperative, not adversary.

The Japanese system of compensation reinforces these goals because it is based on company performance bonuses. Everybody in a Japanese company gets a bonus, from the lowest employee to the highest, twice a year. In good times the bonus is high (up to 50% of their salaries), while in bad times there may be no bonus. As a result of this, the employees have an attitude that says, "If the company does well, I do well," which is important from the standpoint of soliciting their help to improve productivity.

ATTITUDE TOWARD WORKERS

The attitude of management toward the workers is also critical. The Japanese do not look at people as human machines. As a matter of fact, they believe that if a machine can do a job then a person shouldn't do it because it's below his dignity. In the United States, we all believe in the value of human worth, but when it comes to the shop floor we don't necessarily practice it. A corollary concept says that if workers are really as important as people you must also believe that they can do much more than you are now giving them the opportunity to do. We normally have to see a person in a job for some time before we accept their competence. What the Japanese says is, "What they're doing today is only tapping their capability. We must give them an opportunity to do more." Thus, a third and most significant attitude, requires that the management system provide every worker with an opportunity to display his maximum capabilities. These things are practiced, not just discussed, and the Japanese spend more for employee training and education - at all levels - than any other industrial nation.

AUTOMATION/ROBOTICS

When people feel secure, identify with the company, and believe that they are being given an opportunity to fully display their talents, then the introduction of automation and robotics are not considered efficiency moves. The Japanese feel that this is a way to eliminate dull jobs so people can do more important things, and they have been making major capital investments in these areas. Interestingly enough, Japan has invested one-third of its gross national product in capital improvements for the last fifteen years, compared to about 19% for the U.S. during the same period. In automation, they have invested first in low cost enhancements to existing and/or standard equipment, using some clever approaches. In the capital area they have begun to concentrate on programmable robots. A recent survey showed that Japan had approximately 45,000 programmable robots (some of them quite simple) while the United States had only 5,000. Most of those robots were built here. Again, we shipped our technology to Japan where it was utilized to build products to compete with us. Today, Japan is building its own robots at a rapid pace and has become both the leading robot producer and robot user in the world. Since they honestly believe that robots free people for more important tasks, there is little worker resistance to the implementation. In fact, workers go out of their way to figure out how to eliminate their job, if they find it dull, because they know the company will find something better and more interesting for them to do.

JIDOKA

When management demonstrates that degree of confidence in people, it is possible to implement a quality concept which the Japanese call Jidoka. The word means "Stop everything when something goes wrong." It can be thought of as controlling quality at the source. Instead of using inspectors to find the problems that somebody else may have created, the worker in a Japanese factory becomes his or her own inspector. This concept was developed by Taiichi Ohno, who was Vice President of Manufacturing for Toyota, in the early fifties. Ohno was convinced that one of the big problems faced by Toyota was bringing quality levels up to the necessary standards to penetrate the world automotive market. He felt that there was too much looking over each others' shoulders and wanted, instead, for every individual to be responsible personally for the quality of the product/component that he produced.

Ohno determined that the best thing to do was to give each person only one part to work on at a time so that under no circumstances would he be able to bury his problems by working on alternate parts. Jidoka push-buttons were installed on the assembly lines. If anything went wrong, if a worker found a defective part, if he could not keep up with production, if production was going too fast according to the pace that was set for the day, or if he found a safety hazard, he was obligated to push the button. When he did, a light flashed, a bell rang, and the entire assembly line came to a grinding halt. People descended upon the spot where the light was flashing. It was something like a volunteer fire department because they were coming from the industrial engineering department, from management, etc., to respond to that particular alarm, and they fixed the problem on the spot. Meanwhile, the workers polished their machines, swept the floor, or did whatever else they could to keep busy, but the line didn't move until the problem was fixed.

Jidoka also encompasses automated inspection, sometimes called Autonomation. Just like automation and robotics, the Japanese believe that if inspection can be done by a machine, because it's faster, easier, more repeatable, or redundant, then a person shouldn't have to do it. However, the inspection step is a part of the production process, does not involve a separate location or person to perform it, and automatically shuts off a machine when a problem arises. This prevents the mass production of defective parts.

Now contrast that with our operations. How long does it take us to find a problem, to convince somebody it's real, to get it solved, and to get the fix implemented? How much do we produce in the meantime that isn't any good? Line shutdowns in Japan are encouraged to protect quality and because management has confidence in the individual worker. No one likes to see a line stopped, but Ohno suggests that a day without a single Jidoka drill can mean people aren't being careful enough.

BOTTOM-ROUND MANAGEMENT

This kind of mutual reliance is a manifestation of the management style the Japanese call "bottom-round management." It's also been identified as "consensus management" or "committee management." It is innate to the Japanese culture because they have grown up with the concept that the importance of the group supercedes that of the individual. Consider that they have more than a hundred million people crowded on a tiny island group about the size of California, 80% of which is mountainous, living very closely together in bamboo and paper houses. In those circumstances, one must have considerable respect for his neighbor or social survival would be impossible. This cultural concept is ideal in a manufacturing facility because the process requires that people work together in a group to make a product. The individual cannot function independently, without concern for others, because all he's going to do is get out of synchronization with the rest of the group and disrupt the process.

Bottom round management is a slow decision making process. In attempting to arrive at a true consensus, not a compromise, the Japanese will involve all potentially interested parties, talk over a problem at great length, often interrupt the process, seek out more information and retalk the problem until everyone finally agrees. While we have often criticized the slowness of this method, the Japanese have an interesting response.

They say, "You Americans will make an instant decision and then you'll take a very long time to implement it. The decision is made so quickly, without consulting many of the people it's going to affect, that as you try to implement it you begin to encounter all sorts of unforeseen obstacles. "Now, in our system," they say, "we take a long time to make a decision, but it only takes us a short time to implement it because by the time we've finally reached a conclusion, everybody involved has had their say. We have tried to consider every possible problem that may have to be surmounted. Suppose that the total duration for the combination of decision and implementation is the same; our way is still better because we implement all of our decisions and you Americans don't. Quick decisions often die partway through the implementation process because you encounter insurmountable obstacles." Maybe they're right. Maybe the process isn't as inefficient as we would like to think. Implementation is certainly much faster and surer.

A key to "bottom-round management" is that decisions are made at the lowest possible level. In essence, the employees recognize a problem, work out a potential solution with their peers, and make recommendations to the next level of management. They, in turn, do the same thing and make the next recommendation up the line. And so it goes, with everyone participating. As a result, top management in Japanese companies makes very few operating decisions, being almost totally devoted to strategic planning. It is important to note, though, that the use of bottom-round management makes it extremely difficult to manage a large, complex manufacturing organization. That's another reason why the Japanese build focused factories, which were discussed earlier.

SUBCONTRACTOR NETWORKS

The specialized nature of Japanese factories has fostered the development of an enormous subcontractor network, the bulk of which have less than 30 employees. More than 90% of all Japanese companies are part of the supplier network, which is many tiers deep, because there is so little vertical integration in Japanese factories.

There are two kinds of suppliers: specialists in a narrow field who serve multiple customers (very much like U.S. suppliers), and captives, who usually make a small variety of parts for a single customer. The latter is more predominant in Japan. Of course, the idea of sole-source suppliers is diametrically opposed to the U.S. multi-source concept. Sole source arrangements work in Japan because the relationships are based on a tremendous amount of mutual trust. They seek long-term partnerships between customer and supplier. Americans who do business with Japanese companies know that the very first stages of negotiation involve an elaborate ceremony of getting to know one another to determine whether there is a mutual, long-term potential relationship in the picture. They're rarely interested in a one-time buy, so it's a different way of doing business for us.

Each of the suppliers in Japan considers itself part of the customer family. Very often key suppliers are invited to company functions like picnics or parties. In return, suppliers deliver high quality parts many times per day, often directly to the customer's assembly line, bypassing receiving and inspection. A typical scenario would have the supplier's truck arriving at a precise time of day, the driver would unload the truck himself, transport the parts into the factory and deliver them to the assembly line at a given station, deposit the parts, pick up his empty containers, load them in the truck, and leave, without any interference. No receiving, no incoming inspection, no paper, no delays. It's an almost paper-free system, all built on mutual trust.

Trust is a two-way street. Because so many of the suppliers are small and undercapitalized, a Japanese customer will advance money to finance them, if necessary. Customer process engineers and quality personnel will help the vendor improve his manufacturing system to meet the rigid quality and delivery standards imposed. Efforts will also be made to help the vendor cost reduce his production process to help insure his profitability. Nevertheless, the customer will still use these vendors as buffers during economic downturns to protect his own work force. He'll bring work back in, leaving the vendors to adjust, because they don't have the permanent, life-time employment guarantees that the major companies do. However, this is known in advance and is an accepted risk to the suppliers.

QUALITY CIRCLES

Another interesting technique, with which many Americans are already familiar, is Quality Circles. The Japanese call them Small Group Improvement Activities (SGIA). A Quality Circle is a group of volunteer employees who meet once a week on a scheduled basis to discuss their function and the problems they're encountering, to try to devise solutions to those problems and to propose those solutions to their management. The group may be led by a foreman or it may be a production worker. It usually includes people from a given discipline or a given production area, like Assembly Line A or the Turning Department. It can also be multidisciplined, e.g., including all of the material handlers who deliver materials to a department, the IE's who work in that department, etc. It does have to be led, though, by someone who is trained as a group leader. The trainers are called facilitators and each one may coordinate the activities of a member of Quality Circles. Westinghouse, for example, has 275 Quality Circles and about 25 facilitators.

It's an elaborate process to initiate. Circle members are taught brain-storming techniques, how to define a problem, how to evaluate solutions, how to prepare flow charts, etc. They learn how to make a presentation to management so their proposals will sell. This takes time, effort and money. Some companies do this all on company time while others allow a half-hour on company time and a half-hour of personal time.

It really works because it's an open forum. It takes some skills to prevent it from becoming a "gripe" session, but that's where the trained group leaders come in. Interestingly enough, only about one third of the proposals generated turn out to be quality related. More than half are productivity oriented. It's really amazing how many good ideas these motivated employees can contribute toward the profitability and the improved productivity of their companies. Quality Circles are actually a manifestation of the consensus, "bottom-round" management approach but limited to these small groups.

Practical results have been impressive. In 1960, when Toyota had the equivalent of an American suggestion system, the company averaged one proposal per employee per year, about four times as good as the U.S. national average. Toyota subsequently initiated a Quality Circle program, and ten years later they had increased the number of proposals to two-and-a-half per employee and the acceptance rate jumped to 70%. This was a five-fold improvement in acceptable ideas in a ten year span (see Figure 5). In 1976, the program averaged 15 proposals per person per year with an 83% acceptance ratio. It is interesting to note that many of the suggestions produced small individual savings, but the aggregate from 380,000 ideas was considerable.

Q. C. CIRCLES
EFFECTIVENESS AT TOYOTA

YEAR	TOTAL PROPOSALS	PROPOSALS PER CAPITA	PERCENT ACCEPTED
1960	9,000	1.0	39%
1970	40,000	2.5	70%
1973	247,000	12.2	76%
1976	380,000	15.3	83%

Figure 5

Quality Circles is the kind of program that can be initiated quickly and which can help set the stage for the introduction of other concepts. However, full realization of its benefits will take time (it took 10 years at Toyota) and should not be embarked upon as this year's catchy, "gee whiz" program.

JUST-IN-TIME PRODUCTION

The Japanese system is based on a fundamental concept which they call Just-In-Time Production. It requires the production of precisely the necessary units in the necessary quantities at the necessary time, with the objective of achieving plus or minus ZERO performance to schedule. It means that producing one extra piece is just as bad as being one piece short. In fact, anything over the minimum amount necessary is viewed as WASTE, since effort and material expended for something not needed now cannot be utilized now. (Later requirements are handled later.) That's another different idea for us, since our measure of good performance has always been to meet or exceed the schedule. It will be a most difficult concept for American manufacturing management to accept because it is contrary to our current practice, which is to stock extra material "Just-In-Case" something goes wrong.

The Just-In-Time concept applies primarily to a repetitive manufacturing process. It does not necessarily require large volumes, but is restricted to those operations that produce the same parts over and over again. Ideally, the finished product would be repetitive in nature. However, as a Westinghouse team learned during a recent visit to Mitsubishi Inazawa, a Japanese elevator manufacturer, the repetitive segments of the business may only appear several levels down the product structure. Even so, applying Just-In-Time concepts to a portion of the business produced significant improvements for them.

Under Just-In-Time, the ideal lot size is ONE PIECE. The Japanese view the manufacturing process as a giant network of interconnected work centers, wherein the perfect arrangement would be to have each worker complete his task on a part and pass it directly to the next worker just as that person was ready for another piece. The idea is to drive all queues toward zero in order to:

o minimize inventory investment,

o shorten production lead times,

o react faster to demand changes, and

o uncover any quality problems.

Figure 6 is a graphic that the Japanese use to explain the last idea. They look upon inventory as the water level in a pond and at the rocky bottom as a representation of problems that might occur in a shop. Lots of water in that pond will cover up the problems and one can sit happily in self-delusion. The problems, however, are still there. Invariably, the water level goes down at the worst possible time, like during an economic downturn. Then one must address the problems without having the needed resources to solve them. The Japanese say it is better to force the water level down on purpose, especially in good times, expose the problems and fix them now, before they cause trouble.

INVENTORY HIDES
PROBLEMS

| PROBLEMS HIDDEN | PROBLEMS EXPOSED |

Figure 6

The zeal with which the Japanese hammer at inventories is incredible. To begin with, inventory is viewed as a negative thing, not an asset. According to Toyota, "The value of inventory is disavowed." Nippondenso's attitude is even more severe, calling inventory "the root of all evil."

Almost universally, the Japanese see inventory as a deterrent to product quality. Finally, since the shop floor is programmed to have very little inventory, the slightest aberration in the process which results in extra parts is readily visible and serves as a red flag to which immediate response is required.

Since it is impossible to have every worker in a complex manufacturing process adjacent to one another, and since the network also includes outside suppliers, the Japanese recognize that the system must allow for transit time between centers. However, transfer quantities are kept as small as possible. Typical internal lot sizes are 1/10 of a day's production, vendors ship several times a day to their customers, and constant pressure is exercised to reduce the number of lots in the system.

Just-In-Time production makes no allowances for contingencies. Every piece is expected to be correct when received. Every machine is expected to be available to produce parts. Every delivery commitment is expected to be honored at the precise time it is scheduled. Consequently, the Japanese heavily emphasize quality, preventive maintenance and a high degree of mutual trust between all participants in the manufacturing enterprise. The process is gospel and everyone conscientiously adheres to it.

UNIFORM PLANT LOADING

To use the Just-In-Time production concept, it is necessary that production flow as smoothly as possible in the shop. The starting point is what the Japanese call Uniform Plant Loading. Its objective is to dampen the reaction waves that normally occur in response to schedule variations. For example, when a significant change is made in final assembly, it creates changed requirements in feeder operations that are usually amplified because of lot sizing rules, set ups, queues and waiting time. By the time the impact is felt at the start of the supply chain, a 10% change at the assembly could easily result in a 100% change at the front end.

The Japanese tell us the only way to eliminate that problem is to make the perturbations at the end as small as possible so that we get ripples going through the shop, not shock waves. They accomplish it by setting up a firm monthly production plan for which the output rate is frozen. Most U.S. manufacturing people have been trying to achieve that for years, without success, because they've tried to freeze a specific sequential configuration. The Japanese circumvent this issue by planning to build the same mix of products every day, even if the total quantities are small. For example, if they're only building a hundred pieces a month, they'll build five each day. Since they expect to build some quantity of everything that's on the schedule daily, they always have a total mix available to respond to variations in demand.

Going even further, they'll take those five units and intermix them on the assembly line. An example of how Toyota would do this is shown in Figure 7. Presume three kinds of vehicles being made in an assembly plant; sedans, hard tops and station wagons. The monthly rates shown are then reduced to daily quantities (presuming a 20-day month) of 250, 125 and 125, respectively. From this, the Japanese compute the necessary <u>cycle times</u>. Cycle time in Japan is the period of time between two identical units coming off the production line. The Japanese use this figure to adjust their resources to produce precisely the quantity that's needed, no more, no less.

The Japanese do not concern themselves with achieving the rated speeds of their equipment. In American shops, a given machine will be rated at a thousand pieces per hour so if we need five thou-

sand pieces we'll run it five hours to obtain this month's requirement. The Japanese will produce only the needed quantity each day, as required. To them, cycle time is an indicator which defines how to assemble their resources to meet this month's production. If the rate for next month changes, the resources will be reconfigured.

TOYOTA EXAMPLE:

MODEL	MONTHLY QTY.	DAILY QTY.	CYCLE TIME
SEDAN	5,000	250	2 MIN.
HARDTOP	2,500	125	4 MIN.
WAGON	2,500	125	4 MIN.

SEQUENCE: SEDAN, HARDTOP, SEDAN, WAGON, SEDAN, HARDTOP, SEDAN, WAGON, ETC.

Figure 7

KANBAN PRODUCTION CONTROL SYSTEM

This kind of an approach calls for a control system that is simple, self-regulating and which will provide good management visibility. The shop floor/vendor release and control system is called Kanban (kahn-bahn), from the Japanese word meaning card. It is a paperless system, using dedicated containers and recycling traveling requisitions/cards, which is quite different from our old, manual shop packet systems. Kanban is a "pull" type of reorder system in that the authority to produce or supply comes from down-stream operations. While work centers and vendors plan their work based on schedules, they execute based on Kanbans, which are completely manual.

There are two types of Kanban cards. The Production Kanban authorizes the manufacturing of a container of material. The Withdrawal Kanban authorizes the withdrawal and movement of that container. The number of pieces in a container never varies for a given part number.

When production rates change, containers will be added or deleted from the system, according to a simple formula. The idea of safety stock is included in the basic calculation but is limited to 10% of a single day's demand. This gives the theoretical number of Kanban/containers required. In practice, efforts are made to reduce the number in circulation to keep inventories to a minimum.

The flow of Kanban cards between two work centers is shown in Figure 8. The machining center shown is making two parts, a and b, and they are stored in standard containers next to the work center. When the assembly line starts to use Part a from a full container, a worker takes the Withdrawal Kanban from the container and travels to the machining center storage area. He finds a container of Part a, removes the Production Kanban and replaces it with his Withdrawal Kanban card, which authorizes him to move the container. The liberated Production Kanban is then placed in a rack by the machining center as a work authorization for another lot of material. Parts are manufactured in the order in which cards are places on the rack (the Japanese call this the Kanban hanging) which makes the set of cards in the rack a dispatch list.

FLOW OF TWO KANBANS

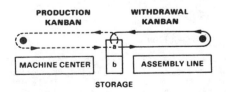

STORAGE

Figure 8

If it turns out that the demand for Part a is greater than planned and less than planned for Part b the system self regulates to these changes since there can be no more parts built than called for by the Kanban cards in circulation. Mix changes of 10% to 20% can easily be accommodated because the shifts are gradual and the increments are small. The ripple effect upstream is similarly dampened.

The same approach is used to authorize vendor shipments. When both the customer and the vendor are using the Kanban System, the Withdrawal Kanban serves as the vendor release/shipping document while the Production Kanban at the vendor's plant regulates his production.

The whole system hinges on everyone doing exactly what is authorized and following procedures explicitly. In fact, the Japanese use no production coordinators on the shop floor, relying solely on foremen to insure compliance. Cooperative worker attitudes are essential to its success.

Results can be impressive. Jidosha Kiki, a Bendix braking components affiliate in Japan, installed the Kanban/Just-In-Time system in 1977 with the help of their customer, Toyota. Within two years they had doubled productivity, tripled inventory turnover (see Figure 9) and substantially reduced overtime and space requirements. They have stated that this was a slow and difficult learning process for their employees, even considering the Japanese culture, because all the old rules of thumb had to be tossed out the window and deep rooted ideas had to be changed.

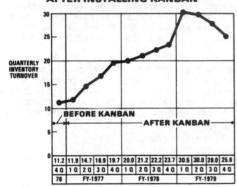

JIDOSHA KIKI CORP.
QUARTERLY INVENTORY TURNOVER
AFTER INSTALLING KANBAN

Figure 9

MINIMIZED SET UP TIMES

The Japanese approach to productivity demands that small lots be run in production. This is impossible to do if machine setups take hours to accomplish. In fact, we use the economic order quantity (EOQ) formula in the United States to determine what quantity we should run to absorb a long and costly setup time.

The Japanese have the same formula, but they've turned it around. Instead of accepting setup times as fixed numbers, they fixed the lot sizes (very small) and went to work to reduce setup time.

That is the fourteenth point (and a very crucial one) in the Japanese approach. Their success in this area has received widespread acclaim. Many Americans have been to Japan and witnessed a team of press operators change an eight-hundred ton press in ten minutes. Compare those data with ours as shown in Figure 10. The Japanese aim for single digit setup times (i.e., less than 10

minutes) for every machine in their factories. They've addressed not only big things, like presses, but small molding machines and standard machine tools, as well.

MINIMIZING SET-UP TIME
HOOD AND FENDER PRESS COMPARISON
(800 TON PRESS)

	TOYOTA	U.S.A.	SWEDEN	W. GERMANY
SET-UP TIME	10 MIN.	6 HR.	4 HR.	4 HR.
SET-UPS/DAY	3	1	—	1/2
LOT SIZE	1 DAY*	10 DAYS	1 MONTH	—

*FOR LOW DEMAND ITEMS (LESS THAN 1000/MONTH). AS LARGE AS 7 DAYS

Figure 10

Successful setup reduction is easily achieved when approached from a methods engineering perspective. The Japanese separate setup time into two segments: internal - that part which must be done while a machine is stopped, and external - that part which can be done while the machine is operating. Simple things, like the staging of replacement dies, fall into the external category which, on the average, represents half of the usual setup time.

Another 50% reduction can be achieved by the application of time and motion studies and practice. (It is not usual for a Japanese setup team to spend a full Saturday practicing changeovers). Time saving devices like hinged bolts, roller platforms and folding brackets for temporary die staging are commonly seen, all of which are low cost items.

Only then is it necessary to spend larger sums, to reduce the last 15% or so, on things like automatic positioning of dies, rolling bolsters, duplicate tool holders, etc. The result is that 90% or MORE of present setup times can be eliminated if we have a desire to do so.

Referring again to Jidosha Kiki Corporation, Figure 11 shows the remarkable progress they made in just four years. These data related to all the machines in their factory. It's interesting that while we are quite impressed that two thirds of their equipment can be changed over in less than two minutes, they are embarrassed that 10% still takes more than 10 minutes.

The savings in setup time are used to increase the number of lots produced, with a corollary reduction in lot sizes. This makes the use of Just-In-Time production principles feasible which, in turn, makes the Kanban control system practical. All the pieces fit together.

SET-UP REDUCTION
RESULTS AT JKC

SET-UP TIME	1976	1977	1980
>60 MIN.	30%	0	0
30 - 60 MIN.	19%	0	0
20 - 30 MIN.	26%	10%	3%
10 - 20 MIN.	20%	12%	7%
5 - 10 MIN.	5%	20%	12%
100 SEC. - 5 MIN.	0	17%	16%
<100 SEC.	0	41%	62%

Figure 11

WHAT WE CAN DO

The best managed manufacturing companies in Japan have clearly shown us the viability of their approach to productivity, many elements of which were borrowed from America. We can now borrow back many of their modified approaches and may very likely adjust them to meet our environment.

What is important is that we recognize the value of what they're doing, gain an understanding of how they do it, realize that most of the techniques are NOT culturally restricted, and apply applicable innovations to our business so we can enhance our own productivity and be competitive with them.

The keys to making these things happen in American companies are attitude and time. While much has been made of renewing the American work ethic and developing a better working partnership between labor and management, the most significant issue may well be American management attitude. Our manufacturing management is, by necessity, driven by short term objectives and, as a consequence, is extremely conservative and tactically oriented. Methods learned over a lifetime of experience are not easily given up, especially when they've been successful by past standards. The point is the standards are changing. What the Japanese have really given us is hard proof that their techniques really work, so we're not just talking about theory. American manufacturing management needs to understand that.

We can't even get started if we don't accept the rationale that Japanese productivity methods can work in the U.S. and must be implemented if we are to successfully compete in the future. Yet there are undercurrents today of a "Japanese backlash." Many managers claim they are "tired of hearing about it," as if refusing to acknowledge the problem will make it go away. Others are opting for import restrictions, local content legislation or subsidies as cures. But, none of these things will help us meet the competitive challenge in world markets. We need better productivity, not protection.

During the last five years, Japan has been able to offset its inflation rate by productivity improvements so the cost-per-unit-output has remained relatively flat, as shown in Figure 12. By contrast, with sometimes negative productivity changes combined with high inflation rates, U.S. manufacturing costs-per-unit-output are now 35% higher than they were five years ago. Shall we let that trend continue or shall we make the changes necessary to reverse it?

The kinds of changes we are talking about here are long term in nature, because they involve the changing of fundamental concepts. It took the best Japanese companies more than thirty years to get where they are. It may take decades for us. There are no miracles or quick fixes. The Japanese say that American visitors are always looking for "tricks and secret weapons," but there aren't any. There are just good principles applied rigorously in the right management environment over a long period of time. The time to start is now.

THE CHALLENGE IS REAL

UNIT LABOR COSTS IN THE UNITED STATES AND JAPAN
INDEX: 1975 = 100

Figure 12

BIOGRAPHICAL SKETCH

KENNETH A. WANTUCK

Kenneth A. Wantuck is the Corporate Director-Advanced Manufacturing Facilities for the Bendix Corporation, where he is responsible for strategic location planning, project coordination, productivity enhancements and integrated control systems in new manufacturing facilities.

His twenty-four years of industrial experience include management positions in engineering, manufacturing, material, producement and business planning for Bendix, Westinghouse, Reeves-Hoffman, CTS Knights and Milgo Electronics.

He has been directly responsible for the implementation of mechanized manufacturing control systems, including MRP, Master scheduling, purchasing, forecasting and automated stores. His research on Japanese production methods includes visits to numerous facilities, both here and abroad. He has authored many articles, presentations and a videotape on these topics.

Mr. Wantuck is a member of the Society of Manufacturing Engineers, The American Production and Inventory Control Society, and the Industrial Development Research Council. He also serves on the Plossl Manufacturing Controls Council and the Automotive-Industries Action Group.

Ken received his B.S. in Electrical Engineering from the University of Florida and did post-graduate work in Engineering Administration at George Washington University. He is an APICS Certified Fellow in Production and Inventory Management (CPIM*) and an NAPM Certified Purchasing Manager (CPM).

LEONARD J. RICARD

Leonard J. Ricard was named director of Inventory Management-Production Control for General Motors Materials Management Staff in July, 1982.

In this newly-established position, Mr. Ricard has responsibility for the coordination of inventory management programs and the implementation of a 'Just-in-Time' inventory system corporatewide.

Mr. Ricard began his GM career at the Research Laboratories in 1962. The following year he was named to Chevrolet Motor Division, where he held a number of financial assignments, including supervisor of Hourly Payroll and general supervisor, General Accounting.

In 1972 Mr. Ricard, who holds a bachelor's degree in mathematics from Wayne State University, was assigned to GM Assembly Division, where he held various assignments in the Financial and Industrial Engineering staffs.

He joined GMC Truck and Coach Division, where he was named staff systems analyst in late 1974.

In 1977, Mr. Ricard was named manager-Systems Development for GM Overseas Corporation in Japan. Three years later he was named director of Schedules and Systems on GM's Materials Management Staff, the post he held prior to his current assignment.

FUNDAMENTALS OF SHOP FLOOR CONTROL

William R. Wassweiler
MRM, Inc.

INTRODUCTION

The objective of this presentation is to provide an overview of the basic prerequisites, features and functions necessary to operate an effective Shop Floor Control System. The discussion relates to a Shop Floor Control System that operates within a closed loop manufacturing control system driven by a master production schedule and material requirements planning. The paper begins with a review of the data base required to support the system and then proceeds to discuss the sequence of activities involved in Shop Floor Control, along with the tools necessary to do the job.

DATA BASE REQUIREMENTS

In addition to bills of material, on-order status and part masters, the major elements of a shop floor control data base are routings and work center definition. Exhibit 1 is a typical example of a routing.

ROUTING

PART NUMBER	DESCRIPTION	ORDER NUMBER	QUANTITY
8875	SIDE	53151	200

OPERATION NUMBER	DESCRIPTION	DEPT.	WORK CENTER	MACH. NBR.	LABOR GRADE	RUN HR/PC	SET-UP HOURS	TOOLS TOOLS
10	CUT OFF	10	11	623	05	.020	.5	1012
20	SHAPE	10	12	127	05	.030	2.10	601
30	DRILL	20	21	500	08	.060	.20	500
40	INSPECT	49	22		02	.000	.00	
50	HEAT TREAT	H.T.	4		00	.000	.00	
60	INSPECT	49	32		00	.000	.00	

EXHIBIT 1

When implementing a shop floor control system, it becomes readily apparent that the routing is as critical to shop floor control as the bill of material is to MRP. Routings must be accurate, for they are the "road maps" the factory follows to get the job done. Routings must indicate where the work is to be performed, the sequence of the work, how to build the product, the movement of the job, the specific tools needed, the amount of set-up time required, and a time, either estimated or a standard, must be assigned each operation. Routings are typically used as shop travelers and accompany the work from operation to operation. The traveler contains no schedule information whatsoever, only quantity and shop order number.

The purpose of the work center file (Exhibit 2) is to assemble in one place all relevant data related to a work center, such as status, capacity, load and performance.

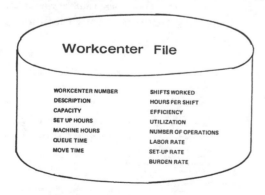

Workcenter File

WORKCENTER NUMBER	SHIFTS WORKED
DESCRIPTION	HOURS PER SHIFT
CAPACITY	EFFICIENCY
SET UP HOURS	UTILIZATION
MACHINE HOURS	NUMBER OF OPERATIONS
QUEUE TIME	LABOR RATE
MOVE TIME	SET-UP RATE
	BURDEN RATE

EXHIBIT 2

Work centers usually contain machines or equipment that are either identical or similar in capability or process. The work center file supports data processing programs that use information in the file for standard cost, routings and work center where-used reports.

MATERIAL REQUIREMENTS PLANNING

The major advantage of a Shop Floor Control System driven by MRP is the inherent capability of MRP to establish priorities and then maintain them. This important characteristic can easily be communicated to the factory through a dispatch list indicating the relative priority of all work-in-process by a routed operation and work center. This feature is the primary reason why MRP-driven Shop Floor Control Systems can improve customer service and reduce work-in-process inventory. MRP indicates to the factory what product to build, how many of the product to build, and when the product is needed. MRP is the interface which indicates shop order release dates and quantities, along with subsequent revisions as needed to due dates and/or quantities. In conjunction with Shop Floor Control, MRP is a scheduling device rather than an order launching tool. Exhibit 3 is an example of an MRP print which contains a number of features that support Shop Floor Control.

MRP PRINT

Part No.	Description	Lead Time	Queue Time	Shrink Qty.	Shrink Pct.	Safety Stk.	Family	Lot Size	Tool NBR	Lower Level
297810	Housing	25	17.5	0	5%		Yes	As Req'd.	T-5	397810

Total Qty. On Hand	On Hand Stk. Rm.	On Hand Receiving	Qty. In Flr. Stk.	Qty. Loan to Mfg.	Qty. Held Stk. Room	Product Line	Minimum Ord. Qty.	Maximum Ord. Qty.	Stk. Loc.
150	100		50	0	0	T-5	25	800	A4

	2/20/79	2/27/79	3/6/79	3/13/79	3/20/79	3/27/79	4/3/79	4/10/79	4/17/79	4-24/79	5/1/79
Gross Reqrnt.	25		75		50		300			250	20
Sch. Receipt											
OH/Available	125	125	50	50	0		300-	300-	300-	550-	570-
Planned Order		315			263	21					

PEGGED REQUIREMENTS

Parent Part Number	Order Number	Date Required	Quantity Required
8866	C5080	2/20/79	25
8866	C7511	3/6/79	75
8868		3/20/79	50

EXHIBIT 3

The total on-hand quantity is broken down to show material on hand in the stockroom, receiving, floor stock, loan to manufacturing, or held for re-inspection. To effectively control material, you must know where it is. Queue time is indicated so the planner can relate its relative compression to a reduction of the total lead time when expediting is necessary. A shrink quantity or percent is a useful feature when planning material that is subject to yield or scrap conditions. The minimum and maximum run quantity that the routing for the part can handle is indicated for timely coordination with Industrial Engineering. Another MRP feature that is critical to a dynamic shop environment is net change versus regeneration. This environment requires an MRP system that can react to change on a timely basis. Net change has this quality, for it is change-driven, which means it can respond to scrap, lead time changes, bill of material changes, inventory adjustments, order cancellations, master schedule changes, material receipts and issues as frequently as the user requires. This characteristic keeps the information in the Shop Floor Control System up to date and, therefore, provides more capability than a weekly regeneration. For MRP to be effective, it must accurately reflect what is happening on the factory floor, and net change provides that feature.

COMPONENT AVAILABILITY CHECKING

Before a planned order from MRP is released to the factory for fabrication or assembly, component material availability must be confirmed prior to release to the stockroom and shop floor. There is no need to stage material to determine part shortages, because a material availability checking program can easily be added to an MRP system. This feature allows a planner to check the availability and status of components prior to the release of a production order to the stockroom for picking. The program indicates either the order is complete - or the part numbers and quantities short are listed (Exhibit 4).

MANUFACTURING ORDER RELEASE STATUS

Start	Part Number	Order Number	Due Date	Available Stk. Room	Allocated	Order Quantity
5/24/79	A10503	C-0003	6/5/79	744	744	150

Short	Available Stk. Room	Allocated	Required Quantity	Short Quantity	Part Type
10001	500	500	150	1	P

RELEASE BY PASSED — SHORTAGE

Start	Part Number	Order Number	Due Date	Available Stk. Room	Allocated	Order Quantity
5/28/79	13-6951	S-1505	6/8/79	963	963	50

RELEASED

EXHIBIT 4

If appropriate, this feature can be programmed to automatically release orders based on the start date for an order. At the planned order release time, the availability of all components will be checked, based on the on-hand plus on-order, minus committed balances for each part. If shortages exist, the order paperwork will not be prepared unless the planner issues a forced release transaction. A by-product of this exercise is an availability report (or mechanized shortage list (Exhibit 5), which indicates the due date of the shortage, along with previous claims of other production orders that have the same shortage.

ORDER RELEASE
SUMMARIZED SHORTAGE REPORT

Component Part Number	Part Type	Available Stk. Room	Req'd This Release	Available Quantity
10001	P	500	1156	656-

Required On	Part Number	Order Number	Start Date	Qty. Required
	A10503	C-0003	5/24/79	1
	A10536	C-0008	5/24/79	100
	A10850	C-0011	6/5/79	200
	A10999	C-0037	6/12/79	256

Scheduled Receipts	Order Number	Date Due	Order Qty.	Balance On Order	Part Type
	P-0004	5/17/79	1000	500	P
	P-0009	5/24/79	1000	1000	P
	P-0100	7/31/79	1000	1000	P

EXHIBIT 5

DISPATCH LIST

MRP provides the priority planning information that establishes the need dates and quantities of work-in-process, which is communicated to the shop floor in the form of a dispatch list. Exhibit 6 is an example of a basic dispatch list.

Daily Work Center Job Schedule

EXHIBIT 6

The report is a listing by operation of all the jobs available to be run in the work center. The ranking of the work is by a relative priority index. In this example, the priority is the result of a critical ratio calculation which is the time remaining for a shop order over the work remaining. The time remaining comes from the requirement line of MRP and the work remaining is developed by re-calculating the lead time left for each job in process by considering transit, queue time, setup and run time. The arithmetic will indicate that priorities less than 1.0 are behind schedule, priorities of 1.0 are on schedule, and an index greater than 1.0 is ahead of schedule. As an example:

$$\frac{\text{Time Remaining} = 10 \text{ Days}}{\text{Work Remaining} = 20 \text{ Days}} = .5 \text{ behind schedule}$$

$$\frac{\text{Time Remaining} = 10 \text{ Days}}{\text{Work Remaining} = 10 \text{ Days}} = 1.0 \text{ on schedule}$$

$$\frac{\text{Time Remaining} = 20 \text{ Days}}{\text{Work Remaining} = 10 \text{ Days}} = 2.0 \text{ ahead of schedule}$$

Critical ratio is a dynamic technique that is ideally suited to a net change MRP system, but the use of start and due date by operation is also very effective.

The primary objective of both operation due date and critical ratio is to communicate to the shop foreman the schedule needs so that jobs can be completed on time. At the top of Exhibit 6 the jobs at the work center are indicated, whereas the bottom portion of the report shows work that is coming into the center. Work coming information is helpful to the foreman, for the visibility provides planning and coordination of capacity, tools, machines, and people before the fact. The dispatch list, by itself, creates many benefits, such as providing the foreman with information to do a better job of managing his department, the dynamics of MRP has been transferred to the shop floor, and schedules are truly current, plus the need for stockchasers is eliminated. The dispatch list fulfills the basic characteristics of a good schedule: It is simple; it is understandable. This is important, since it is Production Control's basic means of communicating with the factory.

PRODUCTION REPORTING

After an order has been released, it will appear on the dispatch list for the first operation on the routing which means a reporting mechanism must be in place to continue to monitor the status and movement of a job until it is completed. The typical methods of reporting include the use of timekeepers, job card racks, control centers, work station terminals, and on-line data entry. The most effective technique is on-line data entry, for it provides the advantages of timely updating of the files and immediate error correction through edits that indicate invalid transactions. Regardless of the method of data collection used, the key consideration revolves around discipline. The system will not operate properly without accurate reporting of scrap, rework, production counts, labor reporting, material receipts, and issues. Without proper discipline, the best designed system is doomed to failure.

CAPACITY REQUIREMENTS PLANNING

In addition to using the dispatch list as a capacity control tool, capacity requirements planning (Exhibit 7) provides more visibility, for it looks ahead as far as the time span that covers MRP.

Capacity Requirements Planning

EXHIBIT 7

CRP refers to an intermediate range of planning by relating how much capacity is required by work center, what the load will be (considering both released and planned orders), and when the load will occur by time period. The hours are created by the standard hours on the routing extended by the order quantity of released and unreleased work to arrive at the total load hours by time period by work center. (Without MRP, this report cannot be generated.) Because of its early recognition of capacity requirements, this report provides management an opportunity to do a better job of re-deploying labor and making better decisions concerning the material plan. Remedial action can be taken by using alternate routings, sub-contracting overloaded work centers, adding additional tooling, and reallocating the work force.

TOOL REQUIREMENTS PLANNING

The flexibility and potential of MRP is further demonstrated by its ability to plan tool requirements by time period (Exhibit 8).

TOOL REQUIREMENTS PLANNING

Tool NBR	Part Number	Order NBR	Tool/Pcs.	2/20/79	2/27/79	3/6/79	3/13/79	3/20/79	3/27/79	4/3/79	4/10/79
T-251	A3580	S-5035	10000				1500			1000	
T-300	A3580	S-5035	10000				1500			1000	
T-410	80060	S-8010	5000			4000				4000	
T-500	297810	S-7080	8000		315			203	21		
T-600	81010	S-6050	20000	5000					5000		
T-600	81011	S-6051	20000		5000					5000	
T-600	81012	S-6052	20000			20000					20000

EXHIBIT 8

Insuring the availability of tools to support shop order schedules can be improved by using the planned order start dates of MRP to indicate a need date for tooling. As planned orders in MRP generate requirements for lower components, they also can indicate a time-phased requirement for tooling. Exhibit 8 relates the tool numbers to the part number and order number. The tool/pieces is an indication of the number of total pieces that can be run on a tool before it must be re-sharpened or repaired. Projected usage and activity on the planning horizon provides the tool room foreman with the needed visibility to schedule tool repair, plan manpower and justify duplicate tooling. A problem with tooling can destroy a schedule as easily as a part shortage.

CONCLUSION

When a company utilizes the features/functions and techniques outlined in this Shop Floor Control presentation, it will follow that the key objectives of maximum manufacturing efficiency, improved customer service, and reduced work-in-process will occur.

ABOUT THE AUTHOR

William R. Wassweiler is a Vice President of MRM, Inc., a Milwaukee based consulting firm. He is the former Manager of Materials for Twin Disc, Inc. Mr. Wassweiler has over twenty years of experience in Production and Inventory Control plus Purchasing. He is a member of NAPM and member and past President of Milwaukee APICS. He is an instructor for the University of Wisconsin and Marquette University. Also, Director of University of Wisconsin Extension Division Advisory Board and Chairman of Committee that developed Shop Floor Certification program. He was the winner of APICS Communication Award for 1974. Author of the article entitled "Material Requirements Planning - The Key to Critical Ratio Effectiveness", which appeared in the 1972 issue of Production and Inventory Management. Mr. Wassweiler is a frequent lecturer for AMA, AIIE and APICS chapters and national conferences. He has recently participated in the rewrite of the APICS Dictionary and the development of the Shop Floor Control Training Aid.

Reprinted from *Production and Inventory Management*, Vol. 11, No. 3 (1970).

INPUT/OUTPUT CONTROL
A REAL HANDLE ON LEAD TIME

OLIVER WIGHT

Symptoms of Uncontrolled Lead Time

The Board of Directors of the Manufacturing Association of a midwest city got together recently to plan their programs for the coming year. They decided to try to arrive at common problems first and then have their speaking program address these problems. Five of the problems that were universal to each company represented weren't problems at all. They were *symptoms:*

1. Excessive inventories of parts and finished material combined with poor off-the-shelf service.
2. Inability to make realistic delivery promises and meet them.
3. Excessive expediting.
4. Chronic lack of space in the plant.
5. Plants that are always behind schedule.

Why should serious problems like these go unsolved for years in manufacturing plants even with the advent of much improved inventory management techniques, better scheduling techniques, and computers to implement them? The answer is simple:

With all the fancy tools that have been developed, industry has failed to learn the fundamentals of lead time control.

Most books on scientific inventory management, for example, start out by saying, "Lead time is assumed to be known". They then proceed to develop scientific approaches to inventory management that will certainly not be able to generate anything like their potential benefits if lead times are long and erratic.

Why don't people like to address the lead time problem? Perhaps because it is almost totally ignored in the literature of production and inventory control; perhaps because it is not a problem that a convenient set of mathematical equations can solve. The lead time problem, as it manifests itself in most American manufacturing companies, is basically a problem of management. The solutions to it are not difficult to understand; in fact, they are deceptively simple. The biggest difficulty in making these solutions work is in changing the traditional thinking of manufacturing people. The Board of Directors of the Association mentioned earlier *should be* concerned about this problem: a dramatic change in the way a company operates can only be implemented if top management understands the principles and educates other members of the company to be sure they are observed religiously.

What is Lead Time?

Before discussing some of the principles of lead time control, it is worth reviewing the basic concepts. Lead time can be defined as that time that elapses between the moment it is determined that an item is needed and ordered to be replenished and that moment when the item is available for use. Lead time can include all the elements of order entry time, such as preparing input data for the computer, waiting for the computer to process batches of input data, review of orders for credit check, engineering, etc. Often there is a fertile area for lead time improvement in order entry. Among other elements in the lead time cycle that can be excessively long are backlogs in production scheduling. Particularly in make-to-order plants, it is traditional to run with consistent backlogs behind starting operations in the factory. This is ostensibly because the amount of work coming in each week cannot be predicted and tends to be erratic. Most companies, however, seldom measure this incoming work rate or know how erratic it is and they usually carry excessive backlogs to "protect" themselves. An example of the application of the basic principles of lead time control to this type of situation will be given below.

But what about the manufacturing lead time itself? The actual amount of elapsed time in the factory takes place from the moment that a shop order is released to the factory to the time it is completed. This lead time can be broken into the following elements:

LEAD TIME = SET-UP TIME + RUNNING TIME + MOVE TIME + WAIT TIME + QUEUE TIME

Set-up time is the time when the job is sitting behind the machine and the machine is being set up with the proper tooling for this job.

Running time is the actual time the job is at the machine and being worked on.

Move time is the actual time that a job spends in transit. In most job shops, this could be defined as the time the job actually spends on the fork of the forklift truck.

Wait time has been separated from Queue Time so that it could be arbitrarily associated with move time since, in many factories, the dispatching job is not highly organized and the forklift truck operators usually don't get to a job as soon as it is ready to move. In some plants, an operator of a forklift truck may "clean out" one department once a day. This could mean an average wait time of half a day and if there were 10 moves in the operation sequence, 5 days of time could be expended in waiting for a move.

Queue time is that time that the job spends waiting to be worked on because another job is already being run on that machine center.

Elapsed lead times are always far greater than actual set-up and running time. It is hard to believe that any substantial amount of the elapsed lead time is truly spent "in transit"—on the forks of the forklift truck. A substantial amount of the time *could* be spent waiting for moves. In actual practice, most of the lead time turns out to be queue time. A simple experiment can verify this for any company. Taking some samples from completed shop orders, determine the date the job started in the first department and the number of elapsed working hours that took place in the first department (counting only *manned* shifts during the week). If, for example, Job A takes one week to go through Department No. 1, this amounts to forty hours of elapsed manned time. If Job A has two hours of set-up and two hours of run time, then the set-up and running time are 10% of the elapsed time.

A continuing survey of manufacturing companies indicates that ten per cent—or less—of the total lead time in the average company is actual working time! How can that be? It would seem that queues are completely out of control. And, of course, in practice *they are!* There is overwhelming evidence in most manufacturing companies to indicate that the amount of backlog that exists is as much as the company can possibly tolerate. Backlogs on the factory floor are in evidence everywhere and there seems to be a variation of Parkinson's Law at work in the typical manufacturing shop, since:

"work-in-process normally tends to expand to fill the space available".

What plant foreman doesn't feel that he is crowded for space? What shop doesn't occasionally run out of skids, pallets, shop boxes? What shop has open spaces out on the factory floor? In the typical job shop, work-in-process tends to be piled everywhere and the oldest jobs always seem to get up against the wall so that the newer ones are the only ones that can be worked on. This "Last-in-first-out" effect tends to keep customer service low, in spite of high inventories and high expediting efforts. In most shops, even a small capacity bottleneck will cause some queueing and as queues build, expediting becomes frantic.

Backlogs are the problem

Since backlog is a fundamental cause of long lead time and lead time can only be controlled if backlog is controlled, lets look at the three major causes of large backlogs.

1. Lead time inflation.
2. Erratic input to the plant.
3. Inability to plan and control output effectively.

No. 1 *LEAD TIME INFLATION*—Take the example of a company that plans to have its product manufactured in a six week lead time. As business picks up they manage to put more into the factory than they take out. This builds up the shop backlogs and, as a result, they find that their lead times are increasing from six weeks to eight weeks. The plant always feels that if they had just a little more lead time it would be a simple matter to get jobs completed on schedule. They cite the fact that many jobs come through two weeks after their schedule date as a reason for allowing two weeks more in the lead time. When the historical "facts" show that lead time is actually closer to eight weeks, they assume that this lead time should be built back into the inventory planning. Any inventory system assumes some length of lead time in its re-ordering mechanism. An order point system tries to forecast demand over *lead time* plus some safety stock. A requirements planning system tries to determine *when* requirements will fall, and then, in backing off in time to account for the *lead time*, it determines when orders should be placed. Either basic type of inventory system relies heavily on lead time estimates.

Ironically, *as planned lead times are increased, orders will be generated sooner, thus increasing backlogs in the shop.*

In our example, an increase in the planning lead time from six weeks to eight weeks would immediately generate an extra two weeks worth of work for the shop which would increase the backlogs and thus increase the lead times. If the actual lead times are observed now, they will be longer than ever. If they are once again built into the inventory plans, orders will be generated sooner again thus increasing backlogs and increasing lead times once again. This, then, is one of the most dangerous and most common misconceptions in the industry, yet many companies have even developed sophisticated computer programs to average historical lead times so that these can be built into their planning systems! Unfortunately, a computer is amoral; it can be used to do the wrong thing faster than it was ever possible to do it manually.

An even worse situation exists between vendors and their customers. It is aggravated by the fact that purchasing people often have no real understanding of the ill effects of long lead times. Some even encourage vendors to quote longer lead times in the belief that these longer lead times will be more reliable. They seldom are. Unfortunately, even if they were, the people generating the orders, usually in inventory control in the company purchasing material, find that their ability to forecast their needs accurately goes down dramatically as they forecast farther in advance. Thus they have to carry higher safety stocks and/or reschedule frequently to protect against forecast error as vendors increase their lead time. This can readily be seen in most companies by examining their open purchase order file. The bulk of the orders are late, but *are not needed*, while other orders, some of which were just placed recently, are being expedited because they *are* needed! Part of this problem could be caused by an ineffective inventory system, but even this is going to be aggravated if lead times are long and unreliable.

Many vendors quote longer lead times in the belief that this will give them a better chance to get the product out the door on time. It never works that way. In fact, when a vendor quotes longer lead times to his customer, he almost always winds up with a bigger backlog of orders. If, for example, a vendor had been quoting a ten week lead time and now quotes a fifteen week lead time, his customers will have to plan to cover all of their requirements five weeks farther out than they normally did. This will result in sending the vendor an extra five weeks worth of purchase orders, thus increasing the vendor's backlog and his lead time. If he once again quotes a longer lead time, most of his customers will send him more purchase orders until they get throughly disgusted with him and start going to his competition. In many industries, however, such as the gray iron foundries in the United States, capacity is often tight. As one foundry increases its lead time and customers start placing orders with competitors, the competitors wind up in a capacity squeeze and then start increasing their lead time. A small increase in lead time can easily be escalated into a total lead time that is patently absurd. It is not uncommon for gray iron foundries to be quoting lead times of 36 to 48 weeks to make castings that can easily be produced in five working days!

What happens to the vendor when this small capacity bottleneck is finally eliminated? Under extreme pressure from his sales department, he reduces his quoted lead time from 48 weeks to 40 weeks. The salesman is delighted to convey this information to the customer's purchasing department. They convey it to production and inventory control who then build it back into their inventory control system. Since lead time is shorter than it was before, there is really very little they need to order right now!

Back at the vendor, the flow of incoming orders slows down. The sales department is panic stricken and decides that the competition must be getting the business. They insist upon a further reduction in lead time. When this is relayed to the customers inventory control group, they further reduce their planned lead times. This generates fewer orders and reduces the input to the vendor which further reduces his backlog of orders! One bearing manufacturer was quoting a forty-eight week lead time in one product line and twelve months later could quote a three week lead time in the same line. Three weeks is probably pretty realistic for assembling a bearing from stocked parts, but what happened to the forty-five week backlog? It seems difficult to believe that this company could have produced fifty-two weeks of normal production and also produced enough to eliminate forty-five weeks work of backlogs. This would be equivalent to ninety-seven normal weeks of production in a year! They really went through the lead time "deflation" cycle after having previously had their lead times inflated to forty-eight weeks (probably because of a *small* capacity bottleneck).

The role of lead time inflation has never been thoroughly explored in the study of business cycles. It certainly has made an important contribution, particularly since the increase in backlog tends to increase the real volume that a company has to handle because as people try to forecast their requirements farther and farther out into the future, they are less and less accurate. They suddenly find things that they need very quickly that they were not able to anticipate. When they go to order these from their suppliers, the suppliers quote them extremely long lead times *principally because they currently have backlogs made up of other items that this customer and other customers tried to forecast far in advance of requirements.*

Most systems have good expediting capability but very little "unexpediting" capability. Since the customer seldom has a good enough inventory system so that he can see what he doesn't need today, he almost always winds up adding the new item that he knows he needs to an existing backlog which has many items in it that he no longer needs. The result is a very real increase in volume just when capacity is tightest. The correct technique to handle this problem will be discussed below, but certainly one thing should be obvious to the reader:

if the reaction to longer lead times is to order material farther in advance, this will only increase backlogs and increase lead times.

No. 2 *ERRATIC PLANT INPUT*—Releasing jobs to the manufacturing floor as the system generates requirements always results in a highly erratic input to the shop. Witness these figures from a company that has an extremely stable assembly production rate. These figures represent the number of standard hours of work generated over a ten week period for parts made on one particular group of screw machines:

Week	Standard Hours
1	286 hours
2	50 hours
3	147 hours
4	176 hours
5	695 hours
6	531 hours
7	139 hours
8	321 hours
9	61 hours
10	284 hours

This is truly random input and consists of total hours generated each week. No attempt has been made to show the number of pieces or the number of shop orders created each week, since that is not relevant to the discussion. The important point to see is the tremendous variation in input rate. If a foreman is to run his department on schedule, he should produce fifty hours worth of work in one week and in another week he should make 695 hours worth of work. This type of thinking might have been reasonable during the 30's. Indeed, much of our production control technology being used today—even that being implemented on computers—dates back to the 30's when dramatic changes in capacity were not only possible but were quite economical because there was such a large surplus of available labor. Obviously, no plant today could produce the hours as input in this example. Any foreman in his right mind would try to run a fairly stable production rate. But how could he possibly run at a stable rate with this erratic input? The obvious answer is that he cannot; therefore, he does the best he can: he tries to run at a stable rate by running in a perpetual behind schedule condition. Obviously, in a week like Week No. 5, when 695 hours are required, somebody will have to make a decision as to which hours are required first. When the inventory planner passes that burden to the foreman, he has insured that an expediter will have to come into the picture to straighten out the mess which production and inventory control should have straightened out in the first place by recognizing the necessity to run the plant at a fairly stable rate. Erratic input of this type makes it necessary for the foreman to run in a constant behind schedule condition and, since he is never sure how much work is coming to him in the future, he always feels that large backlogs are necessary and the best guarantee of steady work rates in the future.

This belief coupled with production control's usual abdication of responsibility for keeping work flowing to the foreman at a steady rate, tends to aggravate the problem of backlogs out on the factory floor. This is where backlogs really cause the most problems. *How many expediters would really be necessary in a company where there was only one job behind each operation?* In most companies, expediters are constantly reshuffling the backlog that never should have been allowed to get into the factory in the first place.

In fact, as production control continues to put jobs into a plant that is already far behind schedule, their entire scheduling system ceases to function with any degree of effectiveness. Whenever there is a capacity bottleneck, the most important question to ask is, "Which job should be done first?" The production and inventory control system in many companies would be able to give only one answer under these circumstances, "They're all late—we need them all". This is why expediting has become such a frantic effort in most manufacturing companies. The cycle can be predicted very reliably: any small capacity bottleneck will be followed by an aggravation of the backlog situation in the factory and this will be followed by increasing amounts of expediting. Expediting seems to fit one definition of fanaticism:

"A fanatic is a man who redoubles his efforts when all hope of reaching the goal has been lost".

Obviously, putting orders into a shop on the date when they are supposed to be started, regardless of capacity, doesn't really make a great deal of sense. If the shop is behind on capacity, and input exceeds output, the orders will all show up late and it will be very difficult to determine what the real priorities are, particularly since these are quite likely to have changed since the orders were originally released. If the inventory system doesn't generate orders one week, it behooves people in production and inventory control to try to smooth out the input. If they don't, the foremen will have to. A brief acquaintance with any foreman, or for that matter, any production worker, will convince the observer that he has no confidence that anything but big backlogs out in the factory will guarantee a steady flow of work for him. A low level of shop backlog can be maintained only if jobs are released to the plant at a steady rate. This means that some jobs will have to be started somewhat earlier than their normal release dates and occasionally some will have to be started somewhat later. The calculations that are made to determine lead time are approximate and it is reasonable and right to juggle the actual starting time of an order to smooth the input.

No. 3 *INABILITY TO PLAN AND CONTROL OUTPUT RATES*—Figure 1 shows a typical machine load report. There would usually also be detailed load information showing order by order the jobs that constitute the load in each week. While the format has been simplified, nothing has been left out that would bear on the current discussion. Note that the load shows the weekly capacity. This is usually adjusted to reflect the shop's ability to convert actual working hours into standard hours. For example, if it takes forty hours of actual time to produce thirty-two standard hours of work, the shop is said to be working at 80% of capacity and that figure

```
┌─────────────────────────────────────────┐
│                                          │
│         MACHINE LOAD REPORT              │
│                                          │
│         Work Center 5910                 │
│    (All figures in standard hours)       │
│                                          │
│                                          │
│    WEEKLY CAPACITY  240 HR.              │
│    PRODUCTION LAST WEEK  205 HR.         │
│                                          │
│  Week Ending    Load    Over/Under Load  │
│                                          │
│  Past Due       824        + 584         │
│     706         286        +  46         │
│     711          50        − 190         │
│     716         247        +   7         │
│     721         196        −  64         │
│     726         690        + 450         │
│     731         130        − 110         │
│     734         139        − 101         │
│     739          27        − 213         │
│     744          68        − 172         │
│     749          84        − 156         │
│                                          │
└─────────────────────────────────────────┘
```

Figure 1

is reflected in the capacity figure shown on the machine load report. Note that the machine load report also shows the production for last week, which, in this case, was quite a bit below what is obviously required. It shows a very erratic workload with the load tapering off dramatically after the bulge in Week 726. This report in its raw form is practically useless for the following reasons:

1 It doesn't project capacity requirements far enough into the future to be of real value to the foreman in making economical changes in capacity; i.e., hiring and training of people, buying new machinery, etc.

2. It shows work scheduled to be produced at widely varying rates week to week with a limited number of machines and a limited number of men. Because this is certainly not the way production will actually run, it is not a realistic plan for the foreman.

3. It does not provide a workable "norm" against which a department's performance can be measured. Since we don't really expect the foreman to produce at these weekly rates, how do we measure him?

4. It doesn't really tell us very much about what the actual capacity is. It tells us the theoretical capacity and the actual output for one week, typically.

5. It is almost impossible to learn anything about the input/output relationship that actually controls the backlog (and, in turn, controls the lead time) from a machine load report.

Machine load reports are a tool that was probably moderately effective in the past. In the 30's, manpower was readily available and capacity could be expanded or contracted on very short notice. During the 40's and 50's, large backlogs of orders existed. Even though manpower was not readily available, plenty of time was available to make significant adjustments in capacity. Today, the need to keep people working at a stable rate is recognized by practically every company. We have two conflicting pressures:

the pressure to plan farther ahead at the same time that there is less backlog that can be used for planning purposes.

These, then, are three problems that aggravate the backlog—and thus the lead time—problem:

1. Lead time inflation.
2. Erratic input.
3. Inability to plan and control output rates.

Our classical production control techniques were not designed to address these problems. Machine loading has been adopted and discarded by many companies. Yet, machine loading approaches, particularly if done by computer, *can* be used effectively to plan and control capacity—but only if they are used in conjunction with a new kind of report—the input/output report.

Input/Output Controls

There is one simple rule for controlling backlogs and thus controlling lead time and that is:

THE INPUT TO A SHOP MUST BE EQUAL TO OR LESS THAN THE OUTPUT.

There is practically nothing in any of the classical production or inventory control systems that focuses anyone's attention on the relationship of *input* to *output*, yet it is this fundamental relationship that is the most important one, not only in getting production under control but in stabilizing lead times so that inventories can be managed effectively. Input/output control is the only way to control backlogs and thus control lead time.

This tool *has* been developed by some companies. But not enough manufacturing executives today have even recognized how critical it is to have a tool that:

1. Projects capacity requirements far into the future.
2. Shows them at a level rate.
3. Shows the relationship between input and output.

Figure 2 shows an input/output report. The work rate at a work center has been planned and in the planning, the rate has been levelled out. Note that this was planned without actually scheduling individual orders. If schedule dates were put on orders far in advance, the dates would be meaningless by the time these orders were due to be released. Because it is possible to do a reasonable job of forecasting when larger groups are forecast, the total production rate required for a work center can usually be predicted with reasonable accuracy. In Figure 2, the output rate has been pegged at 300 hours per week for the first four weeks

INPUT/OUTPUT CONTROLS

Work Center 0138
(All figures in standard hours)

	Week Ending	505	512	519	526	533	540	547	554	561	568
Unreleased Backlog **0**	Planned Input	270	270	270	270	270	270	270	270	270	270
	Actual Input	270	265	250							
	Cumulative Deviation		−5	−25							
Released* **Backlog** **120 HR.**	Planned Output	300	300	300	300	270	270	270	270	270	270
	Actual Output	305	260	280							
	Cumulative Deviation	+5	−35	−55							

*Above desired level of work-in-process (standard queue) at this work center as of start of plan.

Figure 2

and then 270 hours per week. Note that the input rate is planned to be 270 hours per week as far out as the plan goes. (These plans have been abbreviated. Most of them would tend to go out twelve to twenty-five weeks into the future to give an adequate planning horizon to enable foremen to adjust capacity.) The planned output is higher than the planned input for the first four weeks. This is intended to reduce the existing released backlog by 120 standard hours.

Note that this input/output report shows the planned output at a fairly level rate. It also shows the actual output rather than the theoretical capacity and the output for one week as the machine load report did. We can get a far better idea from it of whether or not we have adequate capacity in this particular work center. The report also clearly indicates whether or not backlog, and consequently, lead time in this work center is building up. If this work center is a starting work center and it is fed by the inventory control or scheduling system, the input can be regulated to meet the planned rate. There is no need to continue to put work into the shop at a faster rate than they are taking it out. Many production control people tend to do this because *their present systems only show a capacity deficit when they have actually overloaded the shop.* Note that the input/output report will show that output has been insufficient *even if load has not been released to the shop.*

One of the rules that is usually used with this type of report is that input in any given week cannot exceed output the previous week. Note that in Week 519, the scheduler looking at the output from the previous week released only 250 hours of work (theoretically, he would have released 260, the same rate that was put out the previous week, but lot sizes will generally make it necessary to adjust this slightly upward or downward in real life). He can hold back work—as he should when the shop cannot produce it—and still see that the shop is not producing on schedule. By holding orders in production control, he can be sure that the priority on orders when they are released is the very latest. This will also avoid building the large in-plant queues that *always* generate excessive expediting.

The input/output report meets all the requirements for good lead time control. It shows a production plan far out into the future, since it shows it in total only. It measures capacity in terms of total hours rather than late orders out in the shop.

What's the "input" to the input/output report? The same computer program that is used to create the classical machine load can be used to create the input/output planning information. This planning information consists of a forecast of the usage of parts over the next few months. The planning horizon can be at the company's option. Most companies like to see an idea of what they're going to need in the way of manpower at least twelve to thirteen weeks ahead of time; therefore, production plans are usually reviewed monthly and extended out ninety days into the future. This does not include the less frequent, usually quarterly, production plans that are used to plan facilities requirements and extend out one to two years.

A company that has a time phased requirements planning system can periodically put their best estimate of future schedules into the computer program and then put the planned orders into a machine load program to generate a report like that shown in Figure 3. This machine load projection isn't a real load report—it's a *forecast* of the total amount of work that will be required in a work center over a period of time. The objective is *not* to schedule and load the individual orders. Capacity will be *planned in total hours* and then this plan will be levelled out to give the planned output rate for a work center. With input/output control, the machine load report has two functions:

1. When forecasts are put into the machine loading program, the average required production rate can be set up as the "planned output" requirement.

2. Once input/output control reports are established, the machine load report *can* be used to show where short term bottlenecks are developing. In most companies, the input/output reports will do this job without additional machine load reports.

Machine loading without input/output control is a poor tool for keeping lead time under control in a manufacturing company. Input/output—used properly—will enable a company to control lead times.

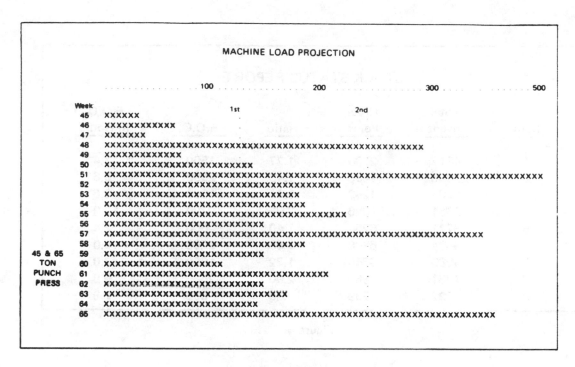

Figure 3

Controlling Input

Once capacity plans have been established, the individual items to be scheduled must be put into the plant *at the planned rate and at the last possible moment* so that their schedule dates can be made more accurate by forecasting over a shorter period of time. This can result in more accurate dates on shop orders. Highly inaccurate dates exist in most companies today because lead times are extremely long and it is, therefore, necessary to forecast individual item completion dates far out into the future. Because of this, it is common to walk into any manufacturing department and find that many jobs are well behind schedule, yet if you ask the foreman about these jobs, he'll tell you that nobody is looking for them. This indicates that the original dates on the orders were forecast sometime in the past and are no longer valid or it would be a symptom of a *very* poor inventory system!

The techniques for controlling input to meet a planned rate are not difficult to implement, particularly when a machine load program is available on a computer. The approach varies depending on the inventory system being used, the availability of a machine load report with planned orders (usually generated by a material requirements planning computer program) shown on it, and the type of work center involved. There are many work centers out in the shop where it is possible to plan the required input/output rates, but it is difficult to control the input since this is fed in from previous work centers. There are other work centers that are the "gateways" to the shop. These are starting operations like turret lathes, screw machines, presses, and work is fed into them from scheduling or often from inventory control itself.

STOCK STATUS REPORT

Item	Total Invent	Order Point	Ratio	E.O.Q.	E.O.Q. in Hours
1	4817	2730	1.77	1500	7.4
2	2056	1436	1.43	2500	8.6
3	5963	4242	1.41	1000	3.6
4	2851	1386	2.06	2700	12.8
5	8771	6250	1.40	500	2.4
6	9894	6768	1.46	2250	10.0
7	4080	3346	1.22	1000	7.0
8	1781	866	2.06	2500	9.8
9	192	239	.80	500	2.8

Figure 4

Figure 4 shows one approach to handling this problem. In this case, the inventory control system is an order point system and the ratio of order point to the inventory on hand and on order ("total" inventory) is shown. This facilitates picking which job to put into production next since it is not at all unusual to have a situation where, due to seasonal inventory build-ups, most items are above order point. The ratio then tells which item ought to be scheduled into production first. In this case, Item 9 should go in first, Item 7 should go in second, etc. The order quantity is shown in pieces and also in hours. Where a planned input rate must be attained, the inventory control man can determine which items to put into production to hit the planned rate. Obviously, if there is not enough capacity to handle all of the items that he would like to run, he must decide which ones are most important. This works out far better in practice than having him order everything he wants and then having expediters trying to sort it out after it has hit a badly overloaded factory.

In a company using a requirements plan generated by computer, the inventory report shows "planned order releases" for past due, current, and future periods. If these planned orders are then put into a machine load program, the detailed load report will show the number of hours that are planned to be released to the gateway work centers each week. When these hours do not meet the planned input rate, the scheduler can go back to the inventory planners and ask them to move some orders up a week or back a week. Since the material requirements plan should have been used to project the planned input rates, any variation in input rates should be purely random. In practice, if this is done well, there are far fewer occasions than most production control people imagine where orders have to be moved up or pushed back more than a week to keep the input rates steady.

Inventory control people frequently rebel at the idea of keeping the input rate steady. Somehow they feel that the starting date on any order is inviolable. Anyone who knows how lead times are calculated in most scheduling systems knows that even in the best run companies they are an approximation at best. Smoothing out the input rates makes a lot more sense than trying to put orders out into a shop that is overloaded or holding orders back from a shop that is running out of work.

Still another approach can be taken to controlling input. It really amounts to controlling input by exception. With this approach, orders are released to the gateway work centers as they come out of the inventory scheduling system, unless the input/output report shows a substantial deviation in actual input from planned input. When this occurs, action is taken to search out orders that can either be held back or pulled up to correct the input deviation.

There's plenty of good reason for smoothing input so that it's not erratic. Erratic input requires large queues of work to absorb the ups and downs in the workload. Many people ask, "How much work-in-process *should* we have?" The answer is that queues exist in the factory primarily to absorb the fluctuations in input rates. One company, for example, sampled the backlogs behind a particular operation over a long period of time and found that the greatest number of containers of work they ever had behind that operation was 125. The smallest number they ever had was 75. This means that the fluctuation rate was within the range of 50; in fact, this is what the normal allowed queue should have been. At a gateway work center, this fluctuation rate can be reduced to practically nothing and *there is no excuse for having large queues of released orders in front of these gateway operations.*.

How can we control the input to intermediate operations? This is a far more difficult proposition since the workload is coming in from many diverse areas typically. Nevertheless, the input/output report can be used to monitor input rates and when these are dropping or falling, the machine load report can be used to pinpoint jobs in preceding operations that should be rescheduled to smooth out the input. One approach that has occurred to a few companies is to analyze their capacity requirements by key work center. They usually find that a little scheduling attention to a small number of items can do quite a bit to take some of the peaks and troughs out of the input to intermediate work centers.

Why all the attention to smoothing input? Obviously, the smoother the input rate, the less backlog the shop must have and the shorter their lead time can be. By not releasing work into the gateway work centers from the scheduling or inventory control systems at a higher rate than previous weeks output, backlogs are held in production and inventory control rather than released to the shop. This reduces expediting and confusion. It places the decision for which item to run when capacity is tight in the hands of the inventory planner who is best equipped to do it. Forcing him to decide how he can best use his limited capacity resources when output is falling behind the plan or what he would like to start first when the inventory system must be forced to generate some input to meet the plan.

Input/output control is a far cry from the classical approaches to production and inventory control. Some companies have applied input/output controls already and the results have been dramatic.

Some Examples of Input/output Control

The General Manager of one medium sized manufacturing company decided that the principles of input/output control made some sense in his plant. Lead time on a particular product line was running six weeks and, while this was not abnormally high or uncompetitive, it seemed to him that it could be reduced. He set up input/output controls and planned the output at a level that would reduce the in-plant backlog from the normal six weeks of work-in-process to five weeks. He then went to the inventory control people and told them that lead time in the future would be five weeks instead of six weeks. In spite of his high position in the company, he was greeted with a degree of skepticism. The inventory people felt that he was tampering with some of the natural laws of nature! One was heard to remark, "The next thing he'll be telling us is that we can't have rainy weather".

By setting his output slightly higher than his input and reducing backlogs, he was able to reduce lead time from six weeks to five weeks, in spite of the skeptics. In fact, by telling inventory control that their lead time was only five weeks, he got an almost perfect reduction in input, since they released very few orders the first week the shorter lead time was in effect. This general manager also charged his inventory control people with keeping a smooth flow of work into the shop. He told them it was their responsibility to decide which orders had to be done first. They couldn't just send them all out into the shop regardless of the shop's capacity, and thus automatically create the need for expediting.

Having been successful in reducing lead time from six weeks to five weeks, he proceeded to reduce it to four weeks by increasing the output rate above the input rate once again. Again, he told the people in inventory control that their lead time would be reduced from five weeks to four weeks. Again, they were skeptical; but again, because he did bring the backlogs down in the factory from a five week level to a four week level, lead time was reduced to four weeks, which to him seemed very satisfactory. He had done it all empirically; he had found that there was really very little increase in the amount of idle time for lack of work out in the shop. Without any attempt to be scientific, he feels now that this 50% reduction in lead time represents a very satisfactory achievement in a few short month's time.

While very few companies have ever done anything scientific to decide on the level of work-in-process that they should have, many manufacturing oriented people within the companies feel that the level of work-in-process they have is just barely adequate. Most foremen are deathly afraid that they will run out of work—and for good reason. The foreman has little or no control over the flow of work into his department. The control of input lies with other departments or with production control itself. Very few foremen have any confidence that production control will keep work flowing to them at a steady rate and they're usually justified in this feeling. Therefore, the presence of physical backlogs in the factory is the only security they know.

Management has aggravated this problem considerably. One of the fundamental rules of management is to measure people on those functions that they truly control. The foreman feels that he is measured on idle time for lack of material. If a man is standing around, a great deal of pressure is on him to get rid of the man. On the other hand, the production control man feels he is responsible for getting work out the door on schedule. *Doesn't it make better sense to put the responsibility for hitting the schedule on the foreman and the responsibility for keeping work flowing through the shop at a steady rate on production control?*

Some companies today charge all idle time for lack of work to production control. Other companies say they never have idle time for lack of work, but the fact of the matter is, they have many indirect charges such as broken tools, looking for skids, etc. that tend to grow drastically when workers see backlogs on the floor decreasing. They would probably be better off to pay these people for standing around than to hide their heads in the sand over the very real problem of idle time for lack of material. By the same token, trying to carry enough work-in-process so that there will never by any idle time generates excessively long lead times. It is discouraging to see company policies that are aimed at making it impossible to have a man occasionally standing idle for lack of material while they spend large amounts of money on:

1. Work-in-process inventory.
2. Inventories to protect against the large forecast errors that result when lead times are long.
3. Excessive expediting.
4. Missed schedules because large queues make it so difficult to make the *right* item.

The problem of educating machine operators so that they will not be afraid of running out of work when they see shop floor backlogs decrease is a real one. It is necessary to assure them that the work flow will continue to come or they will tend to slow down. Even companies with an incentive system can have a dramatic slowdown without the employee losing much in wages, as any man who has filled out a time ticket can attest! Some companies have fought this problem by posting on the departmental bulletin board the planned production rates as in-plant backlogs were reduced. Others have done it through education programs and by informing employees that indirect charges were going to be watched very closely as the new program was instituted. Others *pay* operators for idle time due to lack of material. Obviously, education is extremely important when a work-in-process reduction is generated. A serious work slowdown—often unconscious—can result if the education program is neglected.

Let's look at another example to illustrate the input/output relationship. A company installed the Critical Ratio priority system. This priority system is a dynamic priority system which gives a good updated relative priority for every job in the shop. Lead time quickly decreased and jobs seemed to be coming out on schedule far better than they ever had before. They were delighted with the results of Critical Ratio. Unfortunately, a short time later, things started to deteriorate and they couldn't understand it. Analyzing the problem, it was found that at the same time they instituted their Critical Ratio program, they added 40 direct labor people to the second shift. This resulted in an increase in output at the same time that input wasn't increasing dramatically. Later on, an increase in sales caused an increase in input. The increase in input built up backlogs again and lead times once again got longer. As longer queues built up in the shop, job selection became a much more difficult problem and more and more jobs came through behind schedule. The Critical Ratio technique is an excellent priority technique, but this company mistakenly assumed that it could control lead time with a priority technique. Only input/output controls can really control lead time.

Many companies have problems with their vendors. One midwest company, recognizing the importance of input/output controls and the basic principle that capacity should be forecast without committing themselves to actual orders, set up a very effective program with one of their foundries. They commit themselves to run a given number of molds down each line in the foundry as far out as the foundry would like to have this commitment. They do not specify the actual orders they're going to run. Six weeks ahead of time they specify the actual orders they're going to run. In effect, they have blocked out capacity at the foundry and committed themselves to it, but they haven't committed themselves to forecasting far in advance which orders they want to run within that capacity.

This approach also forces their inventory control people to take a look at the requirements for castings every week and determine what they think they need six weeks ahead of time. They're in a position at the present time where they can get any casting they want from this foundry in six weeks. Any of their competition ordering castings from the same foundry would have to wait twenty-two weeks! Ironically, if this company had done what the foundry had originally requested them to do, they would have increased their lead time in their inventory system until they had actual orders out at the foundry twenty two weeks in advance. If they then needed an order in a hurry, the foundry would honestly have told them that it would take twenty-two weeks to get it! The logic of projecting capacity requirements and then scheduling actual orders to meet these plans seems to be hard to get through to manufacturing people, but its benefits are dramatic.

The production control manager of one midwest company was told by one of his vendors that lead time had increased from twelve weeks to twenty weeks. He put this information into his computer and the computer promptly reacted by generating orders for eight additional weeks. The production control manager boxed these orders and shipped them by freight to the vendor. The vendor called and asked where all the orders came from. The production control manager told him that these were orders to cover the extra lead time that had been requested. The vendor indicated that he already had file drawers full of orders and had hired two clerks to file these orders and re-file them as customers called in schedule changes. Our astute production control manager told his vendor that it was his experience that as lead time increased, the number of reschedules went up geometrically! (He was right. This is the result of the inability to forecast in detail far into the future with any degree of accuracy). The production control manager volunteered to give the vendor any "further help" that he might require. He asked if perhaps the vendor would like to have orders covering thirty weeks lead time, or forty weeks, or fifty. It's a simple matter to put this information into a computer and to generate bales of paper representing orders which probably will have to be rescheduled many, many times before they are actually delivered. Yet the number of manufacturing executives who realize the folly of increasing planning lead times when their capacity thightens up is still very small indeed!

The lead time that people use to plan has a very significant effect upon the rate of input itself. Using shorter lead times also helps people to forecast over a shorter period of time and to predict more accurately what their detailed requirements will be.

The production control manager of a sizeable company that makes carpets and carries them in inventory was very unhappy because his plant could not produce according to schedule. The order points on the carpets were based on a lead time given to him by the factory plus a safety stock to cover forecast deviation over lead time. When the loom capacity proved to be inadequate to meet his requirements, a great many orders fell past due in the factory and the actual manufacturing lead time increased. Agreat many people pressured this production control manager to increase his planning lead times. Recognizing that this would only generate more orders to an already overloaded shop, he decided to do exactly the opposite! He decreased his lead times in the inventory control system.

This generated less input, allowed the shop to clear up most of the backlog that they had in-process, and enabled him to predict more accurately the items that he really needed to get through his limited capacity since he was predicting his requirements over a shorter span into the future! Without any increase in capacity or any increase in finished goods inventory, he was able to generate a very substantial increase in customer service level by making more of the *right* items.

Many people would question the logic of reducing lead time to less than the actual manufacturing lead time, but there are really *two lead times* in production and inventory control. One is the *actual lead time* that it takes to produce a product and another one is a *control* that we can use in the system that will enable us to cut back on input and to forecast over a shorter period in the future what we actually need. When lead times in the factory increase because of inadequate capacity, the solution is not to increase planning lead times, since this will simply increase backlog. Increasing backlogs will increase expediting. This problem will be aggravated because we will be predicting less accurately what we actually need. The real answer is to introduce input/output controls, and a reduction in the planned lead time can help by getting the *right* items into production.

The relationship of lead time to backlog is seldom really understood, but it was brought into sharp focus in one company with the introduction of input/output controls. One significant manufacturing process had a lead time of six weeks. There was two weeks of backlog behind a badly bottlenecked starting operation. By using the input/output controls, they held back work and put in no more than the operation had turned out in the previous week. They showed the deficiency in capacity through the input/output report rather than through backlogs of actual orders. After a short period of time, they found their actual manufacturing lead time was not six weeks as they originally thought but was, in fact, two weeks. The input/output control had reduced the in-plant backlog so dramatically that, in spite of the capacity bottleneck, the work that was released to the shop was going through in a shorter period of time. Since lead time had been reduced to two weeks, they reflected this back into their inventory control system. As a result the inventory control system then did not release any substantial number of orders over a four week period of time and the company found that an operation that they thought had a two week backlog of unreleased work behind it, in fact, had no work behind it. They had to force orders out of their inventory control system to keep work flowing into what had been a badly bottlenecked operation a few weeks before! Obviously, when capacity is really needed, holding input down does not really solve the capacity problem; it does enable you to do a better job of getting the *right* items. Too often, however, the lack of input/output controls and lead time inflation can create artificial backlogs. Many companies sub-contract, work overtime, and add people just to handle backlogs created by lead time inflation.

Another company that manufactures a product sold almost exclusively to customer order found that their 8 1/2 week quoted lead time consisted of four weeks for scheduling and four and 1/2 weeks for manufacturing. By measuring the *rate* of incoming orders from customers, they found that there wasn't a very substantial variation in input rate. The random variations really tended to cancel each other over a short period of time. By monitoring the input rate, they could see trends up or down and actually plan and control their capacity more effectively than by holding big backlogs of customer orders. They also found that when they needed to make work because incoming orders were low, they could pull ahead orders for many of their larger customers who gave them schedules well into the future. The result in this company was to reduce their lead time from 8 1/2 weeks to five weeks. They found that they only needed to maintain 1/2 week of backlog of orders when they started using input/output controls to control capacity rather than using backlogs. There is an important concept here: our classical approaches to production control muddle the problems of getting "enough" and getting the "right ones". Input/output control forces us to look at each separately.

The Basic Principles of Input/output Control

There are really only two basic questions to be addressed in production control.

1. ARE WE GETTING *ENOUGH?*
2. ARE WE GETTING THE *RIGHT ONES?*

Think about the typical job shop with 30 or 40% of the jobs past due—yet no one is even expediting most of them—they aren't really needed! When this kind of situation exists we don't know where we stand. Are we really short of capacity—then why don't we seem to need the late jobs? Are we getting the right ones—if they are late and not needed it doesn't even seem that we are *asking* for the right ones!

The solutions to these two problems—"enough" and the "right ones" are very different. If we are not getting enough output, we need more capacity. If we are not getting the right ones, either our inventory control system is poor (not an uncommon problem) or we don't work on the right jobs in the plant. If we don't know which problem we have, the odds are great we won't solve it very effectively.

At the root of the input/output concept are two forecast characteristics (Figure 5).

Forecasts are more accurate over short periods of time and less accurate over long periods of time. If we try to predict our sales for next week, we can do this with a greater degree of

	ACCURATE	INACCURATE
HORIZON	SHORT	LONG
GROUP	LARGE	SMALL

Figure 5

accuracy than we can predict sales for a week, six months out into the future. Forecasting is like aiming a gun—the closer you get to the target, the closer you are likely to come to the bullseye.

Forecasts are more accurate for larger groups of items than they are for smaller groups of items. If you were to try to forecast the height of the next man you might meet, your chances of being accurate would be considerably less than if you tried to forecast the height of the next ten men that you might meet.

The marketing department, for example, can always do a better job of forecasting total dollars of sales than they can of forecasting individual items.

In practically every company, trying to determine how much is "enough" and which ones are the "right ones" implies some sort of forecasting. Obviously, then, we ought to recognize these forecast characteristics in the design of our inventory and production management systems. A second glance at the forecast characteristics above makes it obvious that when we are trying to plan capacity ("enough") where we must, by definition, extend our forecast out over a fairly long horizon, we should never try to firm up our plans for manufacturing individual items over that same horizon. The chart shows us that long horizon forecasts tend to be inaccurate. The worst possible situation is to try and forecast small groups of items over a long horizon, or individual items over a long horizon. Far better to forecast a large group of items over the long horizon. The group being the items that go through a particular work center, for example.

Let's try to express, then, the basic principles of input/output control:

1. *Separate the planning and control of capacity from the planning and control of mix.*
2. *Plan capacity requirements in the largest possible groups of items.*
3. *Put the required date on individual items at the last possible moment, i.e., forecast over the shortest possible horizon.*
4. *Never put into a manufacturing facility or to a vendor's facility more than you believe that he can produce. Hold backlogs in production and inventory control.*

The reasons behind these principles should be apparent to the reader at this point. The fourth principle in particular will be hard to teach to many inventory control people. It is difficult for them to understand that when a shop is behind they should not release their backlogs to it. The minute they do, they lose control over getting the right ones through. Expediters must take over and the result is expense, chaos, and confusion. This doesn't say that we shouldn't do our best to have the plant meet our capacity requirements. It does say that using the input/output concept, we can measure capacity deficiencies without releasing backlog to the shop. It also recognizes that when capacity is tight, nobody is in a better position than the inventory planner or scheduler to determine exactly which items should be run within the limited capacity.

Any executive who assumes that these principles are understood in his production and inventory control department or even by higher level manufacturing executives should first look at the literature and education available to manufacturing people. Little of it has ever discussed lead time! He should then look at his production and inventory control system quickly. Are there input/output controls? Are there techniques that show this vital relationship clearly or are the production control techniques classical techniques that tend to obscure the relationship of input and output and to allow backlogs to develop and to get out onto the factory floor where they can't really be controlled but can only generate excessive expediting?

He should be particularly on guard when people tell him that lead time should be increased. Increasing lead times used to order inventory will only result in the increased backlog and expediting. As inventory people try to forecast farther in advance to cover the longer lead times, their guesses get worse. This means more wrong items get made. When capacity is tight, it's *essential* to get the *right* items made or purchased.

The executive should be particularly concerned when computer systems are being applied. Many computer technicians feel that putting any system on a computer will improve it. They pick up "cookbook" techniques and apply them blindly. Unfortunately, unsound applications on computers tend to be as bad or worse than unsound applications manually and to draw attention away from the real problems.

Because an article must necessarily be brief, it is easy to leave the impression that the solution proposed is the complete solution to a problem. Let me hasten to emphasize that, while lead time control is essential to good inventory control, a good inventory control system is also needed. Far too many companies that make assembled products, for example, try to order parts based on historical averages rather than projected assembly requirements. This approach can also contribute to having many "late" jobs in process that are not really needed. Input/output control without a good inventory control system is only half a loaf.

Dramatic new approaches require management understanding and support if they are to work. Plant supervision that is used to living with big in-plant backlogs, workers who are afraid of layoffs when work piles dwindle, and production control people who are used to classical concepts like machine loading will have to be educated, directed, and reassured as lead times are reduced. They will have to be reminded that they cannot really cite any instance where lengthening lead times really made things better and taught to understand what lead time really is.

Control of lead time is vital to any scheduling and to any form of inventory control. Every inventory control system has as its foundation some assumption as to what the actual lead time will be. Very few production control systems actually have the tools in them to bring backlogs sharply into focus and to keep them under control. The introduction of input/output controls and the training of people to use these effectively can be a major step in improving customer service, reducing inventory, and stabilizing production rates in a manufacturing company.

Reprinted from the APICS *1981 Conference Proceedings.*

PRACTICAL DISPATCHING

Jan B. Young
Data Systems Division
A. O. Smith Corporation

This paper is intended to acquaint the reader with the importance of dispatching and to suggest some ideas that may be useful. We will review the state of the art briefly, list some needs and potentials, and present some practical ideas.

We will be concerned only with job shops. For several reasons, the dispatching of process shops is fundamentally different and is beyond our scope.

THE "DISPATCHER"

"What do I do next, Boss?"

That one question defines the dispatcher's role as the individual responsible for assigning work. In more formal words, the dispatcher:

1) Selects, among competing jobs, the one which is to be done next,

2) Allocates personnel, equipment, materials, tooling and supplies and,

3) Gives the work direction necessary to move the selected job through one more step in the production process.

In many plants, dispatching is a part time duty of the supervisor or "lead man". In other cases, there are full time people who are responsible for both dispatching and timekeeping. Sometimes dispatching is centralized with one person or a small group responsible for all work assignment throughout the plant. Or, it may be decentralized with each work group or department making its own decisions.

All too often, management fails to understand the importance of dispatching in a successful business. Even P&IC professionals often think of it as a mechanical, semi-clerical function which has little real impact on the bottom line. We should begin by emphasizing that dispatching is far more than a clerical function.

The individual dispatching decision - whether to dispatch job A or job B - is not normally critical to the success or failure of the company. If job A should go first, but job B accidentally gets put in front, we can usually compensate for the error elsewhere.

But, remember this: In a typical job shop each employee will be assigned work between 4 and 10 times per day. Let's assume that we are working in a $100 million dollar business with 400 hourly employees. In this shop there could easily be 2000 dispatching decisions made per day.

If dispatching decisions have an average impact of $2, they aren't very important by themselves. Certainly few of us can justify much time to worry about a $2 decision. But, taken all together, the dispatching process in this hypothetical plant is worth $4,000 per day. If the plant works 240 days per year, the total value is $1 million per year. Can we afford to ignore that kind of opportunity?

Of course these numbers include some very broad assumptions. Just because you work in a $100 million business, there is no guarantee of a million-dollar savings. But, obviously, dispatching can be important.

THE DISPATCHING DECISION

The dispatching process revolves around the decision made when an employee reports the completion of one job and becomes available for more work. If we can improve the way that this decision is made, we automatically improve the entire dispatching process.

Dispatching has three reasonable objectives:

1) To meet schedules as best possible, given the situation as of the moment,

2) To utilize people, equipment, tooling, materials and supplies to the best advantage, and

3) To avoid problems in areas such as quality, labor relations, customer service, and others.

If these objectives are to be met, dispatching has to be a planning process. When a job is dispatched, the dispatcher's mental processes involve many of the same elements that we use on a more aggregate basis in master scheduling and MRP. For instance, there is concern for material availability, for lead times and economical lot sizes, and for equipment capacity.

In most businesses the dispatcher only has visibility into the next shift or two. The horizon is limited by the rate at which things change in the shop and the amount of time which the dispatcher can afford to spend planning. Since a large amount of detailed information is required to do a good job of dispatch planning, it can be a time-consuming job. Limiting the planning horizon limits the time spent.

Some examples of the things that a good dispatcher has to know about are:

1) The status - now and in the short term future - of people, machines, tools, materials and supplies.

2) Schedule dates and the relative importance of meeting those dates for all orders. Included is a sensitivity to the needs of other departments, of the customers, and of the boss.

3) Problems of all kinds which affect production. For instance, quality problems, shortages, engineering changes, etc.

4) Flexibilities. Ways that the dispatcher can "cheat" to make the shop run more efficiently and to improve quality and delivery performance.

A "bad" dispatching decision, in some cases, may have no effect on the business. For instance, suppose that order X should be dispatched, but it isn't. If the customer cancels the order that same day, then the "bad" decision may turn out to actually have been "good".

But, we can't rely on luck. Poor dispatching can dramatically increase cost. For instance, a poor dispatching job can cause considerable inefficiencies in the next department by creating shortages. Most decentralized dispatchers are measured on meeting schedules and on beating efficiency targets only within their own department. So, this is a common problem.

Another "cost" of bad dispatching is expediting, overtime, and extra work. Failure to dispatch a hot job is likely to create chaos later when the business tries to compensate. More overtime may result, jobs may be interrupted on the machines, more material movement will occur, and the ultimate result may be an unhappy customer or even an ex-customer.

In less dramatic cases, poor dispatching simply reduces employee and equipment utilization. Eventually, the business will have to either improve its dispatching or compensate with more employees and equipment. Since we measure utilization, but don't measure dispatch effectiveness, we are often unaware that the source of the problem may be dispatching.

Poor dispatching can also significantly increase work-in-process inventories by failing to move material through the shop. This extends lead times. P&IC may respond by increasing the lead times in the MRP computer system, which causes extra material to be started. If the shop capacity doesn't change, the extra material can only end up sitting on the floor and adding to inventory.

STATE OF THE ART - THEORY

Factory dispatching has been, and still is, a seat-of-the-pants art. Although a great deal of theoretical work has been done, very little of the theory has been successfully applied in real practice. In fact, few practitioners are aware of the theory and of the useful ideas within it.

Existing theory is based on the idea of a "priority rule". A priority rule is simply a way of calculating a number which allows the dispatcher to line up jobs in order of their importance. If all the available work is lined up in order of its importance, dispatching is simply a matter of picking the job that is on top of the pile. Obviously -- according to the theory -- if we knew how to calculate a priority number which would really put jobs in the "right" sequence, the computer could do the arithmetic for us and dispatching would truly become a clerical function.

Over the years, many rules have been proposed and some of them have actually been tried out in real shops. Let's review a few of the more important ones, beginning with the simplest:

1) First-in-First-Out
The FIFO priority rule says that the most important jobs are the ones that arrive first in the department or at the machine.

There is a certain element of "fairness" to the FIFO priority rule. It does guarantee that spart parts and stock orders receive attention. But most of us will reject it as a way of actually dispatching our shops because it does nothing to help move late jobs through the plant quickly.

2) Shortest Processing Time
The SPT priority rule says that the most important jobs are the ones that can be completed most quickly.

Mathematically, putting the short jobs first minimizes the number of jobs on the shop floor. This can be very helpful because it simplifies the management of the shop and helps control material movement costs. But, the big jobs end up getting delayed time after time. Since the big jobs often represent the most sales revenue, the SPT rule can create more problems than it resolves.

3) Due Date
The due date priority rule assigns priorities in due date sequence, putting the orders that are due first at the front of the line.

Setting priorities based on due dates is natural and seems reasonable. Many shops attempt to dispatch based on due dates. But, there can be problems. For instance, suppose there are two jobs to be dispatched: one due today and the other due tomorrow. If the one due today requires two days of work to finish it, and the one due tomorrow requires one day of work, then following the due date rule, both will be late. But, if we violate the rule and dispatch the shorter job first, it can be completed on time.

4) Critical Ratio
This rule is more sophisticated, since it considers not only the order due date, but also the amount of work remaining. The "critical ratio" is the number of working hours left before a job is due, divided by the number of standard hours of work that remains to be done. The smaller this ratio is, the hotter the job is considered to be. As time goes by, if no work is done on a job, its critical ratio continues to fall until, eventually, it becomes the hottest job in the shop.

The critical ratio is appealing and there are shops which use it for dispatching every day. The primary problem with critical ratio dispatching is that jobs are considered to be completely independent of each other. Why dispatch a job if it is going to be held up at the next operation because parts haven't arrived from the vendor, or because there are still hotter jobs (ones with even lower critical ratios) already on the equipment?

And, there are many others that have been proposed, theoretically investigated, and even tr.ed out in a real factory. They share the common problem that, although they each achieve something, no single rule can achieve everything. It seems that an experienced person can always improve on the mathematical priorities with paper and pencil. A mathematical rule requires an objective that can be mathematically stated, and we don't know how to write a formula that reflects everything that we want to accomplish.

Considering that priority rules generally address only one objective at a time, there has also been some work done on "hybrids". A hybrid rule is simply a combination of several priority rules, usually using weighting factors to blend several numbers into a single number.

For instance, suppose a business wanted to accomplish three things in dispatching: meeting dates, minimizing the largest queue times, and providing for special priorities in emergency situations. That business could program its computer to calculate a priority like this:

- If an order qualifies as an emergency, set the priority to zero (in this scheme, a low priority number gets dispatched first).

- If not, calculate the critical ratio for the order and divide it by the length of time that the order has been in this queue. The result of that division is the priority.

The idea is that a hybrid rule will balance all of the conflicting needs and produce a realistic priority. Unfortunately, experience has shown that hybrids, rather than combining multiple objectives to arrive at a good priority, tend to combine multiple objectives to arrive at a poor priority. No one ever seems to be satisfied with the results. And, hybrid rules quickly get complex and hard to understand. If the dispatchers don't understand the priorities, we can't expect them to believe in the rules or to make much use of them.

STATE OF THE ART - PRACTICE

Real life is very different from the theory. The person who does the dispatching in most plants is likely to be harried and working with incomplete information. When a decision is to be made, the real life "priorities" are likely to go like this:

1) First, the dispatcher will consider the availability of material, tooling, machines, personnel and supplies. A really competent dispatcher will often consider alternative uses for these resources and the impact of selecting them for use on a job right now. But generally the information won't be complete and few dispatchers are well enough trained or motivated to do a really good job of allocation.

2) Then, given several jobs available for dispatching, the "squeaky wheel" will be dispatched first. The job highest on the hot list, or the one most recently discussed with an expeditor goes first.

3) Next, if there are no squeaky wheels to be dispatched, the choice will be made based on the utilization of people and the "fair" distribution of "good" work around the shop.

4) Finally, if there is no other basis for a decision, job due dates and production schedules will rule.

The obvious problem is that this way of dispatching is not repeatable; after the fact, we can't figure out why we dispatched the way we did. And, we have no assurance that the dispatching objectives are being met.

It's easy to be critical. But real life is a lot harder than reading (or writing) a paper. Is this really wrong? What do we really want? Is there any significant financial benefit to doing a better job? How can we do better? As managers of our businesses and as the designers of the systems that our people use every day, it is our job to answer these questions.

WHAT WE NEED

Three things are needed to do a really excellent and effective job of dispatching:

1) Thought. You, the P&IC professional, have to answer the questions posed above. Hard as it may be, we really do need to decide what we want the dispatcher to do and how we want it done.

   The method that you work out need not be mathematical. But, it has to be realistic. Consider how you would answer questions like, "When should I interrupt a running job?", "How should I take into account different people's skills?", "How can I tell what the effect of a decision will be on the downstream departments and the customers?", "When should I leave a person idle, waiting for a hot job to arrive?".

   The "human side" skills are critical. To be effective, your dispatching method has to take them into account.

2) Education. It may be that the best thing you can do will be to get the dispatchers to think about how they should do their jobs, what the most important things are, and how they can be more effective. If you can motivate them by talking with them and listening to them, you might achieve something really worthwhile. And, teaching the dispatchers some of the ideas that have been presented in this paper willl almost certainly help.

3) Discipline. In the positive sense of the word, we need discipline. That is, we need dispatching decisions which are repeatable and measurable. We need a way of knowing when we have done a good job. And, when we have done a poor job, we need to know why so we can do better next time.

Meeting these needs isn't easy. There certainly is no cookbook approach. But, the practictioner who is willing to put time and effort into it, can make some real progress.

WHAT YOU CAN DO

In concrete, practical terms there are four things that you can do right now which will almost certainly improve the results of dispatching in your plant:

1) First, if you haven't already done it, give your dispatchers the training that they need. Don't limit the training to only their own function, but give them a complete picture of how your shop is (or should be) planned and run. Make sure that they understand the goals of your business, how P&IC works to meet those goals, and, in detail, how the schedules they work with every day are created. In particular, make sure that the people doing the dispatching understand how they can contribute to the success of the business.

   Most important, tell your dispatchers what you are doing and why you are spending so much time with them. Listen to their comments. Remember that they know more about the realities of dispatching than you do. Take their gripes and requests into serious consideration.

2) Second, make sure that a written procedure exists for dispatching and that the dispatchers agree to it. The written procedure gives you repeatability and the opportunity to learn from mistakes.

   The written procedure should include a statement of the objectives of dispatching, a statement of the reasons why a consistent, written procedure is necessary, and a listing of the rules and exceptions to the rules. Make sure that the procedure covers the exceptional cases and specifies how and when setups should be broken, what to do when quality problems come up, when to hold a person idle waiting for work, etc.

3) Then, make sure that your dispatchers have all the information that they need. Are they told when an important piece of equipment goes down in another department? Are they aware of current and upcoming engineering changes and quality problems? Do they get this information fast enough to make effective use of it?

4) And, finally, provide the dispatchers with a formal measurement and the incentives to do a really excellent job. Respond, in other words, to the question "What's in it for me?" If the dispatchers want to do well, and if you give them some real help, they almost certainly will do well.

SUMMARY

Dispatching is a frequently ignored, but important, part of the production planning process in many job shops. Although a great deal of theoretical work has been done on mathematical dispatching formulas, they haven't proven to be particularly valuable in the real world except as a source of ideas and inspiration for those of us on the firing line.

Significant improvement in real-life dispatching can be made. Since dispatching remains at least partly "art", the improvements are made through people, rather than through mathematics or computers. Providing your dispatchers with the knowledge and information that is needed, and giving them the incentive to do well, will almost certainly result in a better job and a more successful business.

ABOUT THE AUTHOR:

Jan B. Young is a consultant working for the Data Systems Division of A. O. Smith in Milwaukee, Wisconsin. He has been a frequent speaker at APICS chapter meetings and seminars. He holds master's degrees in both business administration and operations research and is an APICS fellow.

Jan has nine years of experience in line responsibility in both job and process flow shops. He has been a foreman, a general foreman, a P&IC manager, and has held other positions directly involved with the shop floor. He has both dispatched and has managed dispatchers. He now spends full time assisting users of the A. O. Smith manufacturing system and consulting on manufacturing systems problems.